UNIVERSITY CASEBOOK SERIES®

2018 SUPPLEMENT TO

CONSTITUTIONAL LAW

CASES AND MATERIALS

FIFTEENTH EDITION

JONATHAN D. VARAT

Professor of Law Emeritus and Former Dean
University of California, Los Angeles

VIKRAM D. AMAR

Dean and Iwan Foundation Professor of Law
University of Illinois College of Law

FOUNDATION PRESS

University Casebook Series is a trademark registered in the U.S. Patent and Trademark Office.

© 2017 LEG, Inc. d/b/a West Academic
© 2018 LEG, Inc. d/b/a West Academic
444 Cedar Street, Suite 700
St. Paul, MN 55101
1-877-888-1330

Printed in the United States of America

ISBN: 978-1-64020-936-7

PREFACE

October Term 2017 was notable both for important constitutional decisions across a wide range of topics, and for a potentially major shift in the Court's future direction following Justice Anthony M. Kennedy's announcement a few hours after the Term's last opinions were issued on June 27, 2018, that he would retire from active Court service as of July 31. Justice Kennedy's decision to retire provided President Donald J. Trump the opportunity to fill a second Supreme Court vacancy a year after filling his first. President Trump's first Court appointment, Justice Neil Gorsuch, joined the Court on April 8, 2017 at the age of 49. Justice Gorsuch filled the seat that was created by Justice Antonin Scalia's death in February 2016 and that remained open for over a year after the Republican-led Senate refused to process President Obama's March 2016 nominee, Judge Merrick Garland of the United States Court of Appeals for the D. C. Circuit. Justice Kennedy, appointed by President Ronald Reagan in 1987, was the last Justice to serve who joined the Court before 1990.

Shortly after Justice Kennedy's announcement, the Trump administration informed the media that the President would announce his choice for the vacancy at a prime-time televised event on the evening of July 9, 2018. The President did just that, nominating 53-year-old Brett Michael Kavanaugh of Maryland, who (like Judge Garland) has served for many years on the U.S. Court of Appeals for the D. C. Circuit, where he has authored some 300 opinions. Like Justice Gorsuch, Judge Kavanaugh served as a law clerk to Justice Kennedy a quarter century ago, in the October 1993 Term. (Justice Gorsuch also served as a clerk that Term to recently retired Justice Byron R. White.)

As this Supplement is being prepared for publication, the confirmation hearings for Judge Kavanaugh have yet to begin. Democratic Senators, still smarting over the Republicans' refusal to hold hearings for, or a vote on, Judge Garland's nomination, and distrustful of Judge Kavanaugh's past rulings and public writings, are planning to mount a fierce opposition, though even some within their party who are up for reelection this fall in States where President Trump is popular may be unwilling to risk voting against someone with Judge Kavanaugh's strong academic and professional pedigree. For their part, Republicans still hold a majority of Senate seats, and while a few Republican Senators say they will not vote for a nominee who plans to overrule *Roe v. Wade*, that stance may have little meaning if Judge Kavanaugh, like so many of the other recent nominees to the Court, is able to avoid answering meaningful Senate questions concerning contentious cases like *Roe*. While no confirmation is a done deal until after the deal is done, the general expectation is that Judge Kavanaugh will join the Court before the beginning of the October 2018 Term.

If he does, the effect his replacement of Justice Kennedy will have on constitutional jurisprudence is open to some question. Justice Kennedy often served, since Justice Sandra Day O'Connor's retirement in 2006, as the Court's pivot between its "liberal" and "conservative" wings. Justice O'Connor (like Justice Lewis Powell before her) represented one kind of "middle" Justice, occasionally adopting a position in a given case between the "liberal" and "conservative" approaches. Justice Kennedy could be perceived as different; on any particular area of law he might join the "conservatives" or "liberals" wholeheartedly, but his position would fluctuate from issue to issue. As for a Justice Kavanaugh, most analysts expect—based on his record so far—that as a general matter he will be more consistently "conservative" than Justice Kennedy was on many constitutional issues concerning the right to privacy, and likely also on the permissibility of race-based affirmative action. As to structural issues, there is some reason to believe Justice Kavanaugh might be more protective of the unitary executive than was Justice Kennedy, yet equally concerned about state autonomy from federal domination. With regard to electoral reform—e.g., public finance of elections, federal judicial oversight of partisan gerrymandering, use of direct democracy to circumvent state legislatures, etc.—it is hard to predict with a high degree of confidence that Justice Kavanaugh will vote differently than Justice Kennedy did. But of course much remains to be seen.

One thing that does seem clear, however, is that the addition of Justice Kavanaugh would continue to keep the membership of the Court homogeneous on several dimensions. Both of President Trump's picks so far attended the same high school. Both are, like Justice Kennedy (and Justice Scalia), Catholic. So the Court would remain devoid of any Protestant members. Justice Kavanaugh attended Yale Law School and would join three other Yale Law graduates on the Court (Justices Thomas, Alito and Sotomayor), to go along with four Harvard Law School graduates (Chief Justice Roberts and Justices Breyer, Kagan and Gorsuch) and one Columbia Law graduate who transferred to Columbia Law from Harvard (Justice Ginsburg). Justice Kavanaugh's addition would also mark the first time a majority of the Justices (Chief Justice Roberts and Justices Breyer, Kagan, Gorsuch and Kavanaugh) themselves clerked at the Court early in their legal career.

Looking back on the last Term rather than forward to the next, the materials in this 2018 Supplement reflect a considerable amount of new constitutional doctrine, including the explicit overruling of two of the Court's longstanding prior decisions. This year's Supplement features additions to Chapters 2, 4, 5, 6, 7, and 15, which had no reported cases in the 2017 Supplement, as well as additions that were set forth in other Chapters in last year's Supplement.

The First Amendment continues to be a particularly active area for significant opinions, focusing specifically on freedom of speech and the religion clauses. The Court was sharply divided 5–4 or 6–3, as to outcomes and methodologies, in many important rulings this past year—a considerably higher percentage than in recent years—and we have tried to capture those divisions in useful pedagogical detail in many instances as well.

TABLE OF CONTENTS

PART 4. CONSTITUTIONAL PROTECTION OF EXPRESSION AND CONSCIENCE

TABLE OF CASES

The principal cases are in bold type.

UNIVERSITY CASEBOOK SERIES®

2018 SUPPLEMENT TO

CONSTITUTIONAL LAW

CASES AND MATERIALS

FIFTEENTH EDITION

PART 1

THE CONSTITUTION AND THE COURTS: THE JUDICIAL FUNCTION IN CONSTITUTIONAL CASES

CHAPTER 2

JUDICIAL REVIEW

2. CONGRESSIONAL CONTROL OF JUDICIAL REVIEW BY THE FEDERAL COURTS

Page 41. Add after Note (3) and change the numbering of what are currently Notes (4)–(8):

(4)   Patchak v. Zinke, 585 U.S. ___, 138 S.Ct. 897 (2018), involved a federal statute dealing with a particular piece of land (known as the Bradley Property) on which an Indian tribe wished to build a casino. The statute, passed while litigation was pending in the District Court, reaffirmed the land as "trust land" under the Indian Reorganization Act and, in section 2(b), provided that "an action . . . relating to [that] land shall not be filed or maintained in a Federal court and shall be promptly dismissed." In assessing § 2(b), the Supreme Court could not generate a majority opinion. But in announcing the judgment of the Court and speaking for himself and three others, Justice Thomas observed: "Section 2(b) strips federal jurisdiction over suits relating to the Bradley Property. The statute uses jurisdictional language. It states that an 'action' relating to the Bradley Property 'shall not be filed or maintained in a Federal court.' It imposes jurisdictional consequences: Actions relating to the Bradley Property 'shall be promptly dismissed.' [It] has no exceptions. And it applies '[n]otwithstanding any other provision of law,' including the general grant of federal-question jurisdiction, 28 U. S. C. § 1331. Although § 2(b) does not use the word 'jurisdiction,' this Court does not require jurisdictional statutes to 'incant magic words.' . . . Statutes that strip jurisdiction 'chang[e] the law' for the purpose of Article III, . . . [and] reflect the so-called Madisonian Compromise, which resolved the Framers' disagreement about creating lower federal courts by leaving that decision to Congress. . . . Thus, when Congress strips federal courts of jurisdiction, it exercises a valid legislative power no less than when it lays taxes, coins money, declares war, or invokes any other power that the Constitution grants it." He went on to say that "this Court has held that Congress generally does not violate Article III when it strips federal jurisdiction over a class of cases. . . . Patchak compares § 2(b) to the statute this Court held unconstitutional in *Klein.* . . . This Court has since explained that 'the statute in *Klein* infringed the judicial power, not because it left too little for courts to do, but because it attempted to direct the result without altering the legal standards governing the effect of a pardon—standards Congress was powerless to prescribe.' . . . Congress had no authority to declare that pardons are not evidence of loyalty, so it could not achieve the same result by stripping jurisdiction whenever claimants cited pardons as evidence of loyalty. Nor could Congress confer jurisdiction to a federal court but then strip jurisdiction from that same court once the court concluded that a pardoned claimant should prevail under the statute. Patchak's attempts to compare § 2(b) to the statute in *Klein* are unpersuasive. Section 2(b) does not attempt to exercise a power that

the Constitution vests in another branch. And unlike the selective jurisdiction-stripping statute in *Klein*, § 2(b) strips jurisdiction over every suit relating to the Bradley Property. Indeed, *Klein* itself explained that statutes that do 'nothing more' than strip jurisdiction over 'a particular class of cases' are constitutional. That is precisely what § 2(b) does."

CHAPTER 3

THE JURISDICTION OF FEDERAL COURTS IN CONSTITUTIONAL CASES

1. SUPREME COURT REVIEW OF STATE COURT DECISIONS

A. HISTORY AND STRUCTURE

Page 48. Add before Section B:

Supreme Court Appellate Power to Review Decisions by Non-Article III Courts Other than State Courts

In Ortiz v. United States, 585 U.S. ___, 138 S.Ct. 2165 (2018), the Court addressed its power to review decisions by the Court of Appeals for the Armed Forces (CAAF), which sits atop the court martial system. Although neither the petitioner (an Airman First Class convicted by a court-martial of possessing and distributing child pornography) nor the United States questioned the Court's jurisdiction, an amicus argued that Marbury v. Madison and Article III foreclosed the Court's appellate review. The Court rejected that argument 7–2 (Justice Alito, joined by Justice Gorsuch, dissenting), with Justice Kagan writing for the majority. She explained:

"We begin with a question of our own jurisdiction to review the CAAF's decisions. Congress has explicitly authorized us to undertake such review in 28 U. S. C. § 1259. Both the Federal Government and Ortiz view that grant of jurisdiction as constitutionally proper. But an *amicus curiae* . . . argues that it goes beyond what Article III allows. That position is a new one to this Court: We have previously reviewed nine CAAF decisions without anyone objecting that we lacked the power to do so. Still, we think the argument is serious, and deserving of sustained consideration. That analysis leads us to conclude that the judicial character and constitutional pedigree of the court-martial system enable this Court, in exercising appellate jurisdiction, to review the decisions of the court sitting at its apex.

". . . [Amicus relies on Chief Justice's Marshall's language in *Marbury*.] '[T]he essential criterion of appellate jurisdiction,' the Chief Justice explained, is 'that it revises and corrects the proceedings in a cause already instituted, and does not create that cause.' . . . Marbury's petition, Chief Justice Marshall held, commenced the cause—or, to use the more modern word, the case; hence, it was not a matter for appellate jurisdiction. [Amicus] contends that the same is true of Ortiz's petition.

"On any ordinary understanding of the great Chief Justice's words, that is a surprising claim. Ortiz's petition asks us to 'revise and correct' the latest decision in a 'cause' that began in and progressed through military justice 'proceedings.' . . . Or, as the Government puts the point, this case fits within Chief Justice Marshall's standard because 'it comes to th[is] Court on review of the Court of Appeals for the Armed Forces' decision, which reviewed a criminal proceeding that originated in [a] court[ ]-martial.' . . . So this Court would hardly be the first to render a decision in the case. Unless Chief Justice Marshall's test implicitly exempts cases instituted in a military court—as contrasted, for example, with an ordinary federal court—the case is now appellate.

"The military justice system's essential character—in a word, judicial— provides no reason to make that distinction. Each level of military court decides criminal 'cases' as that term is generally understood, and does so in strict accordance with a body of federal law (of course including the Constitution). The procedural protections afforded to a service member are 'virtually the same' as those given in a civilian criminal proceeding, whether state or federal. And the judgments a military tribunal renders, as this Court long ago observed, 'rest on the same basis, and are surrounded by the same considerations[, as] give conclusiveness to the judgments of other legal tribunals.' . . .

"The jurisdiction and structure of the court-martial system likewise resemble those of other courts whose decisions we review. . . .

"And just as important, the constitutional foundation of courts-martial—as judicial bodies responsible for 'the trial and punishment' of service members—is not in the least insecure. . . .

. . .

". . . [T]his Court's appellate jurisdiction, as Justice Story made clear ages ago, covers more than the decisions of Article III courts. In Martin v. Hunter's Lessee, 1 Wheat. 304 (1816), we considered whether our appellate jurisdiction extends to the proceedings of state courts, in addition to those of the Article III federal judiciary. We said yes, as long as the case involves subject matter suitable for our review. For our 'appellate power,' Story wrote, 'is not limited by the terms of [Article III] to any particular courts.' . . . The decisions we review might come from Article III courts, but they need not.

"The same lesson emerges from two contexts yet more closely resembling this one—each involving a non-Article III judicial system created by Congress. First, in United States v. Coe, 155 U. S. 76 (1894), this Court upheld the exercise of appellate jurisdiction over decisions of federal territorial courts, despite their lack of Article III status. . . .

"Second, we have routinely, and uncontroversially, exercised appellate jurisdiction over cases adjudicated in the non-Article III District of Columbia courts. . . ."

. . .

3. CASES AND CONTROVERSIES AND JUSTICIABILITY

B. STANDING

1. "CONVENTIONAL" STANDING

Page 66. Add the following before Section 2:

Town of Chester v. Laroe Estates, Inc., ___ U.S. ___, 137 S.Ct. 1645 (2017). The Court held, in a case where a real estate development company sought to intervene under Federal Rule of Civil Procedure 24(a)(2) in a takings lawsuit brought by a land developer against a town over an unsuccessful housing subdivision, that a litigant seeking to intervene as a matter of right under Rule 24(a)(2) must meet the requirements of Article III standing—that is, an injury-in-fact that is traceable to defendant's conduct and redressable by a favorable judicial ruling—if the intervenor wishes to pursue relief not requested by the plaintiff. The Court noted that at least one plaintiff must have standing to seek each form of relief sought in the Complaint, and that principle applies also to intervenors of right; for each aspect of relief sought, there must be a litigant with standing, whether that litigant joins the lawsuit as a plaintiff, a co-plaintiff, or an intervenor of right. Thus, when an intervenor seeks relief beyond that requested by any plaintiff in the case—including a separate money judgment for the intervenor—the intervenor must satisfy Article III.

Gill v. Whitford, 585 U.S. ___, 138 S.Ct. 1916 (2018). A group of Democratic voters in Wisconsin sued to challenge partisan gerrymandering vote dilution resulting from the "packing" and "cracking" of Democratic voters into particular state legislative districts by a Republican-controlled legislature. ("Packing" describes concentrating a party's voters in certain districts to deprive that party of the possibility of votes in other parts of the state, whereas "cracking" refers to the related practice of spreading a party's voters strategically throughout different districts so that they will fall just short of being able to elect their party's candidate in each of those districts.) In a unanimous opinion, the Court declined to reach the merits or decide even whether partisan gerrymandering claims like this are justiciable, "because the plaintiffs in this case have not shown standing under the theory upon which they based their claims for relief." The plaintiffs' alleged vote dilution claim was district specific, but none of them sought to prove at trial that they lived in a particular "cracked" or "packed" district, and so they failed to demonstrate the requisite Article III "injury in fact." And as to their claim of "legal injury" in the form of "statewide harm to their interest 'in their collective representation in the legislature,' and in influencing the legislature's overall 'composition and policymaking,'" the Court said that "our cases to date have not found that this presents an individual and personal injury of the kind required for Article III standing." Rather, a "citizen's interest in the overall composition of the legislature is embodied in his right to vote for his representative." Because the case "concern[ed] an unsettled kind of claim this Court has not agreed upon, the contours and justiciability of which are unresolved[,] . . . and in light of . . . allegations that [four plaintiffs] live in districts where Democrats like them have been packed or cracked," the Court (with Justice Thomas, joined by Justice Gorsuch, disagreeing only on this point) declined to follow its usual practice of directing dismissal, instead remanding "so that the plaintiffs may have an opportunity to prove concrete and particularized injuries using evidence. . .that would tend to demonstrate a burden on their individual votes."

A longer report of this case appears infra, at p. 64.

C. MOOTNESS

Page 83. Add at the end of the Section:

In United States v. Sanchez-Gomez, 584 U.S. ___, 138 S.Ct. 1532 (2018), respondents were four criminal defendants who challenged a policy adopted by the United States District Court for the Southern District of California that permitted the use of handcuffs connected to a waist chain, with legs shackled, on most in-custody defendants (including the respondents) who are produced in court for nonjury proceedings by the United States Marshals Service. The district court rejected the challenge, and respondents appealed to the Ninth Circuit. Before the Ninth Circuit could rule on the merits, respondents' underlying criminal cases ended. The Ninth Circuit nonetheless reached the merits, and found the handcuff/shackles policy was unconstitutional. When the United States sought review in the Supreme Court, the Justices ruled 9–0 that the claims were moot, rejecting respondents' arguments that the claims of two of them, Sanchez-Gomez and Patricio-Guzman, fell within the "capable of repetition, yet evading review" exception to mootness. Respondents argued that the exception applied because these two respondents will again violate the law, be arrested, and be subjected to the pretrial full restraint policy. The Court adhered to what it called its consistent position that Article III's case-or-controversy requirement is not satisfied by the possibility that a party "will be prosecuted for violating valid criminal laws." The Court distinguished two civil cases, Honig v. Doe, 484 U. S. 305 (1988), and Turner v. Rogers, 564 U. S. 431 (2011), in which the Court concluded that the expectation that a litigant would repeat the misconduct that gave rise to his claims rendered those claims capable of repetition—holding that the litigants in those cases were unable, for reasons beyond their control, to prevent themselves from transgressing and avoiding recurrence of the challenged conduct. By contrast, the Court observed, Sanchez-Gomez and Patricio-Guzman, are "able—and indeed required by law"—to refrain from further criminal conduct.

PART 2

ALLOCATION OF GOVERNMENTAL POWERS: THE NATION AND THE STATES; THE PRESIDENT, THE CONGRESS, AND THE COURTS

CHAPTER 4

THE SCOPE OF NATIONAL POWER

3. THE SCOPE OF NATIONAL POWER TODAY

F. OTHER FEDERAL POWERS

3. REGULATION OF ALIENS

Page 217. Add after Kleindienst v. Mandel:

Trump v. Hawaii
585 U.S. ___, 138 S.Ct. 2392, ___ L.Ed.2d ___ (2018).

[The report of this case appears infra, at p. 129.]

CHAPTER 5

STATE SOVEREIGNTY AND FEDERAL REGULATION

1. STATE IMMUNITY FROM FEDERAL REGULATION

Page 241. Add after Reno v. Condon:

Murphy v. National Collegiate Athletic Association, 585 U.S. ___, 138 S.Ct. 1461 (2018). The federal Professional and Amateur Sports Protection Act (PASPA) makes it "unlawful" for a State or any of its subdivisions "to sponsor, operate, advertise, promote, license, or authorize by law or compact . . . a lottery, sweepstakes, or other betting, gambling, or wagering scheme based . . . on" competitive sporting events. § 3702(1). In a separate provision relevant to but not directly at issue in the case, Congress has made it "unlawful" for "a person to sponsor, operate, advertise, or promote" those same gambling schemes— provided the person has done any of these things "pursuant to the law or compact of a governmental entity." . . . PASPA does not criminalize sports gambling under federal law but does allow the Attorney General, as well as professional and amateur sports organizations, to bring civil actions to enjoin violations.

When PASPA was passed, some jurisdictions allowed some types of sports gambling, and these activities were grandfathered so as to be unaffected by PASPA. Another provision allowed New Jersey to legalize sports gambling in Atlantic City if New Jersey chose to do so within a year of PASPA's enactment. New Jersey did not invoke that option, but many years later, in 2012 and again in 2014, it did seek to decriminalize some sports gambling that was prohibited at the time of PASPA's passage. The 2014 New Jersey Act, the one in controversy in the case, "declares that it is not to be interpreted as causing the State to authorize, license, sponsor, operate, advertise, or promote sports gambling. Instead, it is framed as a repealer. Specifically, it repeals the provisions of state law prohibiting sports gambling insofar as they concern[ ] the 'placement and acceptance of wagers' on sporting events by persons 21 years of age or older at a horseracing track or a casino or gambling house in Atlantic City. The new law also specified that the repeal was effective only as to wagers on sporting events not involving a New Jersey college team or a collegiate event taking place in the State." . . .

The 2014 Act was challenged in federal court by the National Collegiate Athletic Association and others as violating PASPA's prohibition on a state "authoriz[ing]" and "licens[ing]" sports gambling. New Jersey defended on the ground that PASPA's prohibitions on authorization and licensing of sports gambling by states and their subdivisions constituted impermissible "commandeering" of state legislatures by the federal government in violation of the Tenth Amendment and the principles laid out under it in New York v. United States, 505 U.S. 144 (1992), and Printz v. United States. 521 U.S. 898 (1997). The lower courts rejected this commandeering argument, but the Supreme Court reversed, 7–2, with Justice Alito writing for the Court:

"Before considering the constitutionality of the PASPA provision prohibiting States from 'author[izing]' sports gambling, we first examine its meaning. The parties advance dueling interpretations, and this dispute has an important bearing on the constitutional issue that we must decide. Neither respondents nor the United States, appearing as an *amicus* in support of respondents, contends that the provision at issue would be constitutional if petitioners' interpretation is correct. Indeed, the United States expressly concedes that the provision is unconstitutional if it means what petitioners claim. Brief for United States 8, 19.

"Petitioners argue that the anti-authorization provision requires States to maintain their existing laws against sports gambling without alteration. One of the accepted meanings of the term 'authorize,' they point out, is 'permit.' . . . They therefore contend that any state law that has the effect of permitting sports gambling, including a law totally or partially repealing a prior prohibition, amounts to an authorization. . . . Respondents interpret the provision more narrowly. They claim that the *primary* definition of 'authorize' requires affirmative action. . . . To authorize, they maintain, means '[t]o empower; to give a right or authority to act; to endow with authority.' . . . And this, they say, is precisely what the 2014 Act does: It empowers a defined group of entities, and it endows them with the authority to conduct sports gambling operations. Respondents do not take the position that PASPA bans all modifications of old laws against sports gambling, Brief for Respondents 20, but just how far they think a modification could go is not clear. They write that a State 'can also repeal or enhance [laws prohibiting sports gambling] without running afoul of PASPA' but that it 'cannot 'partially repeal' a general prohibition for only one or two preferred providers, or only as to sports-gambling schemes conducted by the state. . . .

"The United States makes a similar argument. PASPA, it contends, does not prohibit a State from enacting a complete repeal because 'one would not ordinarily say that private conduct is "authorized by law" simply because the government has not prohibited it.' Brief for United States 17. But the United States claims that '[t]he 2014 Act's selective and conditional permission to engage in conduct that is generally prohibited certainly qualifies' as an authorization. . . .

"In our view, petitioners' interpretation is correct: When a State completely or partially repeals old laws banning sports gambling, it 'authorize[s]' that activity. . . .

. . .

"The respondents and United States argue that even if there is some doubt about the correctness of their interpretation of the anti-authorization provision, that interpretation should be adopted in order to avoid any anti-commandeering problem that would arise if the provision were construed to require States to maintain their laws prohibiting sports gambling. . . . [B]ut even if the law could be interpreted as respondents and the United States suggest, it would still violate the anticommandeering principle, as we now explain.

. . .

"The legislative powers granted to Congress are sizable, but they are not unlimited. The Constitution confers on Congress not plenary legislative power but only certain enumerated powers. Therefore, all other legislative power is reserved for the States, as the Tenth Amendment confirms. And conspicuously absent from the list of powers given to Congress is the power to issue direct orders to the governments of the States. The anticommandeering doctrine simply represents the recognition of this limit on congressional authority.

"Although the anticommandeering principle is simple and basic, it did not emerge in our cases until relatively recently, when Congress attempted in a few isolated instances to extend its authority in unprecedented ways. The pioneering case was *New York*. . . .

"Five years after *New York*, the Court applied the same principles to a federal statute requiring state and local law enforcement officers to perform background checks and related tasks in connection with applications for handgun licenses. *Printz*,. . . .

"Our opinions in *New York* and *Printz* explained why adherence to the anticommandeering principle is important. Without attempting a complete survey, we mention several reasons that are significant here. First, the rule serves as 'one of the Constitution's structural protections of liberty.' . . . 'The Constitution does not protect the sovereignty of States for the benefit of the States or state governments as abstract political entities.' . . . 'To the contrary, the Constitution divides authority between federal and state governments for the protection of individuals.' . . . '[A] healthy balance of power between the States and the Federal Government [reduces] the risk of tyranny and abuse from either front.' . . .

"Second, the anticommandeering rule promotes political accountability. When Congress itself regulates, the responsibility for the benefits and burdens of the regulation is apparent. Voters who like or dislike the effects of the regulation know who to credit or blame. By contrast, if a State imposes regulations only because it has been commanded to do so by Congress, responsibility is blurred.

"Third, the anticommandeering principle prevents Congress from shifting the costs of regulation to the States. If Congress enacts a law and requires enforcement by the Executive Branch, it must appropriate the funds needed to administer the program. It is pressured to weigh the expected benefits of the program against its costs. But if Congress can compel the States to enact and enforce its program, Congress need not engage in any such analysis. . . .

"The PASPA provision at issue here—prohibiting state authorization of sports gambling—violates the anticommandeering rule. That provision unequivocally dictates what a state legislature may and may not do. And this is true under either our interpretation or that advocated by respondents and the United States. In either event, state legislatures are put under the direct control of Congress. It is as if federal officers were installed in state legislative chambers and were armed with the authority to stop legislators from voting on any offending proposals. A more direct affront to state sovereignty is not easy to imagine.

"Neither respondents nor the United States contends that Congress can compel a State to enact legislation, but they say that prohibiting a State from enacting new laws is another matter. Noting that the laws challenged in *New York* and *Printz* 'told states what they must do instead of what they must not do,' respondents contend that commandeering occurs 'only when Congress goes beyond precluding state action and affirmatively commands it.'

"This distinction is empty. It was a matter of happenstance that the laws challenged in *New York* and *Printz* commanded 'affirmative' action as opposed to imposing a prohibition. The basic principle—that Congress cannot issue direct orders to state legislatures—applies in either event.

"Here is an illustration. PASPA includes an exemption for States that permitted sports betting at the time of enactment, but suppose Congress did not adopt such an exemption. Suppose Congress ordered States with legalized sports betting to take the affirmative step of criminalizing that activity and ordered the remaining States to retain their laws prohibiting sports betting. There is no good reason why the former would intrude more deeply on state sovereignty than the latter.

"Respondents and the United States claim that prior decisions of this Court show that PASPA's anti-authorization provision is constitutional, but they misread those cases. In none of them did we uphold the constitutionality of a federal statute that commanded state legislatures to enact or refrain from enacting state law. . . .

". . . Reno v. Condon, 528 U. S. 141 (2000), . . . concerned a federal law restricting the disclosure and dissemination of personal information provided in applications for driver's licenses. The law applied equally to state and private actors. It did not regulate the States' sovereign authority to 'regulate their own citizens.'

. . .

"Respondents and the United States defend the anti-authorization prohibition on the ground that it constitutes a valid preemption provision, but it is no such thing. Preemption is based on the Supremacy Clause, and that Clause is not an independent grant of legislative power to Congress. Instead, it simply provides 'a rule of decision.' It specifies that federal law is supreme in case of a conflict with state law. Therefore, in order for the PASPA provision to preempt state law, it must satisfy two requirements. First, it must represent the exercise of a power conferred on Congress by the Constitution; pointing to the Supremacy Clause will not do. Second, since the Constitution 'confers upon Congress the power to regulate individuals, not States,' the PASPA provision at issue must be best read as one that regulates private actors.

"Our cases have identified three different types of preemption—'conflict,' 'express,' and 'field,'—but all of them work in the same way: Congress enacts a law that imposes restrictions or confers rights on private actors; a state law confers rights or imposes restrictions that conflict with the federal law; and therefore the federal law takes precedence and the state law is preempted.

"This mechanism is shown most clearly in cases involving 'conflict preemption.' . . .

" 'Express preemption' operates in essentially the same way, but this is often obscured by the language used by Congress in framing preemption provisions. The provision at issue in Morales v. Trans World Airlines, Inc., 504 U. S. 374 (1992), is illustrative. The Airline Deregulation Act of 1978 lifted prior federal regulations of airlines, and '[t]o ensure that the States would not undo federal deregulation with regulation of their own,' the Act provided that 'no State or political subdivision thereof . . . shall enact or enforce any law, rule, regulation, standard, or other provision having the force and effect of law relating to rates, routes, or services of any [covered] air carrier.'

"This language might appear to operate directly on the States, but it is a mistake to be confused by the way in which a preemption provision is phrased. As we recently explained, 'we do not require Congress to employ a particular linguistic formulation when preempting state law.' . . . And if we look beyond the phrasing employed in the Airline Deregulation Act's preemption provision, it is clear that this provision operates just like any other federal law with preemptive effect. It confers on private entities (*i.e.*, covered carriers) a federal right to engage in certain conduct subject only to certain (federal) constraints.

" 'Field preemption' operates in the same way. . .

. . .

"In sum, regardless of the language sometimes used by Congress and this Court, every form of preemption is based on a federal law that regulates the conduct of private actors, not the States.

"Once this is understood, it is clear that the PASPA provision prohibiting state authorization of sports gambling is not a preemption provision because there is no way in which this provision can be understood as a regulation of private actors. It certainly does not confer any federal rights on private actors interested in conducting sports gambling operations. (It does not give them a federal right to engage in sports gambling.) Nor does it impose any federal restrictions on private actors. If a private citizen or company started a sports gambling operation, either with or without state authorization, § 3702(1) would not be violated and would not provide any ground for a civil action by the Attorney General or any other party. Thus, there is simply no way to understand the provision prohibiting state authorization as anything other than a direct command to the States. And that is exactly what the anticommandeering rule does not allow.

. . .

"Having concluded that § 3702(1) violates the anti-commandeering doctrine, we consider two additional questions: first, whether the decision below should be affirmed on an alternative ground and, second, whether our decision regarding the anti-authorization provision dooms the remainder of PASPA.

"Respondents and the United States argue that, even if we disagree with the Third Circuit's decision regarding the constitutionality of the anti-authorization provision, we should nevertheless affirm based on PASPA's prohibition of state 'licens[ing]' of sports gambling. Although New Jersey's 2014 Act does not expressly provide for the licensing of sports gambling operations, respondents and the United States contend that the law effectively achieves that result because the only entities that it authorizes to engage in that activity, *i.e.*, casinos and racetracks, are already required to be licensed.

"We need not decide whether the 2014 Act violates PASPA's prohibition of state 'licens[ing]' because that provision suffers from the same defect as the prohibition of state authorization. It issues a direct order to the state legislature.[29] Just as Congress lacks the power to order a state legislature not to enact a law authorizing sports gambling, it may not order a state legislature to refrain from enacting a law licensing sports gambling."

---

[29] Even if the prohibition of state licensing were not itself unconstitutional, we do not think it could be severed from the invalid provision forbidding state authorization. . . .

The Court went on to hold all the rest of the provisions of the PASPA inseverable and thus invalid. Justice Thomas, who joined the majority opinion, wrote a separate concurrence to express dissatisfaction with the current state of severability doctrine. Justice Breyer, who joined the Court's opinion except for its severability section, wrote separately to say he would have invalidated only the provision of PASPA dealing with "authoriz[ation]" and licens[ing]," and left intact the rest. Justice Ginsburg, joined by Justice Sotomayor, dissented, criticizing the Court's unwarranted severability analysis used to "deploy a wrecking ball destroying" PASPA. The fact that they dissented rather than concurred in part (as did Justice Breyer) could be read to suggest they disagreed with the majority's commandeering analysis as well (and they did refer to that part of the case as "the alleged 'commandeering' " elements of PASPA), but they never explained any disagreement with the majority on this point.

CHAPTER 6

THE SCOPE OF STATE POWER

1. INTRODUCTION

B. TAXATION

Page 252. Replace text (and accompanying footnotes) at the end of Section 1B (Introduction/Taxation) beginning with "Despite *Complete Auto . . .*" with the following:

South Dakota v. Wayfair

585 U.S. ___, 138 S.Ct. 2080, ___ L.Ed.2d ___ (2018).

■ JUSTICE KENNEDY delivered the opinion of the Court.

When a consumer purchases goods or services, the consumer's State often imposes a sales tax. This case requires the Court to determine when an out-of-state seller can be required to collect and remit that tax. All concede that taxing the sales in question here is lawful. The question is whether the out-of-state seller can be held responsible for its payment, and this turns on a proper interpretation of the Commerce Clause, U. S. Const., Art. I, § 8, cl. 3.

In two earlier cases the Court held that an out-of-state seller's liability to collect and remit the tax to the consumer's State depended on whether the seller had a physical presence in that State, but that mere shipment of goods into the consumer's State, following an order from a catalog, did not satisfy the physical presence requirement. National Bellas Hess, Inc. v. Department of Revenue of Ill., 386 U. S. 753 (1967); Quill Corp. v. North Dakota, 504 U. S. 298 (1992). The Court granted certiorari here to reconsider the scope and validity of the physical presence rule mandated by those cases.

I

Like most States, South Dakota has a sales tax. It taxes the retail sales of goods and services in the State. Sellers are generally required to collect and remit this tax to the Department of Revenue. If for some reason the sales tax is not remitted by the seller, then instate consumers are separately responsible for paying a use tax at the same rate.

Many States employ this kind of complementary sales and use tax regime. Under this Court's decisions in *Bellas Hess* and *Quill*, South Dakota may not require a business to collect its sales tax if the business lacks a physical presence in the State. Without that physical presence, South Dakota instead must rely on its residents to pay the use tax owed on their purchases from out-of-state sellers. "[T]he impracticability of [this] collection from the multitude of individual purchasers is obvious." . . . And consumer compliance rates are notoriously low [in the neighborhood of a 4 percent collection rate.] . . . It is estimated that *Bellas Hess* and *Quill* cause the States to lose between $8 and $33 billion every year. . . . In South Dakota alone, the Department of Revenue estimates revenue loss at $48 to $58 million annually. . . . Particularly because South Dakota has no state income tax, it must put substantial reliance on its sales and use taxes for the revenue necessary to fund essential services. Those taxes account for over 60 percent of its general fund.

In 2016, South Dakota confronted the serious inequity *Quill* imposes by enacting S. 106—"An Act to provide for the collection of sales taxes from certain remote sellers, to establish certain Legislative findings, and to declare an emergency." . . . The legislature found that the inability to collect sales tax from remote sellers was "seriously eroding the sales tax base" and "causing revenue losses and imminent harm . . . through the loss of critical funding for state and local services." . . . The legislature also declared an emergency: "Whereas, this Act is necessary for the support of the state government and its existing public institutions, an emergency is hereby declared to exist." . . . Fearing further erosion of the tax base, the legislature expressed its intention to "apply South Dakota's sales and use tax obligations to the limit of federal and state constitutional doctrines" and noted the urgent need for this Court to reconsider its precedents. . . .

To that end, the Act requires out-of-state sellers to collect and remit sales tax "as if the seller had a physical presence in the state." . . . The Act applies only to sellers that, on an annual basis, deliver more than $100,000 of goods or services into the State or engage in 200 or more separate transactions for the delivery of goods or services into the State. The Act also forecloses the retroactive application of this requirement and provides means for the Act to be appropriately stayed until the constitutionality of the law has been clearly established.

Respondents Wayfair, Inc., Overstock.com, Inc., and Newegg, Inc., are merchants with no employees or real estate in South Dakota. Wayfair, Inc., is a leading online retailer of home goods and furniture and had net revenues of over $4.7 billion last year. Overstock.com, Inc., is one of the top online retailers in the United States, selling a wide variety of products from home goods and furniture to clothing and jewelry; and it had net revenues of over $1.7 billion last year. Newegg, Inc., is a major online retailer of consumer electronics in the United States. Each of these three companies ships its goods directly to purchasers throughout the United States, including South Dakota. Each easily meets the minimum sales or transactions requirement of the Act, but none collects South Dakota sales tax.

Pursuant to the Act's provisions for expeditious judicial review, South Dakota filed a declaratory judgment action against respondents in state court, seeking a declaration that the requirements of the Act are valid and applicable to respondents and an injunction requiring respondents to register for licenses to collect and remit sales tax. Respondents moved for summary judgment, arguing that the Act is unconstitutional. South Dakota conceded that the Act cannot survive under *Bellas Hess* and *Quill* but asserted the importance, indeed the necessity, of asking this Court to review those earlier decisions in light of current economic realities.

The trial court granted summary judgment to respondents. The South Dakota Supreme Court affirmed. It stated: "However persuasive the State's arguments on the merits of revisiting the issue, *Quill* has not been overruled [and] remains the controlling precedent on the issue of Commerce Clause limitations on interstate collection of sales and use taxes." This Court granted certiorari. . . .

II

The Constitution grants Congress the power "[t]o regulate Commerce . . . among the several States." Art. I, § 8, cl. 3. The Commerce Clause "reflect[s] a central concern of the Framers that was an immediate reason for calling the Constitutional Convention: the conviction that in order to succeed, the new Union would have to avoid the tendencies toward economic Balkanization that had plagued relations among the Colonies and later among the States under the Articles of Confederation." Hughes v. Oklahoma, 441 U. S. 322, 325–326 (1979). Although the Commerce Clause is written as an affirmative grant of authority to Congress, this Court has long held that in some instances it imposes limitations on the States absent congressional action. Of course, when Congress exercises its power to regulate commerce by enacting legislation, the legislation controls. Southern Pacific Co. v. Arizona ex rel. Sullivan, 325 U. S. 761, 769 (1945). But this Court has observed that "in general Congress has left it to the courts to formulate the rules" to preserve "the free flow of interstate commerce." . . .

To understand the issue presented in this case, it is instructive first to survey the general development of this Court's Commerce Clause principles and then to review the application of those principles to state taxes.

A

From early in its history, a central function of this Court has been to adjudicate disputes that require interpretation of the Commerce Clause in order to determine its meaning, its reach, and the extent to which it limits state regulations of commerce. Gibbons v. Ogden, 9 Wheat. 1 (1824), began setting the course by defining the meaning of commerce. Chief Justice Marshall explained that commerce included both "the interchange of commodities" and "commercial intercourse." . . . A concurring opinion further stated that Congress had the exclusive power to regulate commerce. See id., at 236 (opinion of Johnson, J.). Had that latter submission prevailed and States been denied the power of concurrent regulation, history might have seen sweeping federal regulations at an early date that foreclosed the States from experimentation with laws and policies of their own, or, on the other hand, proposals to reexamine Gibbons' broad definition of commerce to accommodate the necessity of allowing States the power to enact laws to implement the political will of their people.

Just five years after Gibbons, however, in another opinion by Chief Justice Marshall, the Court sustained what in substance was a state regulation of interstate commerce. In Willson v. Black Bird Creek Marsh Co., 2 Pet. 245 (1829), the Court allowed a State to dam and bank a stream that was part of an interstate water system, an action that likely would have been an impermissible intrusion on the national power over commerce had it been the rule that only Congress could regulate in that sphere. . . . Thus, by implication at least, the Court indicated that the power to regulate commerce in some circumstances was held by the States and Congress concurrently. And so both a broad interpretation of interstate commerce and the concurrent regulatory power of the States can be traced to Gibbons and Willson.

Over the next few decades, the Court refined the doctrine to accommodate the necessary balance between state and federal power. In Cooley v. Board of Wardens of Port of Philadelphia ex rel. Soc. for Relief of Distressed Pilots, 12 How. 299 (1852), the Court addressed local laws regulating river pilots who operated in interstate waters and guided many ships on interstate or foreign voyages. The Court held that, while Congress surely could regulate on this subject had it chosen to act, the State, too, could regulate. The Court distinguished between those subjects that by their nature "imperatively deman[d] a single uniform rule, operating equally on the commerce of the United States," and those that "deman[d] th[e] diversity, which alone can meet . . . local necessities." . . . Though considerable uncertainties were yet to be overcome, these precedents still laid the groundwork for the analytical framework that now prevails for Commerce Clause cases.

This Court's doctrine has developed further with time. Modern precedents rest upon two primary principles that mark the boundaries of a State's authority to regulate interstate commerce. First, state regulations may not discriminate against interstate commerce; and second, States may not impose undue burdens on interstate commerce. State laws that discriminate against interstate commerce face "a virtually *per se* rule of invalidity." Granholm v. Heald, 544 U. S. 460, 476 (2005). State laws that "regulat[e] even-handedly to effectuate a legitimate local public interest . . . will be upheld unless the burden imposed on such commerce is clearly excessive in relation to the putative local benefits." Pike v. Bruce Church, Inc., 397 U. S. 137, 142 (1970). Although subject to exceptions and variations, these two principles guide the courts in adjudicating cases challenging state laws under the Commerce Clause.

B

These principles also animate the Court's Commerce Clause precedents addressing the validity of state taxes. The Court explained the now-accepted framework for state taxation in Complete Auto Transit, Inc. v. Brady, 430 U. S. 274 (1977). The Court held that a State "may tax exclusively interstate commerce so long as the tax does not create any effect forbidden by the Commerce Clause." . . . After all, "interstate commerce may be required to pay its fair share of state taxes." D. H. Holmes Co. v. McNamara, 486 U. S. 24, 31 (1988). The Court will sustain a tax so long as it (1) applies to an activity with a substantial nexus with the taxing State, (2) is fairly apportioned, (3) does not discriminate against interstate commerce, and (4) is fairly related to the services the State provides. . . .

Before *Complete Auto*, the Court had addressed a challenge to an Illinois tax that required out-of-state retailers to collect and remit taxes on sales made to consumers who purchased goods for use within Illinois. *Bellas Hess*, 386 U. S., at 754–755. The Court held that a mail-order company "whose only connection with customers in the State is by common carrier or the United States mail" lacked the requisite minimum contacts with the State required by both the Due Process Clause and the Commerce Clause. . . . Unless the retailer maintained a physical presence such as "retail outlets, solicitors, or property within a State," the State lacked the power to require that retailer to collect a local use tax. . . . The dissent disagreed: "There should be no doubt that this large-scale, systematic, continuous solicitation and exploitation of the Illinois consumer market is a sufficient 'nexus' to require Bellas Hess to collect from Illinois customers and to remit the use tax." *Id.*, at 761–762 (opinion of Fortas, J., joined by Black and Douglas, JJ.).

In 1992, the Court reexamined the physical presence rule in *Quill*. That case presented a challenge to North Dakota's "attempt to require an out-of-state mail-order house that has neither outlets nor sales representatives in the State to collect and pay a use tax on goods purchased for use within the State." . . . Despite the fact that *Bellas Hess* linked due process and the Commerce Clause together, the Court in *Quill* overruled the due process holding, but not the Commerce Clause holding; and it thus reaffirmed the physical presence rule. . . .

The Court in *Quill* recognized that intervening precedents, specifically *Complete Auto*, "might not dictate the same result were the issue to arise for the first time today." . . . But, nevertheless, the *Quill* majority concluded that the physical presence rule was necessary to prevent undue burdens on interstate commerce. It grounded the physical presence rule in *Complete Auto*'s requirement that a tax have a " 'substantial nexus' " with the activity being taxed. . . .

Three Justices based their decision to uphold the physical presence rule on *stare decisis* alone. *Id.*, at 320 (Scalia, J., joined by Kennedy and Thomas, JJ., concurring in part and concurring in judgment). Dissenting in relevant part, Justice White argued that "there is no relationship between the physical-presence/nexus rule the Court retains and Commerce Clause considerations that allegedly justify it." *Id.*, at 327 (opinion concurring in part and dissenting in part).

III

The physical presence rule has "been the target of criticism over many years from many quarters." Direct Marketing Assn. v. Brohl, 814 F. 3d 1129, 1148, 1150–1151 (CA10 2016) (Gorsuch, J., concurring). *Quill*, it has been said, was "premised on assumptions that are unfounded" and "riddled with internal inconsistencies." . . . *Quill* created an inefficient "online sales tax loophole" that gives out-of-state businesses an advantage. . . . And "while nexus rules are clearly necessary," the Court "should focus on rules that are appropriate to the twenty-first century, not the nineteenth." . . . Each year, the physical presence rule becomes further removed from economic reality and results in significant revenue losses to the States. These critiques underscore that the physical presence rule, both as first formulated and as applied today, is an incorrect interpretation of the Commerce Clause.

A

Quill is flawed on its own terms. First, the physical presence rule is not a necessary interpretation of the requirement that a state tax must be "applied to an activity with a substantial nexus with the taxing State." *Complete Auto*, 430 U. S., at 279. Second, *Quill* creates rather than resolves market distortions. And third, *Quill* imposes the sort of arbitrary, formalistic distinction that the Court's modern Commerce Clause precedents disavow.

1

All agree that South Dakota has the authority to tax these transactions. S. B. 106 applies to sales of "tangible personal property, products transferred electronically, or services *for delivery into South Dakota*." § 1 (emphasis added). "It has long been settled" that the sale of goods or services "has a sufficient nexus to the State in which the sale is consummated to be treated as a local transaction taxable by that State." Oklahoma Tax Comm'n v. Jefferson Lines, Inc., 514 U. S. 175, 184 (1995); see also 2 C.Trost & P. Hartman, Federal Limitations on State and Local Taxation 2d § 11:1, p. 471 (2003) ("Generally speaking, a sale is attributable to its destination"). The central dispute is whether South Dakota may require remote sellers to collect and remit the tax without some additional connection to the State. The Court has previously stated that "[t]he imposition on the seller of the duty to insure collection of the tax from the purchaser does not violate the [C]ommerce [C]lause." . . . It is a " 'familiar and sanctioned device.' " There just must be "a substantial nexus with the taxing State." *Complete Auto, supra,* at 279.

This nexus requirement is "closely related," *Bellas Hess,* 386 U. S., at 756, to the due process requirement that there be "some definite link, some minimum connection, between a state and the person, property or transaction it seeks to tax." . . . It is settled law that a business need not have a physical presence in a State to satisfy the demands of due process. Burger King Corp. v. Rudzewicz, 471 U. S. 462, 476 (1985). Although physical presence " 'frequently will enhance' " a business' connection with a State, " 'it is an inescapable fact of modern commercial life that a substantial amount of business is transacted . . . [with no] need for physical presence within a State in which business is conducted.' " *Quill,* 504 U. S., at 308. *Quill* itself recognized that "[t]he requirements of due process are met irrespective of a corporation's lack of physical presence in the taxing State." . . .

When considering whether a State may levy a tax, Due Process and Commerce Clause standards may not be identical or coterminous, but there are significant parallels. The reasons given in *Quill* for rejecting the physical presence rule for due process purposes apply as well to the question whether physical presence is a requisite for an out-of-state seller's liability to remit sales taxes. Physical presence is not necessary to create a substantial nexus.

The *Quill* majority expressed concern that without the physical presence rule "a state tax might unduly burden interstate commerce" by subjecting retailers to tax collection obligations in thousands of different taxing jurisdictions. . . . But the administrative costs of compliance, especially in the modern economy with its Internet technology, are largely unrelated to whether a company happens to have a physical presence in a State. For example, a business with one salesperson in each State must collect sales taxes in every jurisdiction in which goods are delivered; but a business with 500 salespersons in one central location and a website accessible in every State need not collect sales taxes on otherwise identical nationwide sales. In other words, under *Quill,* a small company with diverse physical presence might be equally or more burdened by compliance costs than a large remote seller. The physical presence rule is a poor proxy for the compliance costs faced by companies that do business in multiple States. Other aspects of the Court's doctrine can better and more accurately address any potential burdens on interstate commerce, whether or not *Quill*'s physical presence rule is satisfied.

2

The Court has consistently explained that the Commerce Clause was designed to prevent States from engaging in economic discrimination so they would not divide into isolated, separable units. See Philadelphia v. New Jersey, 437 U. S. 617, 623 (1978). But it is "not the purpose of the [C]ommerce [C]lause to relieve those engaged in interstate commerce from their just share of state tax burden." *Complete Auto, supra,* at 288. And it is certainly not the purpose of the Commerce Clause to permit the Judiciary to create market distortions. "If the Commerce Clause was intended to put businesses on an even playing field, the [physical presence] rule is hardly a way to achieve that goal." *Quill, supra,* at 329 (opinion of White, J.). *Quill* puts both local businesses and many interstate businesses with physical presence at a competitive disadvantage relative to remote sellers. Remote sellers can avoid the regulatory burdens of tax collection and can offer *de facto* lower prices caused by the widespread failure of consumers to pay the tax on their own. This "guarantees a competitive benefit to certain firms simply because of the organizational form they choose" while the rest of the Court's jurisprudence "is all about preventing discrimination between firms." *Direct Marketing*, 814 F. 3d, at 1150–1151 (Gorsuch, J., concurring). In effect, *Quill* has come to serve as a judicially created tax shelter for businesses that decide to limit their physical presence and still sell their goods and services to a State's consumers—something that has become easier and more prevalent as technology has advanced.

Worse still, the rule produces an incentive to avoid physical presence in multiple States. Distortions caused by the desire of businesses to avoid tax collection mean that the market may currently lack storefronts, distribution points, and employment centers that otherwise would be efficient or desirable. The Commerce Clause must not prefer interstate commerce only to the point where a merchant physically crosses state borders. Rejecting the physical presence rule is necessary to ensure that artificial competitive advantages are not created by this Court's precedents. This Court should not prevent States from collecting lawful taxes through a physical presence rule that can be satisfied only if there is an employee or a building in the State.

3

The Court's Commerce Clause jurisprudence has "eschewed formalism for a sensitive, case-by-case analysis of purposes and effects." West Lynn Creamery, Inc. v. Healy, 512 U. S. 186, 201 (1994). *Quill*, in contrast, treats economically identical actors differently, and for arbitrary reasons.

Consider, for example, two businesses that sell furniture online. The first stocks a few items of inventory in a small warehouse in North Sioux City, South Dakota. The second uses a major warehouse just across the border in South Sioux City, Nebraska, and maintains a sophisticated website with a virtual showroom accessible in every State, including South Dakota. By reason of its physical presence, the first business must collect and remit a tax on all of its sales to customers from South Dakota, even those sales that have nothing to do with the warehouse. But, under *Quill*, the second, hypothetical seller cannot be subject to the same tax for the sales of the same items made through a pervasive Internet presence. This distinction simply makes no sense. So long as a state law avoids "any effect forbidden by the Commerce Clause," . . . courts should not rely on anachronistic formalisms to invalidate it. The basic principles of the Court's Commerce Clause jurisprudence are grounded in functional, marketplace dynamics; and States can and should consider those realities in enacting and enforcing their tax laws.

B

The *Quill* Court itself acknowledged that the physical presence rule is "artificial at its edges." 504 U. S., at 315. That was an understatement when *Quill* was decided; and when the day-to-day functions of marketing and distribution in the modern economy are considered, it is all the more evident that the physical presence rule is artificial in its entirety. Modern e-commerce does not align analytically with a test that relies on the sort of physical presence defined in *Quill*. In a footnote, *Quill* rejected the argument that "title to 'a few floppy diskettes' present in a State" was sufficient to constitute a "substantial nexus," *id*., at 315, n. 8. But it is not clear why a single employee or a single warehouse should create a substantial nexus while "physical" aspects of pervasive modern technology should not. For example, a company with a website accessible in South Dakota may be said to have a physical presence in the State via the customers' computers. A website may leave cookies saved to the customers' hard drives, or customers may download the company's app onto their phones. Or a company may lease data storage that is permanently, or even occasionally, located in South Dakota. What may have seemed like a "clear," "bright-line tes[t]" when *Quill* was written now threatens to compound the arbitrary consequences that should have been apparent from the outset. . . .

The "dramatic technological and social changes" of our "increasingly interconnected economy" mean that buyers are "closer to most major retailers" than ever before—"regardless of how close or far the nearest storefront." . . . Between targeted advertising and instant access to most consumers via any internet-enabled device, "a business may be present in a State in a meaningful way without" that presence "being physical in the traditional sense of the term." . . . A virtual showroom can show far more inventory, in far more detail, and with greater opportunities for consumer and seller interaction than might be possible for local stores. Yet the continuous and pervasive virtual presence of retailers today is, under *Quill*, simply irrelevant. This Court should not maintain a rule that ignores these substantial virtual connections to the State.

C

The physical presence rule as defined and enforced in *Bellas Hess* and *Quill* is not just a technical legal problem—it is an extraordinary imposition by the Judiciary on States' authority to collect taxes and perform critical public functions. Forty-one States, two Territories, and the District of Columbia now ask this Court to reject the test formulated in *Quill*. *Quill*'s physical presence rule intrudes on States' reasonable choices in enacting their tax systems. And that it allows remote sellers to escape an obligation to remit a lawful state tax is unfair and unjust. It is unfair and unjust to those competitors, both local and out of State, who must remit the tax; to the consumers who pay the tax; and to the States that seek fair enforcement of the sales tax, a tax many States for many years have considered an indispensable source for raising revenue.

In essence, respondents ask this Court to retain a rule that allows their customers to escape payment of sales taxes—taxes that are essential to create and secure the active market they supply with goods and services. An example may suffice. Wayfair offers to sell a vast selection of furnishings. Its advertising seeks to create an image of beautiful, peaceful homes, but it also says that " '[o]ne of the best things about buying through Wayfair is that we do not have to charge sales tax.' " Brief for Petitioner 55. What Wayfair ignores in its subtle offer to assist in tax evasion is that creating a dream home assumes solvent state and local governments. State taxes fund the police and fire departments that protect the homes containing their customers' furniture and ensure goods are safely delivered; maintain the public roads and municipal services that allow communication with and access to customers; support the "sound local banking institutions to support credit transactions [and] courts to ensure collection of the purchase price," and help create the "climate of consumer confidence" that facilitates sales. According to respondents, it is unfair to stymie their tax-free solicitation of customers. But there is nothing unfair about requiring companies that avail themselves of the States' benefits to bear an equal share of the burden of tax collection. . . .

In the name of federalism and free markets, *Quill* does harm to both. The physical presence rule it defines has limited States' ability to seek long-term prosperity and has prevented market participants from competing on an even playing field.

IV

"Although we approach the reconsideration of our decisions with the utmost caution, *stare decisis* is not an inexorable command." . . . Here, *stare decisis* can no longer support the Court's prohibition of a valid exercise of the States' sovereign power. If it becomes apparent that the Court's Commerce Clause decisions prohibit the States from exercising their lawful sovereign powers in our federal system, the Court should be vigilant in correcting the error. While it can be conceded that Congress has the authority to change the physical presence rule, Congress cannot change the constitutional default rule. It is inconsistent with the Court's proper role to ask Congress to address a false constitutional premise of this Court's own creation. Courts have acted as the front line of review in this limited sphere; and hence it is important that their principles be accurate and logical, whether or not Congress can or will act in response. It is currently the Court, and not Congress, that is limiting the lawful prerogatives of the States.

. . . Though *Quill* was wrong on its own terms when it was decided in 1992, since then the Internet revolution has made its earlier error all the more egregious and harmful.

The *Quill* Court did not have before it the present realities of the interstate marketplace. In 1992, less than 2 percent of Americans had Internet access. Today that number is about 89 percent. When it decided *Quill*, the Court could not have envisioned a world in which the world's largest retailer would be a remote seller, [Amazon]. . . .

. . . Last year, e-commerce grew at four times the rate of traditional retail, and it shows no sign of any slower pace. . . .

This expansion has also increased the revenue shortfall faced by States seeking to collect their sales and use taxes. In 1992, it was estimated that the States were losing between $694 million and $3 billion per year in sales tax revenues as a result of the physical presence rule. Now estimates range from $8 to $33 billion. . . .

The argument, moreover, that the physical presence rule is clear and easy to apply is unsound. Attempts to apply the physical presence rule to online retail sales are proving unworkable. States are already confronting the complexities of defining physical presence in the Cyber Age. For example, Massachusetts proposed a regulation that would have defined physical presence to include making apps available to be downloaded by in-state residents and placing cookies on in-state residents' web browsers. . . . Ohio recently adopted a similar standard. . . . Some States have enacted so-called "click through" nexus statutes, which define nexus to include out-of-state sellers that contract with in-state residents who refer customers for compensation. . . . Others still, like Colorado, have imposed notice and reporting requirements on out-of-state retailers that fall just short of actually collecting and remitting the tax. . . . Statutes of this sort are likely to embroil courts in technical and arbitrary disputes about what counts as physical presence.

Reliance interests are a legitimate consideration when the Court weighs adherence to an earlier but flawed precedent. But even on its own terms, the physical presence rule as defined by *Quill* is no longer a clear or easily applicable standard, so arguments for reliance based on its clarity are misplaced. And, importantly, *stare decisis* accommodates only "legitimate reliance interest[s]." . . . Here, the tax distortion created by *Quill* exists in large part because consumers regularly fail to comply with lawful use taxes. Some remote retailers go so far as to advertise sales as tax free. A business "is in no position to found a constitutional right on the practical opportunities for tax avoidance." . . .

Respondents argue that "the physical presence rule has permitted start-ups and small businesses to use the Internet as a means to grow their companies and access a national market, without exposing them to the daunting complexity and business-development obstacles of nationwide sales tax collection." . . . These burdens may pose legitimate concerns in some instances, particularly for small businesses that make a small volume of sales to customers in many States. State taxes differ, not only in the rate imposed but also in the categories of goods that are taxed and, sometimes, the relevant date of purchase. Eventually, software that is available at a reasonable cost may make it easier for small businesses to cope with these problems. Indeed, as the physical presence rule no longer controls, those systems may well become available in a short period of time, either from private providers or from state taxing agencies themselves. And in all events, Congress may legislate to address these problems if it deems it necessary and fit to do so.

In this case, however, South Dakota affords small merchants a reasonable degree of protection. The law at issue requires a merchant to collect the tax only if it does a considerable amount of business in the State; the law is not retroactive; and South Dakota is a party to the Streamlined Sales and Use Tax Agreement.

Finally, other aspects of the Court's Commerce Clause doctrine can protect against any undue burden on interstate commerce, taking into consideration the small businesses, startups, or others who engage in commerce across state lines. For example, the United States argues that tax-collection requirements should be analyzed under the balancing framework of Pike v. Bruce Church, Inc., 397 U. S. 137. Others have argued that retroactive liability risks a double tax burden in violation of the Court's apportionment jurisprudence because it would make both the buyer and the seller legally liable for collecting and remitting the tax on a transaction intended to be taxed only once. Complex state tax systems could have the effect of discriminating against interstate commerce. Concerns that complex state tax systems could be a burden on small business are answered in part by noting that . . . there are various plans already in place to simplify collection; and since in-state businesses pay the taxes as well, the risk of discrimination against out-of-state sellers is avoided. And, if some small businesses with only *de minimis* contacts seek relief from collection systems thought to be a burden, those entities may still do so under other theories. These issues are not before the Court in the instant case; but their potential to arise in some later case cannot justify retaining this artificial, anachronistic rule that deprives States of vast revenues from major businesses.

For these reasons, the Court concludes that the physical presence rule of *Quill* is unsound and incorrect. The Court's decisions in *Quill* . . . and *National Bellas Hess* . . . should be, and now are, overruled.

V

In the absence of *Quill* and *Bellas Hess*, the first prong of the *Complete Auto* test simply asks whether the tax applies to an activity with a substantial nexus with the taxing State. . . . "[S]uch a nexus is established when the taxpayer [or collector] 'avails itself of the substantial privilege of carrying on business' in that jurisdiction." . . . Here, the nexus is clearly sufficient based on both the economic and virtual contacts respondents have with the State. The Act applies only to sellers that deliver more than $100,000 of goods or services into South Dakota or engage in 200 or more separate transactions for the delivery of goods and services into the State on an annual basis. . . . This quantity of business could not have occurred unless the seller availed itself of the substantial privilege of carrying on business in South Dakota. And respondents are large, national companies that undoubtedly maintain an extensive virtual presence. Thus, the substantial nexus requirement of *Complete Auto* is satisfied in this case.

The question remains whether some other principle in the Court's Commerce Clause doctrine might invalidate the Act. Because the *Quill* physical presence rule was an obvious barrier to the Act's validity, these issues have not yet been litigated or briefed, and so the Court need not resolve them here. That said, South Dakota's tax system includes several features that appear designed to prevent discrimination against or undue burdens upon interstate commerce. First, the Act applies a safe harbor to those who transact only limited business in South Dakota. Second, the Act ensures that no obligation to remit the sales tax may be applied retroactively. . . . Third, South Dakota is one of more than 20 States that have adopted the Streamlined Sales and Use Tax Agreement. This system standardizes taxes to reduce administrative and compliance costs: It requires a single, state level tax administration, uniform definitions of products and services, simplified tax rate structures, and other uniform rules. It also provides sellers access to sales tax administration software paid for by the State. Sellers who choose to use such software are immune from audit liability. Any remaining claims regarding the application of the Commerce Clause in the absence of *Quill* and *Bellas Hess* may be addressed in the first instance on remand.

The judgment of the Supreme Court of South Dakota is vacated, and the case is remanded for further proceedings not inconsistent with this opinion.

. . .

■ JUSTICE THOMAS, concurring.

Justice Byron White joined the majority opinion in *National Bellas Hess*. . . . Twenty-five years later, we had the opportunity to overrule *Bellas Hess* in *Quill*. . . . Only Justice White voted to do so. I should have joined his opinion. Today, I am slightly further removed from *Quill* than Justice White was from *Bellas Hess*. And like Justice White, a quarter century of experience has convinced me that *Bellas Hess* and *Quill* "can no longer be rationally justified." . . . The same is true for this Court's entire negative Commerce Clause jurisprudence. Although I adhered to that jurisprudence in *Quill*, it is never too late to "surrende[r] former views to a better considered position." . . .

■ JUSTICE GORSUCH, concurring.

Our dormant commerce cases usually prevent States from discriminating between in-state and out-of-state firms. *National Bellas Hess* and *Quill* do just the opposite. . . . The Court is right to correct the mistake and I am pleased to join its opinion.

My agreement with the Court's discussion of the history of our dormant commerce clause jurisprudence, however, should not be mistaken for agreement with all aspects of the doctrine. The Commerce Clause is found in Article I and authorizes *Congress* to regulate interstate commerce. Meanwhile our dormant commerce cases suggest Article III *courts* may invalidate state laws that offend no congressional statute. Whether and how much of this can be squared with the text of the Commerce Clause, justified by *stare decisis*, or defended as misbranded products of federalism or antidiscrimination imperatives flowing from Article IV's Privileges and Immunities Clause are questions for another day. . . .

■ CHIEF JUSTICE ROBERTS, with whom JUSTICE BREYER, JUSTICE SOTOMAYOR and JUSTICE KAGAN join, dissenting.

In *National Bellas Hess* . . . this Court held that, under the dormant Commerce Clause, a State could not require retailers without a physical presence in that State to collect taxes on the sale of goods to its residents. A quarter century later, in *Quill* . . . this Court was invited to overrule *Bellas Hess* but declined to do so. Another quarter century has passed, and another State now asks us to abandon the physical-presence rule. I would decline that invitation as well.

I agree that *Bellas Hess* was wrongly decided, for many of the reasons given by the Court. The Court argues in favor of overturning that decision because the "Internet's prevalence and power have changed the dynamics of the national economy." . . . But that is the very reason I oppose discarding the physical-presence rule. E-commerce has grown into a significant and vibrant part of our national economy against the backdrop of established rules, including the physical-presence rule. Any alteration to those rules with the potential to disrupt the development of such a critical segment of the economy should be undertaken by Congress. The Court should not act on this important question of current economic policy, solely to expiate a mistake it made over 50 years ago.

I

This Court "does not overturn its precedents lightly." . . . Departing from the doctrine of *stare decisis* is an "exceptional action" demanding "special justification." . . . The bar is even higher in fields in which Congress "exercises primary authority" and can, if it wishes, override this Court's decisions with contrary legislation. *Bay Mills*, 572 U. S., at ___ (slip op., at 16) (tribal sovereign immunity); see, *e.g.,* Kimble v. Marvel Entertainment, LLC, 576 U. S. ___, ___ (2015) (slip op., at 8) (statutory interpretation); Halliburton Co. v. Erica P. John Fund, Inc., 573 U. S. ___, ___ (2014) (slip op., at 12) (judicially created doctrine implementing a judicially created cause of action). In such cases, we have said that "the burden borne by the party advocating the abandonment of an established precedent" is "greater" than usual. . . . Patterson v. McLean Credit Union, 491 U. S. 164, 172 (1989). That is so "even where the error is a matter of serious concern, provided correction can be had by legislation." . . .

We have applied this heightened form of *stare decisis* in the dormant Commerce Clause context. Under our dormant Commerce Clause precedents, when Congress has not yet legislated on a matter of interstate commerce, it is the province of "the courts to formulate the rules." Southern Pacific Co. v. Arizona ex rel. Sullivan, 325 U. S. 761, 770 (1945). But because Congress "has plenary power to regulate commerce among the States," . . . it may at any time replace such judicial rules with legislation of its own, see Prudential Ins. Co. v. Benjamin, 328 U. S. 408, 424–425 (1946).

In *Quill*, this Court emphasized that the decision to hew to the physical-presence rule on *stare decisis* grounds was "made easier by the fact that the underlying issue is not only one that Congress may be better qualified to resolve, but also one that Congress has the ultimate power to resolve." . . .

II

This is neither the first, nor the second, but the third time this Court has been asked whether a State may obligate sellers with no physical presence within its borders to collect tax on sales to residents. Whatever salience the adage "third time's a charm" has in daily life, it is a poor guide to Supreme Court decisionmaking. If *stare decisis* applied with special force in *Quill*, it should be an even greater impediment to overruling precedent now, particularly since this Court in *Quill* "tossed [the ball] into Congress's court, for acceptance or not as that branch elects." . . .

Congress has in fact been considering whether to alter the rule established in *Bellas Hess* for some time. . . . Nothing in today's decision precludes Congress from continuing to seek a legislative solution. But by suddenly changing the ground rules, the Court may have waylaid Congress's consideration of the issue. . . .

The Court proceeds with an inexplicable sense of urgency. It asserts that the passage of time is only increasing the need to take the extraordinary step of overruling *Bellas Hess* and *Quill*: "Each year, the physical presence rule becomes further removed from economic reality and results in significant revenue losses to the States." . . . But evidence . . . indicates that the pendulum is swinging in the opposite direction, and has been for some time. States and local governments are already able to collect approximately 80 percent of the tax revenue that would be available if there were no physical-presence rule. Some companies, including the online behemoth Amazon, now voluntarily collect and remit sales tax in every State that assesses one—even those in which they have no physical presence. To the extent the physical-presence rule is harming States, the harm is apparently receding with time.

. . .

The Court [also] breezily disregards the costs that its decision will impose on retailers. . . .

The burden will fall disproportionately on small businesses. One vitalizing effect of the Internet has been connecting small, even "micro" businesses to potential buyers across the Nation. . . . The Court's decision today will surely have the effect of dampening opportunities for commerce in a broad range of new markets.

A good reason to leave these matters to Congress is that legislators may more directly consider the competing interests at stake. Unlike this Court,

Congress has the flexibility to address these questions in a wide variety of ways. As we have said in other dormant Commerce Clause cases, Congress "has the capacity to investigate and analyze facts beyond anything the Judiciary could match." . . .

    . . .

I respectfully dissent.

CHAPTER 7

SEPARATION OF POWERS

1. THE PRESIDENT'S POWER TO DETERMINE NATIONAL POLICY

B. INTERNATIONAL RELATIONS

Page 348. Add after Zivotofsky v. Kerry:

Trump v. Hawaii

585 U.S. ___, 138 S.Ct. 2392, ___ L.Ed.2d ___ (2018).

[The report of this case appears infra, at p. 129.]

2. CONGRESSIONAL INTERFERENCE WITH PRESIDENTIAL PREROGATIVES

B. APPOINTMENT, DISCHARGE, AND SUPERVISION OF "OFFICERS OF THE UNITED STATES"

Page 387. Add after Free Enterprise Fund v. Public Company Accounting Oversight Board:

NOTE ON WHO COUNTS AS AN "OFFICER OF THE UNITED STATES" SUBJECT TO THE APPOINTMENTS CLAUSE

In Lucia v. Securities and Exchange Commission, 585 U.S. ___, 138 S.Ct. 2044 (2018), the Court confronted the question whether administrative law judges (ALJs) within the Securities and Exchange Commission (SEC) constitute "Officers of the United States"—who, by the terms of the Appointments Clause, can be appointed only by "the President," "Courts of Law," or "Heads of Departments"—or instead employees, who can be appointed by other persons. ALJs within the SEC are not appointed by the Commissioners themselves, but by others within the agency. ALJs are typically given the task of presiding over administrative disciplinary proceedings, and have "authority to do all things necessary and appropriate" to ensure a "fair and orderly" adversarial proceeding. After a hearing is concluded, an ALJ issues an initial decision that the entire Commission may but need not review. If the Commission decides not to review an ALJ's initial decision, that decision becomes final and is "deemed the action of the Commission."

Raymond Lucia was charged by the Commission with various securities laws violations, and his case was assigned to an ALJ who, after a hearing, found a violation and imposed sanctions. Lucia appealed to the Commission, arguing that having an ALJ preside over his hearings violated the Appointments Clause. He lost this argument at the Commission and before the U.S. Court of Appeals for the D.C. Circuit, but prevailed in the Supreme Court 6–3. Writing for the

Court, Justice Kagan relied heavily on Freytag v. Commissioner, 501 U.S. 868 (1991), in which the Court had ruled that special trial judges (STJs) within the United States Tax Court constituted "Officers of the United States" whose appointment needed to comply with the Appointments Clause. Justice Kagan wrote:

"The sole question here is whether the Commission's ALJs are 'Officers of the United States' or simply employees of the Federal Government. The Appointments Clause prescribes the exclusive means of appointing 'Officers.' Only the President, a court of law, or a head of department can do so. See Art. II, § 2, cl. 2. And as all parties agree, none of those actors appointed [the ALJ who] heard Lucia's case; instead, SEC staff members gave him an ALJ slot. So if the Commission's ALJs are constitutional officers, Lucia raises a valid Appointments Clause claim. The only way to defeat his position is to show that those ALJs are not officers at all, but instead non-officer employees—part of the broad swath of 'lesser functionaries' in the Government's workforce. For if that is true, the Appointments Clause cares not a whit about who named them.

"Two decisions set out this Court's basic framework for distinguishing between officers and employees. [United States v. Germaine, 99 U.S. 508 (1879),] held that 'civil surgeons' (doctors hired to perform various physical exams) were mere employees because their duties were 'occasional or temporary' rather than 'continuing and permanent.' Stressing 'ideas of tenure [and] duration,' the Court there made clear that an individual must occupy a 'continuing' position established by law to qualify as an officer. [Buckley v. Valeo, 424 U.S. 1 (1976),] then set out another requirement, central to this case. It determined that members of a federal commission were officers only after finding that they 'exercis[ed] significant authority pursuant to the laws of the United States.' The inquiry thus focused on the extent of power an individual wields in carrying out his assigned functions.

"Both the *amicus* and the Government urge us to elaborate on *Buckley*'s 'significant authority' test, but another of our precedents makes that project unnecessary. The standard is no doubt framed in general terms, tempting advocates to add whatever glosses best suit their arguments. And maybe one day we will see a need to refine or enhance the test *Buckley* set out so concisely. But that day is not this one, because in Freytag v. Commissioner, 501 U. S. 868 (1991), we applied the unadorned 'significant authority' test to adjudicative officials who are near-carbon copies of the Commission's ALJs. [O]ur analysis there (sans any more detailed legal criteria) necessarily decides this case.

. . .

"*Freytag* says everything necessary to decide this case. To begin, the Commission's ALJs, like the Tax Court's STJs, hold a continuing office established by law. . . . Far from serving temporarily or episodically, SEC ALJs 'receive[ ] a career appointment.' . . .

"Still more, the Commission's ALJs exercise the same 'significant discretion' when carrying out the same 'important functions' as STJs do. Both sets of officials have all the authority needed to ensure fair and orderly adversarial hearings—indeed, nearly all the tools of federal trial judges. Consider in order the four specific (if overlapping) powers *Freytag* mentioned. First, the Commission's ALJs (like the Tax Court's STJs) 'take testimony.' More precisely, they '[r]eceiv[e] evidence' and '[e]xamine witnesses' at hearings, and may also take pre-hearing depositions. Second, the ALJs (like STJs) 'conduct trials.' . . . Third, the ALJs (like STJs) 'rule on the admissibility of evidence.' . . . And fourth, the ALJs (like STJs) 'have the power to enforce compliance with discovery orders.' . . . So point for point—straight from *Freytag*'s list—the Commission's ALJs have equivalent duties and powers as STJs in conducting adversarial inquiries.

"And at the close of those proceedings, ALJs issue decisions much like that in *Freytag*—except with potentially more independent effect. As the *Freytag* Court recounted, STJs 'prepare proposed findings and an opinion' adjudicating charges and assessing tax liabilities. Similarly, the Commission's ALJs issue decisions containing factual findings, legal conclusions, and appropriate remedies. And what happens next reveals that the ALJ can play the more autonomous role. In a major case like *Freytag*, a regular Tax Court judge must always review an STJ's opinion. And that opinion counts for nothing unless the regular judge adopts it as his own. By contrast, the SEC can decide against reviewing an ALJ decision at all. And when the SEC declines review (and issues an order saying so), the ALJ's decision itself 'becomes final' and is 'deemed the action of the Commission.' That last-word capacity makes this an *a fortiori* case: If the Tax Court's STJs are officers, as *Freytag* held, then the Commission's ALJs must be too."

Justice Thomas, who joined the majority opinion, wrote a separate concurrence joined by Justice Gorsuch (who also joined the majority) elaborating on situations that might not so easily be covered by *Freytag*. Justice Breyer wrote separately to say he would rule in Lucia's favor on statutory rather than constitutional grounds, and Justice Sotomayor wrote a dissent, joined by Justice Ginsburg.

PART 3

Government and the Individual: The Protection of Liberty and Property Under the Due Process and Equal Protection Clauses

CHAPTER 9

THE DUE PROCESS, CONTRACT, AND JUST COMPENSATION CLAUSES AND THE REVIEW OF THE REASONABLENESS OF LEGISLATION

1. ECONOMIC REGULATORY LEGISLATION

B. THE CONTRACT CLAUSE—WHAT DOES IT ADD TO THE DUE PROCESS LIMITATION?

Page 498. Add the following after Exxon Corp. v. Eagerton:

Sveen v. Melin, 584 U.S. ___, 138 S.Ct. 1815 (2018). A Minnesota law passed in 2002, similar to recent statutory changes in 25 other States, changed the former rule—that divorce did not affect an insured's designation of his or her spouse as the beneficiary of the insurance policy—to a default rule that "the dissolution or annulment of a marriage revokes any revocable[ ] beneficiary designation[ ] made by an individual to the individual's former spouse." The statute is premised on the theory that the policyholder would want that result, but if that is not the case it allows the policyholder after divorce to rename the ex-spouse as beneficiary. With only Justice Gorsuch dissenting, the Court held that the Contracts Clause did not prevent application of the current "revocation-on-divorce law" to a spousal beneficiary designation made before the statute was enacted that the insured, later divorced and now deceased, never changed. Justice Kagan's opinion for the Court included the following:

"[N]ot all laws affecting pre-existing contracts violate the Clause. See El Paso v. Simmons, 379 U.S. 497, 506–507 (1965). To determine when such a law crosses the constitutional line, this Court has long applied a two-step test. The threshold issue is whether the state law has 'operated as a substantial impairment of a contractual relationship.' *Allied Structural Steel Co.*, 438 U.S., at 244. In answering that question, the Court has considered the extent to which the law undermines the contractual bargain, interferes with a party's reasonable expectations, and prevents the party from safeguarding or reinstating his rights. See *id.*, at 246; *El Paso*, 379 U.S., at 514–515; Texaco, Inc. v. Short, 454 U.S. 516, 531 (1982). If such factors show a substantial impairment, the inquiry turns to the means and ends of the legislation. In particular, the Court has asked whether the state law is drawn in an 'appropriate' and 'reasonable' way to advance 'a significant and legitimate public purpose.' Energy Reserves Group, Inc. v. Kansas Power & Light Co., 459 U.S. 400, 411–412 (1983).

"Here, we may stop after step one because Minnesota's revocation-on-divorce statute does not substantially impair pre-existing contractual arrangements. True enough that in revoking a beneficiary designation, the law makes a significant change. As Melin says, the 'whole point' of buying life insurance is to provide the proceeds to the named beneficiary. . . . But three aspects of Minnesota's law, taken together, defeat Melin's argument that the change it effected 'severely impaired' her ex-husband's contract. . . . First, the statute is designed to reflect a policyholder's intent—and so to support, rather than impair, the contractual scheme. Second, the law is unlikely to disturb any policyholder's expectations because it does no more than a divorce court could always have done. And third, the statute supplies a mere default rule, which the policyholder can undo in a moment. . . ."

In her elaboration of these points, Justice Kagan emphasized that "[a]lthough there are exceptions, most divorcees do not aspire to enrich their former partners" and that "the insured's failure to change the beneficiary after a divorce is more likely the result of neglect than choice." Moreover, the statute "is unlikely to upset a policyholder's expectations at the time of contracting . . . because an insured cannot reasonably rely on a beneficiary designation remaining in place after a divorce" given that "divorce courts have wide discretion to divide property between spouses when a marriage ends." And "[f]inally, a policyholder can reverse the effect of the Minnesota statute with the stroke of a pen . . . by the simple act of sending a change-of-beneficiary form to his insurer" or more permanently by "agree[ing] to a divorce settlement continuing his ex-spouse's beneficiary status."

Justice Gorsuch's lone dissent first argued that the "Contracts Clause categorically prohibits states from passing '*any* . . . Law impairing the Obligation of Contracts.' Art. I, § 10, cl. 1 (emphasis added)." He asserted that "[f]or much of its history, this Court construed the Contracts Clause in this light." He then argued that "[e]ven under our modern precedents, . . . when a state alters life insurance contracts by undoing their beneficiary designations it surely 'substantially impairs' them." And he concluded that "[n]o one can offer any reasonable justification for this impairment in light of readily available alternatives." Among such alternatives, "the state could have easily achieved [its] goal without impairing contracts *at all*. It could have required courts to confirm that divorcing couples have reviewed their life insurance designations. . . . It could have instructed insurance companies to notify policyholders of their right to change beneficiary designations. It could have disseminated information on its own. Or it could have required attorneys in divorce proceedings to address the question with affected parties. . . . Yet there's no evidence Minnesota investigated any of them, let alone found them wanting."

C. THE JUST COMPENSATION CLAUSE OF THE FIFTH AMENDMENT—WHAT DOES IT ADD TO DUE PROCESS?

1. RESTRICTIONS ON PROPERTY USE

Page 515. Add the following before Horne v. Department of Agriculture:

Murr v. Wisconsin, 582 U.S. ___, 137 S.Ct. 1933 (2017). Petitioners, family members who owned two adjacent undeveloped lots (known as Lots "E" and "F") along the St. Croix river in Wisconsin, brought suit contending that state governmental entities took their property by enacting burdensome regulations that forbid separate improvement or sale of the parcels. For the area where petitioners' property is located, Wisconsin law contains a "merger" provision specifying that adjacent lots under common ownership may not be "sold or developed as separate lots" unless they meet a certain size requirement.

A decade later after assuming common ownership of the two lots, petitioners became interested in moving a cabin that was located on Lot F to a different portion of the lot and selling Lot E to fund the project. Because of their insufficient size, under state law the lots could not be sold or developed separately, so petitioners then sought variances from the St. Croix County Board of Adjustment to enable the building and improvement plan, including a variance to allow the separate sale or use of the lots. The Board denied the requests, and the state courts affirmed in relevant part. In particular, the Wisconsin Court of Appeals agreed with the Board's interpretation that the local ordinance "effectively merged" Lots E and F, so petitioners "could only sell or build on the single larger [merged] lot."

Petitioners then filed an action in state court, contending that the state and county regulations worked a regulatory taking by depriving them of "all, or practically all, of the use of Lot E because the lot cannot be sold or developed as a separate lot." Both sides submitted appraisal numbers to the trial court. "Respondents' appraisal included values of $698,300 for the lots together as regulated; $771,000 for the lots as two distinct buildable properties; and $373,000 for Lot F as a single lot with improvements[, whereas] Petitioners' appraisal included an unrebutted, estimated value of $40,000 for Lot E as an undevelopable lot, based on the counterfactual assumption that it could be sold as a separate property."

The trial court granted summary judgment to respondents on the ground that notwithstanding the regulations in place petitioners retained "several available options for the use and enjoyment of their property," including preserving or relocating the existing cabin, and eliminating the cabin and building a new residence on Lot E, on Lot F, or across both lots. The court specifically found petitioners had not been deprived of all economic value of their property, because the difference in value between treating the property as two lots versus a single larger lot was less than 10 percent.

The Wisconsin Court of Appeals—observing that it first had to "determine what, precisely, is the property at issue" and observing that the takings analysis should "properly focus[ ] . . . on the Murrs' property as a whole"—affirmed the grant of summary judgment, the Wisconsin Supreme Court denied review, and the Court granted certiorari.

In a 5–3 majority opinion written by Justice Kennedy, and joined by Justices Ginsburg, Breyer, Sotomayor and Kagan, the Court affirmed. Justice Kennedy began the Court's analysis laying out the broader regulatory takings framework:

". . . This area of the law has been characterized by 'ad hoc, factual inquiries, designed to allow careful examination and weighing of all the relevant circumstances.' . . . The Court has, however, stated two guidelines relevant here for determining when government regulation is so onerous that it constitutes a taking. First, 'with certain qualifications . . . a regulation which "denies all economically beneficial or productive use of land" will require compensation under the Takings Clause.' . . . Second, when a regulation impedes the use of property without depriving the owner of all economically beneficial use, a taking still may be found based on 'a complex of factors,' including (1) the economic impact of the regulation on the claimant; (2) the extent to which the regulation has interfered with distinct investment-backed expectations; and (3) the character of the governmental action. . . .

. . .

"A central dynamic of the Court's regulatory takings jurisprudence, then, is its flexibility. This has been and remains a means to reconcile two competing objectives central to regulatory takings doctrine. One is the individual's right to retain the interests and exercise the freedoms at the core of private property ownership. . . . Property rights are necessary to preserve freedom, for property ownership empowers persons to shape and to plan their own destiny in a world where governments are always eager to do so for them.

"The other persisting interest is the government's well-established power to 'adjus[t] rights for the public good.' . . . As Justice Holmes declared, 'Government hardly could go on if to some extent values incident to property could not be diminished without paying for every such change in the general law.' . . . In adjudicating regulatory takings cases a proper balancing of these principles requires a careful inquiry informed by the specifics of the case.

"This case presents a question that is linked to the ultimate determination whether a regulatory taking has occurred: What is the proper unit of property against which to assess the effect of the challenged governmental action? Put another way, '[b]ecause our test for regulatory taking requires us to compare the value that has been taken from the property with the value that remains in the property, one of the critical questions is determining how to define the unit of property "whose value is to furnish the denominator of the fraction."' . . . This Court . . . has explained that the question is important to the regulatory takings inquiry. 'To the extent that any portion of property is taken, that portion is always taken in its entirety; the relevant question, however, is whether the property taken is all, or only a portion of, the parcel in question.'

. . .

"While the Court has not set forth specific guidance on how to identify the relevant parcel for the regulatory taking inquiry, there are two concepts which the Court has indicated can be unduly narrow.

"First, the Court has declined to limit the parcel in an artificial manner to the portion of property targeted by the challenged regulation. . . .

. . .

"The second concept about which the Court has expressed caution is the view that property rights under the Takings Clause should be coextensive with those under state law. . . . The Court [has] explained that States do not have the unfettered authority to 'shape and define property rights and reasonable investment-backed expectations,' leaving landowners without recourse against unreasonable regulations. . . .

. . .

"As the foregoing discussion makes clear, no single consideration can supply the exclusive test for determining the denominator. Instead, courts must consider a number of factors. These include the treatment of the land under state and local law; the physical characteristics of the land; and the prospective value of the regulated land. The endeavor should determine whether reasonable expectations about property ownership would lead a landowner to anticipate that his holdings would be treated as one parcel, or, instead, as separate tracts. The inquiry is objective, and the reasonable expectations at issue derive from background customs and the whole of our legal tradition. . . .

"First, courts should give substantial weight to the treatment of the land, in particular how it is bounded or divided, under state and local law. The reasonable expectations of an acquirer of land must acknowledge legitimate restrictions affecting his or her subsequent use and dispensation of the property. . . . A valid takings claim will not evaporate just because a purchaser took title after the law was enacted. . . . A reasonable restriction that predates a landowner's acquisition, however, can be one of the objective factors that most landowners would reasonably consider in forming fair expectations about their property. . . .

"Second, courts must look to the physical characteristics of the landowner's property. These include the physical relationship of any distinguishable tracts, the parcel's topography, and the surrounding human and ecological environment. In particular, it may be relevant that the property is located in an area that is subject to, or likely to become subject to, environmental or other regulation. . . .

"Third, courts should assess the value of the property under the challenged regulation, with special attention to the effect of burdened land on the value of other holdings. Though a use restriction may decrease the market value of the property, the effect may be tempered if the regulated land adds value to the remaining property, such as by increasing privacy, expanding recreational space, or preserving surrounding natural beauty. A law that limits use of a landowner's small lot in one part of the city by reason of the landowner's nonadjacent holdings elsewhere may decrease the market value of the small lot in an unmitigated fashion. The absence of a special relationship between the holdings may counsel against consideration of all the holdings as a single parcel, making the restrictive law susceptible to a takings challenge. On the other hand, if the landowner's other property is adjacent to the small lot, the market value of the properties may well increase if their combination enables the expansion of a structure, or if development restraints for one part of the parcel protect the unobstructed skyline views of another part. That, in turn, may counsel in favor of treatment as a single parcel and may reveal the weakness of a regulatory takings challenge to the law.

. . .

"The State of Wisconsin and petitioners each ask this Court to adopt a formalistic rule to guide the parcel inquiry. Neither proposal suffices to capture the central legal and factual principles that inform reasonable expectations about property interests. Wisconsin would tie the definition of the parcel to state law, considering the two lots here as a single whole due to their merger under the challenged regulations. That approach, as already noted, simply assumes the answer to the question: May the State define the relevant parcel in a way that permits it to escape its responsibility to justify regulation in light of legitimate property expectations? It is, of course, unquestionable that the law must recognize those legitimate expectations in order to give proper weight to the rights of owners and the right of the State to pass reasonable laws and regulations. . . .

"Petitioners propose a different test that is also flawed. They urge the Court to adopt a presumption that lot lines define the relevant parcel in every instance, making Lot E the necessary denominator. Petitioners' argument, however, ignores the fact that lot lines are themselves creatures of state law, which can be overridden by the State in the reasonable exercise of its power. In effect, petitioners ask this Court to credit the aspect of state law that favors their preferred result (lot lines) and ignore that which does not (merger provision).

"This approach contravenes the Court's case law, which recognizes that reasonable land-use regulations do not work a taking. . . . Among other cases, Agins v. City of Tiburon, 447 U. S. 255 (1980), demonstrates the validity of this proposition because it upheld zoning regulations as a legitimate exercise of the government's police power. . . .

"The merger provision here is likewise a legitimate exercise of government power, as reflected by its consistency with a long history of state and local merger regulations that originated nearly a century ago. . . . Merger provisions often form part of a regulatory scheme that establishes a minimum lot size in order to preserve open space while still allowing orderly development. . . .

. . .

"Petitioners' reliance on lot lines also is problematic for another reason. Lot lines have varying degrees of formality across the States, so it is difficult to make them a standard measure of the reasonable expectations of property owners. Indeed, in some jurisdictions, lot lines may be subject to informal adjustment by property owners, with minimal government oversight. . . . The ease of modifying lot lines also creates the risk of gamesmanship by landowners, who might seek to alter the lines in anticipation of regulation that seems likely to affect only part of their property.

"Under the appropriate multifactor standard, it follows that for purposes of determining whether a regulatory taking has occurred here, petitioners' property should be evaluated as a single parcel consisting of Lots E and F together. First, the treatment of the property under state and local law indicates petitioners' property should be treated as one when considering the effects of the restrictions. As the Wisconsin courts held, the state and local regulations merged Lots E and F. . . . The decision to adopt the merger provision at issue here was for a specific and legitimate purpose, consistent with the widespread understanding that lot lines are not dominant or controlling in every case. . . . Petitioners' land was subject to this regulatory burden, moreover, only because of voluntary conduct in bringing the lots under common ownership after the regulations were enacted. As a result, the valid merger of the lots under state law informs the reasonable expectation they will be treated as a single property.

"Second, the physical characteristics of the property support its treatment as a unified parcel. The lots are contiguous along their longest edge. Their rough terrain and narrow shape make it reasonable to expect their range of potential uses might be limited. . . . The land's location along the river is also significant. Petitioners could have anticipated public regulation might affect their enjoyment of their property, as the Lower St. Croix was a regulated area under federal, state, and local law long before petitioners possessed the land.

"Third, the prospective value that Lot E brings to Lot F supports considering the two as one parcel for purposes of determining if there is a regulatory taking. Petitioners are prohibited from selling Lots E and F separately or from building separate residential structures on each. Yet this restriction is mitigated by the benefits of using the property as an integrated whole, allowing increased privacy and recreational space, plus the optimal location of any improvements. . . .

"The special relationship of the lots is further shown by their combined valuation. Were Lot E separately saleable but still subject to the development restriction, petitioners' appraiser would value the property at only $40,000. We express no opinion on the validity of this figure. We also note the number is not particularly helpful for understanding petitioners' retained value in the properties because Lot E, under the regulations, cannot be sold without Lot F. The point that is useful for these purposes is that the combined lots are valued at $698,300, which is far greater than the summed value of the separate regulated lots (Lot F with its cabin at $373,000, according to respondents' appraiser, and Lot E as an undevelopable plot at $40,000, according to petitioners' appraiser). The value added by the lots' combination shows their complementarity and supports their treatment as one parcel.

"The State Court of Appeals was correct in analyzing petitioners' property as a single unit. Petitioners allege that in doing so, the state court applied a categorical rule that all contiguous, commonly owned holdings must be combined for Takings Clause analysis. . . . This does not appear to be the case, however, for the precedent relied on by the Court of Appeals addressed multiple factors before treating contiguous properties as one parcel. . . . The judgment below, furthermore, may be affirmed on any ground permitted by the law and record. . . . To the extent the state court treated the two lots as one parcel based on a bright-line rule, nothing in this opinion approves that methodology, as distinct from the result.

"Considering petitioners' property as a whole, the state court was correct to conclude that petitioners cannot establish a compensable taking in these circumstances. Petitioners have not suffered a taking under *Lucas*, as they have not been deprived of all economically beneficial use of their property. . . . They can use the property for residential purposes, including an enhanced, larger residential improvement. The property has not lost all economic value, as its value has decreased by less than 10 percent. . . .

"Petitioners furthermore have not suffered a taking under the more general test of *Penn Central*. . . . The expert appraisal relied upon by the state courts refutes any claim that the economic impact of the regulation is severe. Petitioners cannot claim that they reasonably expected to sell or develop their lots separately given the regulations which predated their acquisition of both lots. Finally, the governmental action was a reasonable land-use regulation, enacted as part of a coordinated federal, state, and local effort to preserve the river and surrounding land."

   . . .

Chief Justice Roberts, joined by Justices Thomas and Alito, dissented, saying that the Court's "bottom-line conclusion [finding no taking] does not trouble me; the majority presents a fair case that the Murrs can still make good use of both lots, and that the ordinance is a commonplace tool to preserve scenic areas, such as the Lower St. Croix River, for the benefit of landowners and the public alike.

"Where the majority goes astray, however, is in concluding that the definition of the 'private property' at issue in a case such as this turns on an elaborate test looking not only to state and local law, but also to (1) 'the physical characteristics of the land,' (2) 'the prospective value of the regulated land,' (3) the 'reasonable expectations' of the owner, and (4) 'background customs and the whole of our legal tradition.' . . . Our decisions have, time and again, declared that the Takings Clause protects private property rights as state law creates and defines them. By securing such *established* property rights, the Takings Clause protects individuals from being forced to bear the full weight of actions that should be borne by the public at large. The majority's new, malleable definition of 'private property'—adopted solely 'for purposes of th[e] takings inquiry,' " . . .— undermines that protection.

"I would stick with our traditional approach: State law defines the boundaries of distinct parcels of land, and those boundaries should determine the 'private property' at issue in regulatory takings cases. Whether a regulation effects a taking of that property is a separate question, one in which common ownership of adjacent property may be taken into account. Because the majority departs from these settled principles, I respectfully dissent.

. . .

"Staying with a state law approach to defining 'private property' would make our job in this case fairly easy. The Murr siblings acquired Lot F in 1994 and Lot E a year later. Once the lots fell into common ownership, the challenged ordinance prevented them from being 'sold or developed as separate lots' because neither contained a sufficiently large area of buildable land. . . . The Murrs argued that the ordinance amounted to a taking of Lot E, but the State of Wisconsin and St. Croix County proposed that both lots together should count as the relevant 'parcel.' The trial court sided with the State and County, and the Wisconsin Court of Appeals affirmed. Rather than considering whether Lots E and F are separate parcels under Wisconsin law, however, the Court of Appeals adopted a takings-specific approach to defining the relevant parcel. . . . Relying on what it called a 'well-established rule' for 'regulatory takings cases,' the court explained "that contiguous property under common ownership is considered as a whole regardless of the number of parcels contained therein.' . . . And because Lots E and F were side by side and owned by the Murrs, the case was straightforward: The two lots were one 'parcel' for the regulatory takings analysis. The court therefore evaluated the effect of the ordinance on the two lots considered together.

"As I see it, the Wisconsin Court of Appeals was wrong to apply a takings-specific definition of the property at issue. Instead, the court should have asked whether, under general state law principles, Lots E and F are legally distinct parcels of land. I would therefore vacate the judgment below and remand for the court to identify the relevant property using ordinary principles of Wisconsin property law.

"After making that state law determination, the next step would be to determine whether the challenged ordinance amounts to a 'taking.' . . . "

Justice Thomas wrote a separate dissent, expressing agreement with Chief Justice Roberts' dissent but also urging the Court "to take a fresh look at our regulatory takings jurisprudence, to see whether it can be grounded in the original public meaning of the Takings Clause of the Fifth Amendment or the Privileges or Immunities Clause of the Fourteenth Amendment."

Justice Gorsuch took no part in the consideration or decision of this case.

2. PROTECTION OF PERSONAL LIBERTIES

B. FAMILY AND MARITAL RELATIONSHIPS

Page 572. Add after Obergefell v. Hodges:

Pavan v. Smith, 582 U.S. ___, 137 S.Ct. 2075 (2017). In a per curiam opinion, the Court summarily reversed an Arkansas Supreme Court judgment upholding an Arkansas regulatory scheme that "generally requires the name of the mother's male spouse to appear on the child's birth certificate—regardless of his biological relationship to the child"—but does not require the State to "issue birth certificates including the female spouses of women who give birth in the State." In the majority's view, "that differential treatment infringes *Obergefell's* commitment to provide same-sex couples 'the constellation of benefits that the States have linked to marriage,'" . . . .

The suit was brought by "two married same-sex couples who conceived children through anonymous sperm donation." When they sought birth certificates for their newborns, "the Arkansas Department of Health issued certificates bearing only the birth mother's name." The Court noted that "all parties agree [that] the requirement that a married woman's husband appear on her child's birth certificate applies in cases where the couple conceived by means of artificial insemination with the help of an anonymous sperm donor." The Court's opinion contained these passages:

"... [S]ame-sex parents in Arkansas lack the same right as opposite-sex parents to be listed on a child's birth certificate, a document often used for important transactions like making medical decisions for a child or enrolling a child in school. . . .

"*Obergefell* proscribes such disparate treatment. As we explained there, a State may not 'exclude same-sex couples from civil marriage on the same terms and conditions as opposite-sex couples.' . . . Indeed, in listing those terms and conditions—the 'rights, benefits, and responsibilities' to which same-sex couples, no less than opposite-sex couples, must have access—we expressly identified 'birth and death certificates.' . . . That was no accident: Several of the plaintiffs in *Obergefell* challenged a State's refusal to recognize their same-sex spouses on their children's birth certificates. . . . In considering those challenges, we held the relevant state laws unconstitutional to the extent they treated same-sex couples differently from opposite-sex couples. . . . That holding applies with equal force [here].

"Echoing the court below, the State defends its birth-certificate law on the ground that being named on a child's birth certificate is not a benefit that attends marriage. Instead, the State insists, a birth certificate is simply a device for recording biological parentage—regardless of whether the child's parents are married. But Arkansas law makes birth certificates about more than just genetics. As already discussed, when an opposite-sex couple conceives a child by way of anonymous sperm donation—just as the petitioners did here—state law requires the placement of the birth mother's husband on the child's birth certificate. . . . And that is so even though (as the State concedes) the husband 'is definitively not the biological father' in those circumstances. . . .* Arkansas has thus chosen to make its birth certificates more than a mere marker of biological relationships: The State uses those certificates to give married parents a form of legal recognition that is not available to unmarried parents. Having made that choice, Arkansas may not, consistent with *Obergefell*, deny married same-sex couples that recognition."

Justice Gorsuch, joined by Justices Thomas and Alito dissented, finding this case inappropriate for the "strong medicine of summary reversal." He wrote in pertinent part:

". . . [N]othing in *Obergefell* spoke (let alone clearly) to . . . whether [the Arkansas law], or a state supreme court decision upholding it, must go. The statute in question establishes a set of rules designed to ensure that the biological parents of a child are listed on the child's birth certificate. Before the state supreme court, the State argued that rational reasons exist for a biology based birth registration regime, reasons that in no way offend *Obergefell*—like ensuring government officials can identify public health trends and helping individuals determine their biological lineage, citizenship, or susceptibility to genetic disorders. In an opinion that did not in any way seek to defy but rather earnestly engage *Obergefell*, the state supreme court agreed. And it is very hard to see what is wrong with this conclusion for, just as the state court recognized, nothing in *Obergefell* indicates that a birth registration regime based on biology, one no doubt with many analogues across the country and throughout history, offends the Constitution. . . . Neither does anything in today's opinion purport to identify any constitutional problem with a biology based birth registration regime. So whatever else we might do with this case, summary reversal would not exactly seem the obvious course.

. . .

"[I]f the artificial insemination statute [§ 9–10–201] is the concern, it's still hard to see how summary reversal should follow for at least a few reasons. First, petitioners didn't actually challenge [it] in their lawsuit. Instead, petitioners sought and the trial court granted relief eliminating the State's authority . . . to enforce a birth registration regime generally based on biology. On appeal, the state supreme court simply held that this overbroad remedy wasn't commanded by *Obergefell* or the Constitution. And, again, nothing in today's opinion for the Court identifies anything wrong, let alone clearly wrong, in that conclusion. Second, though petitioners' lawsuit didn't challenge § 9–10–201, the State has repeatedly conceded that the benefits afforded nonbiological parents under § 9–10–201 must be afforded equally to both same-sex and opposite-sex couples. So that in this particular case and all others of its kind, the State agrees, the female spouse of the birth mother must be listed on birth certificates too. Third, further proof still of the state of the law in Arkansas today is the fact that, when it comes to adoption (a situation not present in this case but another one in which Arkansas departs from biology based registration), the State tells us that

---

*   [O]ther factual scenarios (beyond those present in this case) similarly show that the State's birth certificates are about more than genetic parentage. For example, when an Arkansas child is adopted, the State places the child's original birth certificate under seal and issues a new birth certificate—unidentifiable as an amended version—listing the child's (nonbiological) adoptive parents.

adopting parents are eligible for placement on birth certificates without respect to sexual orientation.

". . . [I]t is not even clear what the Court expects to happen on remand that hasn't happened already. . . . Perhaps the state supreme court could memorialize the State's concession on § 9–10–201, even though that law wasn't fairly challenged and such a chore is hardly the usual reward for seeking faithfully to apply, not evade, this Court's mandates."

C. PERSONAL AUTONOMY

Page 608. Add after Planned Parenthood of Southeastern Pennsylvania v. Casey:

National Institute of Family and Life Advocates v. Becerra

585 U.S. ___, 138 S.Ct. 2361, ___ L.Ed.2d ___ (2018).

[The report of this case appears infra, at p. 84.]

Page 636. Add after Obergefell v. Hodges:

Pavan v. Smith, 582 U.S. ___, 137 S.Ct. 2075 (2017).

[The report of this case appears supra, p. 47.]

CHAPTER 10

THE EQUAL PROTECTION CLAUSE AND THE REVIEW OF THE REASONABLENESS OF LEGISLATION

3. SUSPECT CLASSIFICATIONS

A. CLASSIFICATIONS DISADVANTAGING RACIAL MINORITIES

Page 691. Add footnote a after Korematsu v. United States:

ᵃ   In Trump v. Hawaii, 585 U.S. ___, 138 S.Ct. 2392 (2018), the Court, 5–4, rejected an Establishment Clause challenge to an Executive Order signed by President Trump (who had made a number of disparaging statements about Muslims during his presidential campaign and after he took office) that imposed restrictions on entry into the United States by foreign nationals from a number of mostly Muslim-majority countries. The Court concluded that "because there is persuasive evidence that the entry suspension has a legitimate grounding in national security concerns, quite apart from any religious hostility, we must accept that independent justification." At the end of his opinion for the Court, responding to the dissent's invocation of *Korematsu*, Chief Justice Roberts wrote this:

"... *Korematsu* has nothing to do with this case. The forcible relocation of U. S. citizens to concentration camps, solely and explicitly on the basis of race, is objectively unlawful and outside the scope of Presidential authority. But it is wholly inapt to liken that morally repugnant order to a facially neutral policy denying certain foreign nationals the privilege of admission. . . .

"The dissent's reference to *Korematsu*, however, affords this Court the opportunity to make express what is already obvious: *Korematsu* was gravely wrong the day it was decided, has been overruled in the court of history, and—to be clear—'has no place in law under the Constitution.' 323 U.S., at 248 (Jackson, J., dissenting)."

For developments between the *Korematsu* decision and Trump v. Hawaii, see infra p. 692 note "a". For the full report of Trump v. Hawaii, see infra, at p. 129.

C. CLASSIFICATIONS BASED ON GENDER

Page 755. Add after Nguyen v. Immigration and Naturalization Service:

Sessions v. Morales-Santana, 582 U.S. ___, 137 S.Ct. 1678 (2017). Under 8 U. S. C. § 1401(a)(7), a child born abroad to married parents, only one of whom is a U.S. citizen, may acquire citizenship at birth only if the citizen parent had resided in the United States for at least a certain period of time before the child was born. (When Morales-Santana was born the requirement was 10 years, at least five of them after the age of 14, but now the residence requirement is 5 years total, two after 14). Those same rules apply to unwed U.S. citizen fathers under § 1409(a), but § 1409(c) creates an exception in the case of an unwed U.S. citizen mother, who can transmit her citizenship to her child if she has lived in the U.S. for just one year before the birth. In a deportation proceeding, Morales-Santana—who has lived most of his life in the U.S.—claimed citizenship through his biological father's U.S. citizenship, even though his father left Puerto Rico, which is part of the United States, for the Dominican Republic, which is not, 20 days shy of his 19th birthday (and therefore just shy of the 5 year after-turning-14 requirement). Morales-Santana contended that the differential treatment of unwed citizen fathers and mothers reflected in the comparison of §§ 1409(a) and 1409(c) violated the equal protection component of the Fifth Amendment's due process clause. He lost in the Board of Immigration Appeals, but the Second Circuit reversed and also held that he derived citizenship from his father. The Supreme Court affirmed on the merits of the equal protection ruling, but reversed as to the remedy. Justice Ginsburg's opinion for the Court included the following:

III

"Sections 1401 and 1409. . . date from an era when the lawbooks of our Nation were rife with overbroad generalizations about the way men and women are. . . .

"Laws granting or denying benefits 'on the basis of the sex of the qualifying parent,' our post-1970 decisions affirm, differentiate on the basis of gender, and therefore attract heightened review under the Constitution's equal protection guarantee. . . .

"Prescribing one rule for mothers, another for fathers, § 1409 is of the same genre as the classifications we declared unconstitutional in *Reed*, *Frontiero*, *Wiesenfeld*, *Goldfarb*, and *Westcott*. . . . Successful defense of legislation that differentiates on the basis of gender . . . requires an 'exceedingly persuasive justification.' *Virginia*, ...

A

"The defender of legislation that differentiates on the basis of gender must show 'at least that the [challenged] classification serves important governmental objectives and that the discriminatory means employed are substantially related to the achievement of those objectives.' *Virginia*, . . . Moreover, the classification must substantially serve an important governmental interest *today*, for 'in interpreting the [e]qual [p]rotection [guarantee], [we have] recognized that new insights and societal understandings can reveal unjustified inequality . . . that once passed unnoticed and unchallenged.' Obergefell v. Hodges, ...

1

"History reveals what lurks behind § 1409. Enacted in the Nationality Act of 1940 . . ., § 1409 ended a century and a half of congressional silence on the citizenship of children born abroad to unwed parents. During this era, two once habitual, but now untenable, assumptions pervaded our Nation's citizenship laws and underpinned judicial and administrative rulings: In marriage, husband is dominant, wife subordinate; unwed mother is the natural and sole guardian of a non-marital child.

". . . [F]rom 1790 until 1934, the foreign-born child of a married couple gained U. S. citizenship only through the father.

"For unwed parents, the father-controls tradition never held sway. Instead, the mother was regarded as the child's natural and sole guardian. . . .

"In the 1940 Act, Congress discarded the father-controls assumption concerning married parents, but codified the mother-as-sole-guardian perception regarding unmarried parents. . . .

"This unwed-mother-as-natural-guardian notion renders § 1409's gender-based residency rules understandable. Fearing that a foreign-born child could turn out 'more alien than American in character,' the administration believed that a citizen parent with lengthy ties to the United States would counteract the influence of the alien parent. . . . Concern about the attachment of foreign-born children to the United States explains the treatment of unwed citizen fathers, who, according to the familiar stereotype, would care little about, and have scant contact with, their nonmarital children. For unwed citizen mothers, however, there was no need for a prolonged residency prophylactic: The alien father, who might transmit foreign ways, was presumptively out of the picture. . . .

2

. . .

". . . [T]he Court has held that no 'important [governmental] interest' is served by laws grounded, as § 1409(a) and (c) are, in the obsolescing view that 'unwed fathers [are] invariably less qualified and entitled than mothers' to take responsibility for nonmarital children. Caban v. Mohammed, 441 U. S. 380, 382, 394 (1979). Overbroad generalizations of that order, the Court has come to comprehend, have a constraining impact, descriptive though they may be of the way many people still order their lives. . . . In light of the equal protection jurisprudence this Court has developed since 1971, . . . § 1409(a) and (c)'s discrete duration-of-residence requirements for unwed mothers and fathers who have accepted parental responsibility is stunningly anachronistic."

Justice Ginsburg distinguished the *Nguyen* case, on which the Government sought to rely, by first noting that this case did not "renew the contest over § 1409's paternal-acknowledgment requirement[,]" given that "the Government does not dispute that Morales-Santana's father, by marrying Morales-Santana's mother, satisfied that requirement[,]" and also by noting as follows:

"Unlike the paternal-acknowledgment requirement at issue in *Nguyen* . . ., the physical-presence requirements now before us relate solely to the duration of the parent's prebirth residency in the United States, not to the parent's filial tie to the child. As the Court of Appeals observed . . ., a man needs no more time in the United States than a woman 'in order to have assimilated citizenship-related values to transmit to [his] child.' . . . And unlike *Nguyen*'s parental-acknowledgment requirement, § 1409(a)'s age-calibrated physical-presence requirements cannot fairly be described as 'minimal.' "

The Government argued "that the statute serves two important objectives: (1) ensuring a connection between the child to become a citizen and the United States and (2) preventing 'statelessness,' *i.e.*, a child's possession of no citizenship at all." But "[e]ven indulging the assumption that Congress intended § 1409 to serve these interests, . . . neither rationale survives heightened scrutiny." Justice Ginsburg's response included this analysis:

1

". . . The Government does not contend, nor could it, that unmarried men take more time to absorb U. S. values than unmarried women do. Instead, it presents a novel argument . . . .

"An unwed mother, the Government urges, is the child's only 'legally recognized' parent at the time of childbirth. . . . An unwed citizen father enters the scene later, as a second parent. A longer physical connection to the United

States is warranted for the unwed father, the Government maintains, because of the 'competing national influence' of the alien mother. . . .

"Underlying this apparent design is the assumption that the alien father of a nonmarital child born abroad to a U. S.-citizen mother will not accept parental responsibility. For an actual affiliation between alien father and nonmarital child would create the 'competing national influence' that, according to the Government, justifies imposing on unwed U. S.-citizen fathers, but not unwed U. S.-citizen mothers, lengthy physical-presence requirements. Hardly gender neutral, that assumption conforms to the long-held view that unwed fathers care little about, indeed are strangers to, their children. Lump characterization of that kind, however, no longer passes equal protection inspection.

"Accepting, *arguendo*, that Congress intended the diverse physical-presence prescriptions to serve an interest in ensuring a connection between the foreign-born nonmarital child and the United States, the gender-based means scarcely serve the posited end. The scheme permits the transmission of citizenship to children who have no tie to the United States so long as their mother was a U. S. citizen continuously present in the United States for one year at any point in her life *prior* to the child's birth. The transmission holds even if the mother marries the child's alien father immediately after the child's birth and never returns with the child to the United States. At the same time, the legislation precludes citizenship transmission by a U. S.-citizen father who falls a few days short of meeting § 1401(a)(7)'s longer physical-presence requirements, even if the father acknowledges paternity on the day of the child's birth and raises the child in the United States. One cannot see in this driven-by-gender scheme the close means-end fit required to survive heightened scrutiny. . . .

2

"The Government maintains that Congress established the gender-based residency differential in § 1409(a) and (c) to reduce the risk that a foreign-born child of a U. S. citizen would be born stateless. . . . But there is little reason to believe that a statelessness concern prompted the diverse physical-presence requirements. Nor has the Government shown that the risk of statelessness disproportionately endangered the children of unwed mothers.

". . . [N]othing in the congressional hearings and reports on the 1940 and 1952 Acts 'refer[s] to the problem of statelessness for children born abroad.' . . . The justification for § 1409's gender-based dichotomy . . . was not the child's plight, it was the mother's role as the 'natural guardian' of a nonmarital child. . . . It will not do to 'hypothesiz[e] or inven[t]' governmental purposes for gender classifications '*post hoc* in response to litigation.' *Virginia*, ..."

Justice Ginsburg also found "the Government's risk-of-statelessness argument" infected by "an assumption without foundation." Because foreign laws placed "formidable impediments . . . on an unwed mother's transmission of citizenship to her child[,]" experts had concluded that " 'the risk of parenting stateless children abroad was, as of [1940 and 1952], and remains today, substantial for unmarried U. S. fathers, a risk perhaps greater than that for unmarried U. S. mothers.' " Thus, "[o]ne can hardly characterize as gender neutral a scheme allegedly attending to the risk of statelessness for children of unwed U. S. citizen mothers while ignoring the same risk for children of unwed U. S.-citizen fathers.

. . .

"In sum, the Government has advanced no 'exceedingly persuasive' justification for § 1409(a) and (c)'s gender-specific residency and age criteria. Those disparate criteria, we hold, cannot withstand inspection under a Constitution that requires the Government to respect the equal dignity and stature of its male and female citizens."[21]

Despite that holding, the Court decided it was "not equipped to grant the relief Morales-Santana seeks, *i.e.*, extending to his father (and, derivatively, to him) the benefit of the one-year physical-presence term § 1409(c) reserves for unwed mothers." Equal treatment could be achieved either by extending the favorable treatment provided to unwed citizen mothers as an exception, as he requested, or by lengthening the physical-presence requirement for unwed citizen mothers to be the same as that for unwed citizen fathers. The "choice . . . is governed by the legislature's intent, as revealed by the statute[,]" and "striking the discriminatory exception . . . leads here to extending the general rule of longer physical-presence requirements to cover the previously favored group." In general, "a court should ' "measure the intensity of commitment to the residual policy" '—the main rule, not the exception—' "and consider the degree of potential disruption of the statutory scheme that would occur by extension as opposed to abrogation." ' " Justice Ginsburg continued:

"The residual policy here, the longer physical-presence requirement stated in §§ 1401(a)(7) and 1409, evidences Congress' recognition of 'the importance of residence in this country as the talisman of dedicated attachment.' . . . And the potential for 'disruption of the statutory scheme' is large. For if § 1409(c)'s one-year dispensation were extended to unwed citizen fathers, would it not be irrational to retain the longer term when the U. S.-citizen parent is married? Disadvantageous treatment of marital children in comparison to nonmarital children is scarcely a purpose one can sensibly attribute to Congress.

"Although extension of benefits is customary in federal benefit cases, . . . all indicators in this case point in the opposite direction. Put to the choice, Congress, we believe, would have abrogated § 1409(c)'s exception, preferring preservation of the general rule.

". . . Going forward, Congress may address the issue and settle on a uniform prescription that neither favors nor disadvantages any person on the basis of gender. In the interim, as the Government suggests, § 1401(a)(7)'s now-five-year requirement should apply, prospectively, to children born to unwed U. S.-citizen mothers. . . ."

Justice Thomas, joined by Justice Alito, concurred in the judgment in part, taking the position that because the "Court's remedial holding resolves this case[,] . . . it is unnecessary for us to decide whether the 1952 version of the INA was constitutional, . . . or whether other immigration laws (such as the current versions of §§ 1401(g) and 1409) are constitutional."

Justice Gorsuch took no part in the consideration or decision of this case.

---

[21] Justice Thomas, joined by Justice Alito, sees our equal protection ruling as "unnecessary," given our remedial holding. But, "as we have repeatedly emphasized, discrimination itself . . . perpetuat[es] 'archaic and stereotypic notions' " incompatible with the equal treatment guaranteed by the Constitution. Heckler v. Mathews, 465 U. S. 728, 739 (1984) (quoting Mississippi Univ. for Women v. Hogan, 458 U. S. 718, 725 (1982)).

G. WHAT OTHER CLASSIFICATIONS WILL PROVOKE HEIGHTENED SCRUTINY?

2. CLASSIFICATIONS DISADVANTAGING THE RETARDED, HOMOSEXUALS, THE ELDERLY, THE POOR, ETC.

Page 889. Add after Obergefell v. Hodges:

Pavan v. Smith, 582 U.S. ___, 137 S.Ct. 2075 (2017).
[The report of this case appears supra, p. 47.]

4. PROTECTION OF PERSONAL LIBERTIES

B. VOTING AND ELECTIONS

2. LEGISLATIVE DISTRICTING

Page 927. Add after Alabama Legislative Black Caucus v. Alabama:

Bethune-Hill v. Virginia State Board of Elections, 580 U.S. ___, 137 S.Ct. 788 (2017). Once again, the Court found that a three-judge District Court had used incorrect legal standards when evaluating claims of impermissible racial gerrymandering. In the process of redistricting "to ensure proper numerical apportionment for the Virginia House of Delegates" after the 2010 census, the Virginia legislature also drew new district boundaries for 12 districts "with a goal of ensuring that each district would have a black voting age population (BVAP) of at least 55%." Voters in those districts challenged each of them as an unconstitutional racial gerrymander, but the District Court found that as to 11 of them "race did not predominate" in the line-drawing. On appeal, the Supreme Court agreed with the challengers "that the District Court misunderstood the relevant precedents when it required the[m] to establish, as a prerequisite to showing racial predominance, an actual conflict between the enacted plan and traditional redistricting principles." Justice Kennedy's majority opinion elaborated:

"The State's theory in this case is irreconcilable with *Miller* and *Shaw II*. The State insists, for example, that the harm from racial gerrymandering lies not in racial line-drawing *per se* but in grouping voters of the same race together when they otherwise lack shared interests. But 'the constitutional violation' in racial gerrymandering cases stems from the 'racial purpose of state action, not its stark manifestation.' *Miller*, ... The Equal Protection Clause does not prohibit misshapen districts. It prohibits unjustified racial classifications.

"The State contends further that race does not have a prohibited effect on a district's lines if the legislature could have drawn the same lines in accordance with traditional criteria. That argument parallels the District Court's reasoning that a reapportionment plan is not an express racial classification unless a racial purpose is apparent from the face of the plan based on the irregular nature of the lines themselves.... This is incorrect. The racial predominance inquiry concerns the actual considerations that provided the essential basis for the lines drawn, not *post hoc* justifications the legislature in theory could have used but in reality did not.

"Traditional redistricting principles, moreover, are numerous and malleable. The District Court here identified no fewer than 11 race-neutral redistricting factors a legislature could consider, some of which are 'surprisingly ethereal' and 'admi[t] of degrees.' . . . By deploying those factors in various combinations and permutations, a State could construct a plethora of potential maps that look consistent with traditional, race-neutral principles. But if race for its own sake is the overriding reason for choosing one map over others, race still may predominate.

"For these reasons, a conflict or inconsistency between the enacted plan and traditional redistricting criteria is not a threshold requirement or a mandatory precondition in order for a challenger to establish a claim of racial gerrymandering. Of course, a conflict or inconsistency may be persuasive circumstantial evidence tending to show racial predomination, but there is no rule requiring challengers to present this kind of evidence in every case.

"As a practical matter, in many cases, perhaps most cases, challengers will be unable to prove an unconstitutional racial gerrymander without evidence that the enacted plan conflicts with traditional redistricting criteria. . . . [Still,] there may be cases where challengers will be able to establish racial predominance in the absence of an actual conflict by presenting direct evidence of the legislative purpose and intent or other compelling circumstantial evidence."

The Court also agreed with the challengers "that the District Court erred . . . when it considered the legislature's racial motive only to the extent that the challengers identified deviations from traditional redistricting criteria that were attributable to race and not to some other factor[, thereby] foreclos[ing] a holistic analysis of each district [that] led the District Court to give insufficient weight to the 55% BVAP target and other relevant evidence that race predominated." Because the "ultimate . . . inquiry . . . is the legislature's predominant motive for the design of the district as a whole[, a] court faced with a racial gerrymandering claim . . . must consider all of the lines of the district at issue; any explanation for a particular portion of the lines, moreover, must take account of the districtwide context. Concentrating on particular portions in isolation may obscure the significance of relevant districtwide evidence, such as stark splits in the racial composition of populations moved into and out of disparate parts of the district, or the use of an express racial target. A holistic analysis is necessary to give that kind of evidence its proper weight."

As to these 11 districts, the Court remanded for the District Court "to determine in the first instance the extent to which, under the proper standard, race directed the[ir] shape . . . . And if race did predominate, it is proper for the District Court to determine in the first instance whether strict scrutiny is satisfied."

The District Court had found that the challenge to the remaining district—District 75—also failed, despite its conclusion that race did predominate in its configuration, because "the State's predominant use of race in District 75 was narrowly tailored to achieve compliance with § 5" of the Voting Rights Act. The Court upheld that ruling. First, the challengers "do not dispute that compliance with § 5 was a compelling interest at the relevant time. As in previous cases, therefore, the Court assumes, without deciding, that the State's interest in complying with the Voting Rights Act was compelling." Second, under the *Alabama* case, the State is not required "to show that its action was 'actually . . . necessary' to avoid a statutory violation, so that, but for its use of race, the State would have lost in court. . . . Rather, the requisite strong basis in evidence exists when the legislature has '*good reasons* to believe' it must use race in order to satisfy the Voting Rights Act, 'even if a court does not find that the actions were necessary for statutory compliance.' " And third, "[u]nder the facts found by the District Court, the legislature performed th[e right] kind of functional analysis of District 75 when deciding upon the 55% BVAP target." Given the "careful assessment of local conditions and structures, the State had a strong basis in evidence to believe a 55% BVAP floor was required to avoid retrogression." In these cases, "the District Court's factual findings are reviewed only for clear error[,]" and the "record here supports the legislature's conclusion that this was one instance where a 55% BVAP was necessary for black voters to have a functional working majority."

Justice Alito concurred in part and concurred in the judgment, "join[ing] the opinion of the Court insofar as it upholds the constitutionality of District 75" and "concur[ring] in the judgment of the Court insofar as it vacates and remands the judgment below with respect to all the remaining districts." He emphasized, however, that "[u]nlike the Court, . . . I would hold that all these districts must satisfy strict scrutiny."

Justice Thomas concurred in the judgment in part and dissented in part. He "concur[red] in the Court's judgment reversing the District Court's decision to uphold 11 of the 12 districts[,]" but did "not agree . . . with the Court's decision to leave open the question whether race predominated in those districts and, thus, whether they are subject to strict scrutiny." He reiterated his view that once a legislature concedes it has intentionally drawn districts as majority-black districts, strict scrutiny is mandated. And he "disagree[d] with the majority's determination that District 75 satisfies strict scrutiny[, because] . . . the State has neither asserted a compelling state interest nor narrowly tailored its use of race." He "would hold that complying with § 5 of the Voting Rights Act is not a compelling interest" since he has concluded that § 5 is unconstitutional. He retained "serious doubts about the Court's standard for narrow tailoring, as characterized today and in Alabama Legislative Black Caucus v. Alabama, 575 U. S. ___ (2015)[,]" finding "[t]hat approach to narrow tailoring—deferring to a State's belief that it has good reasons to use race—. . . 'strict' in name only. . . ." Accordingly, in his view the State's "efforts fall far short of establishing that a 55% black voting-age population bears a more ' "exact connection" ' to the State's interest than any alternative percentage."

Cooper v. Harris, 581 U.S. ___, 137 S.Ct. 1455 (2017). Again applying a deferential standard of review to the factual findings of a three-judge District Court in its resolution of a racial gerrymandering claim, the Court affirmed a judgment holding unconstitutional North Carolina's drawing, after the 2010 census, of two congressional districts with long time "substantial populations of black voters[.]" Under the never-challenged 2001 redistricting map required by population changes revealed in the 2000 census, "neither District 1 nor District 12 had a black voting-age population (called a 'BVAP') that was a majority of the whole: The former had a BVAP of around 48%, the latter a BVAP of around 43%. . . . Nonetheless, in five successive general elections conducted in those reconfigured districts, all the candidates preferred by most African-American voters won their contests—and by some handy margins." When the 2010 census again required redistricting to conform to the one-person, one-vote standard, the "new map . . . significantly altered both District 1 and District 12":

"The 2010 census had revealed District 1 to be substantially underpopulated: To comply with the Constitution's one-person-one-vote principle, the State needed to place almost 100,000 new people within the district's boundaries. . . . [The Republican mapmakers] chose to take most of those people from heavily black areas of Durham, requiring a finger-like extension of the district's western line. . . . With that addition, District 1's BVAP rose from 48.6% to 52.7%. . . . District 12 . . . had no need for significant total-population changes: It was overpopulated by fewer than 3,000 people out of over 730,000. . . . Still, [they] decided to reconfigure the district, further narrowing its already snakelike body while adding areas at either end . . . . Those changes appreciably shifted the racial composition of District 12: As the district gained some 35,000 African-Americans of voting age and lost some 50,000 whites of that age, its BVAP increased from 43.8% to 50.7%."

With respect to District 1, Justice Kagan's majority opinion first concluded that "[u]ncontested evidence in the record shows that the State's mapmakers, in considering District 1, purposefully established a racial target: African-Americans should make up no less than a majority of the voting-age population." Given the "body of evidence—showing an announced racial target that subordinated other districting criteria and produced boundaries amplifying divisions between blacks and whites—the District Court did not clearly err in finding that race predominated in drawing District 1. Indeed, as all three judges recognized, the court could hardly have concluded anything but."

The "more substantial question" was "whether District 1 can survive the strict scrutiny applied to racial gerrymanders." It could not, despite the continued assumption "that complying with the VRA is a compelling interest." The District's "electoral history provided no evidence that a § 2 plaintiff could demonstrate the third *Gingles* prerequisite—effective white bloc-voting." And, to North Carolina's contention that past experience was of limited value concerning a new district with nearly 100,000 additional people, Justice Kagan responded by stating:

"... True enough, a legislature undertaking a redistricting must assess whether the new districts it contemplates (not the old ones it sheds) conform to the VRA's requirements. And true too, an inescapable influx of additional voters into a district may suggest the possibility that its former track record of compliance can continue only if the legislature intentionally adjusts its racial composition. Still, North Carolina too far downplays the significance of a longtime pattern of white crossover voting in the area that would form the core of the redrawn District 1. . . . And even more important, North Carolina can point to no meaningful legislative inquiry into what it now rightly identifies as the key issue: whether a new, enlarged District 1, created without a focus on race but however else the State would choose, could lead to § 2 liability. The prospect of a significant population increase in a district only raises—it does not answer—the question whether § 2 requires deliberate measures to augment the district's BVAP. (Indeed, such population growth could cut in either direction, depending on who comes into the district.) To have a strong basis in evidence to conclude that § 2 demands such race-based steps, the State must carefully evaluate whether a plaintiff could establish the *Gingles* preconditions—including effective white bloc-voting—in a new district created without those measures. We see nothing in the legislative record that fits that description."

That was "no accident" said Justice Kagan, because the redistricters had effectively (and erroneously) "concluded [that] whenever a legislature *can* draw a majority-minority district, it *must* do so—even if a crossover district would also allow the minority group to elect its favored candidates." Finding that idea "at war with our § 2 jurisprudence[,]" the Court refused to "approve a racial gerrymander whose necessity is supported by no evidence and whose *raison d'être* is a legal mistake."

With respect to North Carolina's District 12, which was before the Court for the fifth time starting in 1992, the State did not defend its line-drawing as an effort to comply with § 5 of the VRA, but claimed rather that the district lines were drawn "to 'pack' District 12 with Democrats, not African-Americans"—an account the District Court rejected. Justice Kagan acknowledged the "special challenges" such a defense raises for a trial court:

"In the more usual case alleging a racial gerrymander—where no one has raised a partisanship defense—the court can make real headway by exploring the challenged district's conformity to traditional districting principles, such as compactness and respect for county lines. . . . But such evidence loses much of its value when the State asserts partisanship as a defense, because a bizarre shape—as of the new District 12—can arise from a 'political motivation' as well as a racial one. *Cromartie I*, 526 U. S., at 547, n. 3. And crucially, political and racial reasons are capable of yielding similar oddities in a district's boundaries. That is because, of course, 'racial identification is highly correlated with political affiliation.' *Cromartie II*, 532 U. S., at 243. As a result of those redistricting realities, a trial court has a formidable task: It must make 'a sensitive inquiry' into all 'circumstantial and direct evidence of intent' to assess whether the plaintiffs have managed to disentangle race from politics and prove that the former drove a district's lines. . . .

"Our job is different—and generally easier. [W]e review a district court's finding as to racial predominance only for clear error, except when the court made a legal mistake. . . . [W]e give singular deference to a trial court's judgments about the credibility of witnesses. . . .[7]

"In light of those principles, we uphold the District Court's finding of racial predominance respecting District 12. The evidence offered at trial, including live witness testimony subject to credibility determinations, adequately supports the conclusion that race, not politics, accounted for the district's reconfiguration. And no error of law infected that judgment: Contrary to North Carolina's view, the District Court had no call to dismiss this challenge just because the plaintiffs did not proffer an alternative design for District 12 as circumstantial evidence of the legislature's intent."

Justice Kagan reviewed the evidence before the District Court, and its conclusions, and then said:

---

[7] . . . [I]f legislators use race as their predominant districting criterion with the end goal of advancing their partisan interests—perhaps thinking that a proposed district is more 'sellable' as a race-based VRA compliance measure than as a political gerrymander and will accomplish much the same thing—their action still triggers strict scrutiny. . . . In other words, the sorting of voters on the grounds of their race remains suspect even if race is meant to function as a proxy for other (including political) characteristics. . . .

". . . Maybe we would have evaluated the testimony differently had we presided over the trial; or then again, maybe we would not have. Either way—and it is only *this* which matters—we are far from having a 'definite and firm conviction' that the District Court made a mistake in concluding from the record before it that racial considerations predominated in District 12's design."

As for North Carolina's contention (which the "dissent echoes") that "[w]hen race and politics are competing explanations of a district's lines, . . . the party challenging the district must introduce . . . 'an alternative [map] that achieves the legislature's political objectives while improving racial balance' "—something the challengers here did not do—the majority disagreed:

"We have no doubt that an alternative districting plan, of the kind North Carolina describes, can serve as key evidence in a race-versus-politics dispute. One, often highly persuasive way to disprove a State's contention that politics drove a district's lines is to show that the legislature had the capacity to accomplish all its partisan goals without moving so many members of a minority group into the district."

But "with or without an alternative map" challengers can satisfy "the plaintiff's burden of proof":

". . . In Bush v. Vera, for example, this Court upheld a finding of racial predominance based on 'substantial direct evidence of the legislature's racial motivations'—including credible testimony from political figures and statements made in a § 5 preclearance submission—plus circumstantial evidence that redistricters had access to racial, but not political, data at the 'block-by-block level' needed to explain their 'intricate' designs. . . . Not a single Member of the Court thought that the absence of a counter-map made any difference. Similarly, it does not matter in this case, where the plaintiffs' introduction of mostly direct and some circumstantial evidence—documents issued in the redistricting process, testimony of government officials, expert analysis of demographic patterns—gave the District Court a sufficient basis, sans any map, to resolve the race-or-politics question.

"A plaintiff's task, in other words, is simply to persuade the trial court—without any special evidentiary prerequisite—that race (not politics) was the 'predominant consideration in deciding to place a significant number of voters within or without a particular district.' *Alabama*, . . .; cf. *Bethune-Hill*, ... The Equal Protection Clause prohibits the unjustified drawing of district lines based on race. An alternative map is merely an evidentiary tool to show that such a substantive violation has occurred; neither its presence nor its absence can itself resolve a racial gerrymandering claim."

The State's, and the dissent's, reliance on Easley v. Cromartie (Cromartie II) was misplaced:

". . . In a case like *Cromartie II*—that is, one in which the plaintiffs had meager direct evidence of a racial gerrymander and needed to rely on evidence of forgone alternatives—only maps of that kind could carry the day.

"But this case is most unlike *Cromartie II*, even though it involves the same electoral district some twenty years on. This case turned not on the possibility of creating more optimally constructed districts, but on direct evidence of the General Assembly's intent in creating the actual District 12, including many hours of trial testimony subject to credibility determinations. That evidence, the District Court plausibly found, itself satisfied the plaintiffs' burden of debunking

North Carolina's 'it was really politics' defense; there was no need for an alternative map to do the same job."

Justice Thomas concurred in the majority opinion and wrote briefly "to explain the additional grounds on which [he] would affirm . . . and to note [his] agreement, in particular, with the Court's clear-error analysis." As to District 1, "North Carolina's concession that it created the district as a majority-black district is by itself sufficient to trigger strict scrutiny[,]" and that could not be satisfied based on "efforts to comply with § 2 of the VRA[,]" because in his view "§ 2 does not apply to redistricting and therefore cannot justify a racial gerrymander." As to District 12, "I agree with the Court that the District Court did not clearly err when it determined that race was North Carolina's predominant motive in drawing the district. This is the same conclusion I reached when we last reviewed District 12" in *Cromartie II*: "The Court reached the contrary conclusion in *Cromartie II* only by misapplying our deferential standard for reviewing factual findings. . . . Today's decision does not repeat *Cromartie II*'s error, and indeed it confines that case to its particular facts. It thus represents a welcome course correction to this Court's application of the clear-error standard."

Justice Alito, joined by Chief Justice Roberts and Justice Kennedy, concurred in the judgment with respect to District 1 and dissented with respect to District 12.* As to the latter, he argued that the "failure to produce an alternative map doomed the challengers in *Cromartie II,* and the same should be true now." And his assessment was that the "record shows" that District 12 was not drawn predominantly because of race. He emphasized that because of " 'the intrusive potential of judicial intervention into the legislative realm,' " *Miller,* . . . we have warned that courts must be very cautious about imputing a racial motive to a State's redistricting plan." His insistence that *Cromartie II* mandated the presentation of an alternative map as "a logical response to the difficult problem of distinguishing between racial and political motivations when race and political party preference closely correlate" was premised on the perception that this "is a problem with serious institutional and federalism implications." Among them is that "if a court mistakes a political gerrymander for a racial gerrymander, it illegitimately invades a traditional domain of state authority, usurping the role of a State's elected representatives." And he warned of "a final, often-unstated danger where race and politics correlate: that the federal courts will be transformed into weapons of political warfare." Moreover, "even if there are cases in which a plaintiff could prove a racial gerrymandering claim without an alternative map, they would be exceptional ones in which the evidence of racial predominance is overwhelming. This most definitely is not one of those cases, . . . and the plaintiffs' failure to produce an alternative map mandates reversal. Moreover, even in an exceptional case, the absence of such a map would still be strong evidence that a district's boundaries were determined by politics rather than race."

Justice Alito also argued that even "set[ting] aside the challengers' failure to submit an alternative map, the District Court's finding that race predominated in the drawing of District 12 is clearly erroneous. The State offered strong and coherent evidence that politics, not race, was the legislature's predominant aim, and the evidence supporting the District Court's contrary

---

* Justice Gorsuch did not participate in this case.

finding is weak and manifestly inadequate in light of the high evidentiary standard that our cases require challengers to meet in order to prove racial predominance." His lengthy review of the record led him to conclude that there was "strong evidence . . . that the changes made to the 2001 map were designed to maximize Republican opportunities"; that "so long as the legislature chose to retain the basic shape of District 12 and to increase the number of Democrats in the district, it was inevitable that the Democrats brought in would be disproportionately black"; that "the increase in the black voting age population of District 12 is easily explained by a coherent (and generally successful) political strategy"; and that the references to racial considerations in the record were too weak to support a finding that race was the "predominant" factor in the drawing of District 12's boundaries. He also offered this summary:

"Reviewing the evidence . . ., two themes emerge. First, District 12's borders and racial composition are readily explained by political considerations and the effects of the legislature's political strategy on the demographics of District 12. Second, the majority largely ignores this explanation, as did the court below, and instead adopts the most damning interpretation of all available evidence.

"Both of these analytical maneuvers violate our clearly established precedent. . . ."[a]

---

[a] In North Carolina v. Covington, 581 U.S. ___, 137 S.Ct. 1624 (2017), the Court's per curiam opinion—which noted that the Court had separately summarily affirmed the District Court's ruling that 28 majority-black state legislative districts drawn by the North Carolina General Assembly in 2011 were unconstitutional racial gerrymanders—vacated and remanded for further proceedings the District Court's remedial order in the case. The District Court's ruling on the merits came in August 2016, and that court "declined to require changes in time for the then-impending November 2016 election, but ordered the General Assembly to redraw the map before North Carolina holds any future elections for that body." Shortly after the election, the court set a March 2017 deadline for the drawing of new districts and ordered that "[t]he term of any legislator elected in 2016" from a district later modified by that remedial plan "shall be shortened to one year" (rather than the regular two):

"Those legislators would then be replaced by new ones, to be chosen in court-ordered special elections in the fall of 2017. The legislators elected in those special elections, too, were then to 'serve a one year term.' . . . Finally, in order to make this regime workable, the court also suspended provisions of the North Carolina Constitution requiring prospective legislators to reside within a district for one year before they may be elected to represent it. To explain why these measures were warranted, the court stated: 'While special elections have costs, those costs pale in comparison to the injury caused by allowing citizens to continue to be represented by legislators elected pursuant to a racial gerrymander.'"

The Court's per curiam response to the State's appeal stated in relevant part:

". . . [I]n the context of deciding whether to truncate existing legislators' terms and order a special election, there is much for a court to weigh. Although this Court has never addressed whether or when a special election may be a proper remedy for a racial gerrymander, obvious considerations include the severity and nature of the particular constitutional violation, the extent of the likely disruption to the ordinary processes of governance if early elections are imposed, and the need to act with proper judicial restraint when intruding on state sovereignty. We do not suggest anything about the relative weight of these factors (or others), but they are among the matters a court would generally be expected to consider in its 'balancing of the individual and collective interests' at stake. Swann v. Charlotte-Mecklenburg Bd. of Ed., 402 U.S. 1, 16 (1971).

". . . [T]he District Court addressed the balance of equities in only the most cursory fashion. . . . [Its] minimal reasoning would appear to justify a special election in *every* racial-gerrymandering case—a result clearly at odds with our demand for careful case-specific analysis. For that reason, we cannot have confidence that the court adequately grappled with the interests on both sides of the remedial question before us."

Page 938. Add after Vieth v. Jubelirer:

Gill v. Whitford, 585 U.S. ___, 138 S.Ct. 1916 (2018). Twelve Democratic voters sued to overturn a Republican-enacted redistricting map for the Wisconsin legislature, asserting that—through "packing" and "cracking" of Democratic voters in the districts the plan created—the plan (Act 43) constituted an act of partisan gerrymandering that violated their equal protection rights and their first amendment rights of association. ("Packing" refers to concentrating one party's voters in certain districts to waste that party's statewide votes unnecessarily, whereas "cracking" refers to spreading one party's voters unnecessarily throughout different districts so that they will fall just short of having a majority capable of electing their party's candidate in each of those districts.) The "plaintiffs argued that, on a statewide level, the degree to which packing and cracking has favored one party over another can be measured by . . . an 'efficiency gap' that compares each party's respective 'wasted' votes across all legislative districts[, and] that Act 43 . . . generated a large and unnecessary efficiency gap in favor of Republicans[.]"

In a unanimous opinion authored by Chief Justice Roberts, the Court declined to decide whether partisan gerrymandering claims are justiciable or to decide the merits, "because the plaintiffs in this case have not shown standing under the theory upon which they based their claims for relief." The plaintiffs' alleged vote dilution claim was district specific, but none of them sought to prove at trial that they lived in a "cracked" or "packed" district, and so they failed to demonstrate the requisite Article III "injury in fact." And as to their claim of "legal injury" in the form of "statewide harm to their interest 'in their collective representation in the legislature,' and in influencing the legislature's overall 'composition and policymaking[,]' . . . our cases to date have not found that this presents an individual and personal injury of the kind required for Article III standing." Rather, a "citizen's interest in the overall composition of the legislature is embodied in his right to vote for his representative. And the citizen's abstract interest in policies adopted by the legislature on the facts here is a nonjusticiable 'general interest common to all members of the public.'" The Court concluded that "on this record [this] is a case about group political interests, not individual legal rights." But because this case "concerns an unsettled kind of claim this Court has not agreed upon, the contours and justiciability of which are unresolved[,] . . . and in light of . . . allegations that [four plaintiffs] live in districts where Democrats like them have been packed or cracked," the Court (with Justice Thomas, joined by Justice Gorsuch, disagreeing only on this point) declined to follow its usual practice of directing dismissal, instead remanding "so that the plaintiffs may have an opportunity to prove concrete and particularized injuries using evidence—unlike the bulk of the evidence presented thus far—that would tend to demonstrate a burden on their individual votes."

A concurring opinion by Justice Kagan, joined by Justices Ginsburg, Breyer, and Sotomayor, suggested that although "standing to bring a partisan gerrymandering claim based on vote dilution . . . entails showing, as the Court holds, that she lives in a district that has been either packed or cracked[,] . . . [i]n many partisan gerrymandering cases, that threshold showing will not be hard to make." A "plaintiff could produce an alternative map (or set of alternative maps)—comparably consistent with traditional districting principles—under which her vote would carry more weight." And because "at some points in this litigation, the plaintiffs complained of a different injury—an infringement of their First Amendment right of association[,]" which they might develop on remand, she also addressed "the standing requirement that would then apply[,]" which would not require "show[ing] that her particular voting district was packed or cracked for standing purposes because that fact would bear no connection to her substantive claim. Indeed, everything about the litigation of that claim—from standing on down to remedy—would be statewide in nature."

Even if plaintiffs only demonstrated standing to redress the former, vote dilution injury in their district, Justice Kagan commented that

"cases like this one might warrant a statewide remedy. Suppose that mapmakers pack or crack a critical mass of State Assembly districts all across the State to elect as many Republican politicians as possible. And suppose plaintiffs residing in those districts prevail in a suit challenging that gerrymander on a vote dilution theory. The plaintiffs might then receive exactly the relief sought in this case. To be sure, remedying each plaintiff's vote dilution injury 'requires revising only such districts as are necessary to reshape [that plaintiff's] district—so that the [plaintiff] may be unpacked or uncracked, as the case may be.' But with enough plaintiffs joined together—attacking all the packed and cracked districts in a statewide gerrymander—those obligatory revisions could amount to a wholesale restructuring of the State's districting plan. The Court recognizes as much. It states that a proper remedy in a vote dilution case 'does not *necessarily* require restructuring all of the State's legislative districts.' . . . (emphasis added). Not necessarily—but possibly. It all depends on how much redistricting is needed to cure all the packing and cracking that the mapmakers have done."

As for the latter, right of association injury, Justice Kagan elaborated at some length in these passages:

". . . [P]artisan gerrymanders may infringe the First Amendment rights of association held by parties, other political organizations, and their members. The plaintiffs here have sometimes pointed to that kind of harm. To the extent they meant to do so, and choose to do so on remand, their associational claim would occasion a different standing inquiry than the one in the Court's opinion.

"Justice Kennedy explained the First Amendment associational injury deriving from a partisan gerrymander in his concurring opinion in *Vieth*, 541 U.S. 267. 'Representative democracy,' Justice Kennedy pointed out, is today 'unimaginable without the ability of citizens to band together' to advance their political beliefs. . . . That means significant 'First Amendment concerns arise' when a State purposely 'subject[s] a group of voters or their party to disfavored treatment.' . . . Such action 'burden[s] a group of voters' representational rights.' . . . And it does so because of their 'political association,' 'participation in the electoral process,' 'voting history,' or 'expression of political views.' . . .

"As so formulated, the associational harm of a partisan gerrymander is distinct from vote dilution. Consider an active member of the Democratic Party in Wisconsin who resides in a district that a partisan gerrymander has left untouched (neither packed nor cracked). His individual vote carries no less weight than it did before. But if the gerrymander ravaged the party he works to support, then he indeed suffers harm, as do all other involved members of that party. This is the kind of 'burden' to 'a group of voters' representational rights' Justice Kennedy spoke of. . . . Members of the 'disfavored party' in the State, . . .

deprived of their natural political strength by a partisan gerrymander, may face difficulties fundraising, registering voters, attracting volunteers, generating support from independents, and recruiting candidates to run for office (not to mention eventually accomplishing their policy objectives). . . . And what is true for party members may be doubly true for party officials and triply true for the party itself (or for related organizations). *Cf. California Democratic Party*, 530 U.S., at 586 (holding that a state law violated state political parties' First Amendment rights of association). By placing a state party at an enduring electoral disadvantage, the gerrymander weakens its capacity to perform all its functions.

"And if that is the essence of the harm alleged, then the standing analysis should differ from the one the Court applies. . . . It is because the Court views the harm alleged as vote dilution that it (rightly) insists that each plaintiff show packing or cracking in her own district to establish her standing. But when the harm alleged is not district specific, the proof needed for standing should not be district specific either. And the associational injury flowing from a statewide partisan gerrymander, whether alleged by a party member or the party itself, has nothing to do with the packing or cracking of any single district's lines. The complaint in such a case is instead that the gerrymander has burdened the ability of like-minded people across the State to affiliate in a political party and carry out that organization's activities and objects. Because a plaintiff can have that complaint without living in a packed or cracked district, she need not show what the Court demands today for a vote dilution claim. Or said otherwise: Because on this alternative theory, the valued association and the injury to it are statewide, so too is the relevant standing requirement.

" . . .

" . . . [P]laintiffs did not sufficiently advance a First Amendment associational theory to avoid the Court's holding on standing. Despite referring to that theory in their complaint, the plaintiffs tried this case as though it were about vote dilution alone. Their testimony and other evidence went toward establishing the effects of rampant packing and cracking on the value of individual citizens' votes. Even their proof of partisan asymmetry was used for that purpose—although . . . it could easily have supported the alternative theory of associational harm. The plaintiffs joining in this suit do not include the State Democratic Party (or any related statewide organization). They did not emphasize their membership in that party, or their activities supporting it. And they did not speak to any tangible associational burdens—ways the gerrymander had debilitated their party or weakened its ability to carry out its core functions and purposes. . . .

"[N]othing in the Court's opinion prevents the plaintiffs on remand from pursuing an associational claim, or from satisfying the different standing requirement that theory would entail. . . . And in particular, it leaves for another day the theory of harm advanced by Justice Kennedy in *Vieth*: that a partisan gerrymander interferes with the vital 'ability of citizens to band together' to further their political beliefs. . . . Nothing about that injury is 'generalized' or 'abstract,' as the Court says is true of the plaintiffs' dissatisfaction with the 'overall composition of the legislature.' A suit raising an associational theory complains of concrete 'burdens on a disfavored party' and its members as they pursue their political interests and goals. *Vieth*, 541 U.S., at 315 (opinion of Kennedy, J.); . . . . And when the suit alleges that a gerrymander has imposed those burdens on a statewide basis, then its litigation should be statewide too—as to standing, liability, and remedy alike.

III

"Partisan gerrymandering ... violates the most fundamental of all democratic principles—that 'the voters should choose their representatives, not the other way around.' . . .

"And the evils of gerrymandering seep into the legislative process itself. Among the *amicus* briefs in this case are two from bipartisan groups of congressional members and state legislators. They know that both parties gerrymander. And they know the consequences. The congressional brief describes a 'cascade of negative results' from excessive partisan gerrymandering: indifference to swing voters and their views; extreme political positioning designed to placate the party's base and fend off primary challenges; the devaluing of negotiation and compromise; and the impossibility of reaching pragmatic, bipartisan solutions to the nation's problems. Brief for Bipartisan Group of Current and Former Members of Congress as *Amici Curiae* . . . . The state legislators tell a similar story. In their view, partisan gerrymandering has 'sounded the death-knell of bipartisanship,' creating a legislative environment that is 'toxic' and 'tribal[ ].' Brief for Bipartisan Group of 65 Current and Former State Legislators as *Amici Curiae* . . . .

" . . .

"And our history offers little comfort. Yes, partisan gerrymandering goes back to the Republic's earliest days; and yes, American democracy has survived. But technology makes today's gerrymandering altogether different from the crude linedrawing of the past. New redistricting software enables pinpoint precision in designing districts. With such tools, mapmakers can capture every last bit of partisan advantage, while still meeting traditional districting requirements (compactness, contiguity, and the like). . . . Gerrymanders have thus become ever more extreme and durable, insulating officeholders against all but the most titanic shifts in the political tides. The 2010 redistricting cycle produced some of the worst partisan gerrymanders on record. . . . The technology will only get better, so the 2020 cycle will only get worse.

"Courts have a critical role to play in curbing partisan gerrymandering. . . . Indeed, the need for judicial review is at its most urgent in these cases. For here, politicians' incentives conflict with voters' interests, leaving citizens without any political remedy for their constitutional harms. Of course, their dire need provides no warrant for courts to disregard Article III. Because of the way this suit was litigated, I agree that the plaintiffs have so far failed to establish their standing to sue, and I fully concur in the Court's opinion. But of one thing we may unfortunately be sure. Courts—and in particular this Court—will again be called on to redress extreme partisan gerrymanders. I am hopeful we will then step up to our responsibility to vindicate the Constitution against a contrary law."

PART 4

CONSTITUTIONAL PROTECTION OF EXPRESSION AND CONSCIENCE

CHAPTER 13

GOVERNMENTAL CONTROL OF THE CONTENT OF EXPRESSION

3. SPEECH CONFLICTING WITH OTHER COMMUNITY VALUES: GOVERNMENT CONTROL OF THE CONTENT OF SPEECH

C. CONTROL OF "FIGHTING WORDS" AND OFFENSIVE SPEECH

Page 1336. Add the following before City of Houston, Texas v. Hill:

Matal v. Tam
582 U.S. ___, 137 S.Ct. 1744, 198 L.Ed.2d 366 (2017).

■ JUSTICE ALITO announced the judgment of the Court and delivered the opinion of the Court with respect to Parts I, II, and III–A, and an opinion with respect to Parts III–B, III–C, and IV, in which THE CHIEF JUSTICE, JUSTICE THOMAS, and JUSTICE BREYER join.

This case concerns a dance-rock band's application for federal trademark registration of the band's name, "The Slants." "Slants" is a derogatory term for persons of Asian descent, and members of the band are Asian-Americans. But the band members believe that by taking that slur as the name of their group, they will help to "reclaim" the term and drain its denigrating force.

The Patent and Trademark Office (PTO) denied the application based on a provision of federal law prohibiting the registration of trademarks that may "disparage . . . or bring . . . into contemp[t] or disrepute" any "persons, living or dead." 15 U. S. C. § 1052(a). We now hold that this provision violates the Free Speech Clause of the First Amendment. It offends a bedrock First Amendment principle: Speech may not be banned on the ground that it expresses ideas that offend.

I

A

"The principle underlying trademark protection is that distinctive marks— words, names, symbols, and the like—can help distinguish a particular artisan's goods from those of others." . . . A trademark "designate[s] the goods as the product of a particular trader" and "protect[s] his goodwill against the sale of another's product as his." . . . It helps consumers identify goods and services that they wish to purchase, as well as those they want to avoid. . . .

"[F]ederal law does not create trademarks." . . . Trademarks and their precursors have ancient origins, and trademarks were protected at common law and in equity at the time of the founding of our country. 3 J. McCarthy, Trademarks and Unfair Competition § 19:8 (4th ed. 2017) (hereinafter

McCarthy); 1 *id.*, §§ 5:1, 5:2, 5:3; Pattishal, The Constitutional Foundations of American Trademark Law, 78 Trademark Rep. 456, 457–458 (1988); Pattishall, Two Hundred Years of American Trademark Law, 68 Trademark Rep. 121, 121–123 (1978); . . . For most of the 19th century, trademark protection was the province of the States. . . . Eventually, Congress stepped in to provide a degree of national uniformity, passing the first federal legislation protecting trademarks in 1870. See Act of July 8, 1870, §§ 77–84, 16 Stat. 210–212. The foundation of current federal trademark law is the Lanham Act, enacted in 1946. See Act of July 5, 1946, ch. 540, 60 Stat. 427. By that time, trademark had expanded far beyond phrases that do no more than identify a good or service. Then, as now, trademarks often consisted of catchy phrases that convey a message.

Under the Lanham Act, trademarks that are "used in commerce" may be placed on the "principal register," that is, they may be federally registered. 15 U. S. C. § 1051(a)(1). And some marks "capable of distinguishing [an] applicant's goods or services and not registrable on the principal register . . . which are in lawful use in commerce by the owner thereof " may instead be placed on a different federal register: the supplemental register. § 1091(a). There are now more than two million marks that have active federal certificates of registration. PTO Performance and Accountability Report, Fiscal Year 2016, p. 192 (Table 15), https://www.uspto.gov/sites/default/files/documents/USPTOFY16PAR.pdf   (all Internet materials as last visited June 16, 2017). This system of federal registration helps to ensure that trademarks are fully protected and supports the free flow of commerce. "[N]ational protection of trademarks is desirable," we have explained, "because trademarks foster competition and the maintenance of quality by securing to the producer the benefits of good reputation." . . .

B

Without federal registration, a valid trademark may still be used in commerce. See 3 McCarthy § 19:8. And an unregistered trademark can be enforced against would-be infringers in several ways. Most important, even if a trademark is not federally registered, it may still be enforceable under § 43(a) of the Lanham Act, which creates a federal cause of action for trademark infringement. . . . Unregistered trademarks may also be entitled to protection under other federal statutes, such as the Anticybersquatting Consumer Protection Act, 15 U. S. C. § 1125(d). See 5 McCarthy § 25A:49, at 25A–198 ("[T]here is no requirement [in the Anticybersquatting Act] that the protected 'mark' be registered: unregistered common law marks are protected by the Act"). And an unregistered trademark can be enforced under state common law, or if it has been registered in a State, under that State's registration system. See 3 *id.*, § 19:3, at 19–23 (explaining that "[t]he federal system of registration and protection does not preempt parallel state law protection, either by state common law or state registration" and "[i]n the vast majority of situations, federal and state trademark law peacefully coexist"); *id.*, § 22:1(discussing state trademark registration systems).

Federal registration, however, "confers important legal rights and benefits on trademark owners who register their marks." . . . Registration on the principal register (1) "serves as 'constructive notice of the registrant's claim of ownership' of the mark," . . . ; (2) "is 'prima facie evidence of the validity of the registered mark and of the registration of the mark, of the owner's ownership of the mark, and of the owner's exclusive right to use the registered mark in commerce on or in connection with the goods or services specified in the certificate,' " . . .; and (3) can make a mark " 'incontestable' " once a mark has been registered for five years," . . . . Registration also enables the trademark holder "to stop the importation into the United States of articles bearing an infringing mark." 3 McCarthy § 19:9, at 19–38; see 15 U. S. C. § 1124.

C

The Lanham Act contains provisions that bar certain trademarks from the principal register. For example, a trademark cannot be registered if it is "merely descriptive or deceptively misdescriptive" of goods, § 1052(e)(1), or if it is so similar to an already registered trademark or trade name that it is "likely . . . to cause confusion, or to cause mistake, or to deceive," § 1052(d). At issue in this case is one such provision, which we will call "the disparagement clause." This provision prohibits the registration of a trademark "which may disparage . . . persons, living or dead, institutions, beliefs, or national symbols, or bring them into contempt, or disrepute." § 1052(a). This clause appeared in the original Lanham Act and has remained the same to this day. See § 2(a), 60 Stat. 428.

When deciding whether a trademark is disparaging, an examiner at the PTO generally applies a "two-part test." The examiner first considers "the likely meaning of the matter in question, taking into account not only dictionary definitions, but also the relationship of the matter to the other elements in the mark, the nature of the goods or services, and the manner in which the mark is used in the marketplace in connection with the goods or services." Trademark Manual of Examining Procedure § 1203.03(b)(i) (Apr. 2017), p. 1200–150, http:// tmep.uspto.gov. "If that meaning is found to refer to identifiable persons, institutions, beliefs or national symbols," the examiner moves to the second step, asking "whether that meaning may be disparaging to a substantial composite of the referenced group." *Ibid.* If the examiner finds that a "substantial composite, although not necessarily a majority, of the referenced group would find the proposed mark . . . to be disparaging in the context of contemporary attitudes," a prima facie case of disparagement is made out, and the burden shifts to the applicant to prove that the trademark is not disparaging. *Ibid.* What is more, the PTO has specified that "[t]he fact that an applicant may be a member of that group or has good intentions underlying its use of a term does not obviate the fact that a substantial composite of the referenced group would find the term objectionable." *Ibid.*

D

Simon Tam is the lead singer of "The Slants." . . . He chose this moniker in order to "reclaim" and "take ownership" of stereotypes about people of Asian ethnicity. . . . The group "draws inspiration for its lyrics from childhood slurs and mocking nursery rhymes" and has given its albums names such as "The Yellow Album" and "Slanted Eyes, Slanted Hearts." . . .

Tam sought federal registration of "THE SLANTS," on the principal register, App. 17, but an examining attorney at the PTO rejected the request, applying the PTO's two-part framework and finding that "there is . . . a substantial composite of persons who find the term in the applied-for mark offensive." . . . The examining attorney relied in part on the fact that "numerous dictionaries define 'slants' or 'slant-eyes' as a derogatory or offensive term." . . . The examining attorney also relied on a finding that "the band's name has been found offensive numerous times"—citing a performance that was canceled because of the band's moniker and the fact that "several bloggers and commenters to articles on the band have indicated that they find the term and the applied-for mark offensive." . . .

Tam contested the denial of registration before the examining attorney and before the PTO's Trademark Trial and Appeal Board (TTAB) but to no avail. Eventually, he took the case to federal court, where the en banc Federal Circuit ultimately found the disparagement clause facially unconstitutional under the First Amendment's Free Speech Clause. The majority found that the clause engages in viewpoint-based discrimination, that the clause regulates the expressive component of trademarks and consequently cannot be treated as commercial speech, and that the clause is subject to and cannot satisfy strict scrutiny. . . . The majority also rejected the Government's argument that registered trademarks constitute government speech, as well as the Government's contention that federal registration is a form of government subsidy. . . . And the majority opined that even if the disparagement clause were analyzed under this Court's commercial speech cases, the clause would fail the "intermediate scrutiny" that those cases prescribe. . . .

. . .

The Government filed a petition for certiorari, which we granted in order to decide whether the disparagement clause "is facially invalid under the Free Speech Clause of the First Amendment." . . .

II

Before reaching the question whether the disparagement clause violates the First Amendment, we consider Tam's argument that the clause does not reach marks that disparage racial or ethnic groups. The clause prohibits the registration of marks that disparage "persons," and Tam claims that the term "persons" "includes only natural and juristic persons," not "non-juristic entities such as racial and ethnic groups." . . .

. . .

Tam's argument is refuted by the plain terms of the disparagement clause. The clause applies to marks that disparage "persons." A mark that disparages a "substantial" percentage of the members of a racial or ethnic group, Trademark Manual § 1203.03(b)(i), at 1200–150, necessarily disparages many "persons," namely, members of that group. Tam's argument would fail even if the clause used the singular term "person," but Congress' use of the plural "persons" makes the point doubly clear.

. . .

III

Because the disparagement clause applies to marks that disparage the members of a racial or ethnic group, we must decide whether the clause violates the Free Speech Clause of the First Amendment. And at the outset, we must consider three arguments that would either eliminate any First Amendment protection or result in highly permissive rational-basis review. Specifically, the Government contends (1) that trademarks are government speech, not private speech, (2) that trademarks are a form of government subsidy, and (3) that the constitutionality of the disparagement clause should be tested under a new "government-program" doctrine. We address each of these arguments below.

A

The First Amendment prohibits Congress and other government entities and actors from "abridging the freedom of speech"; the First Amendment does not say that Congress and other government entities must abridge their own ability to speak freely. And our cases recognize that "[t]he Free Speech Clause . . . does not regulate government speech." . . .

As we have said, "it is not easy to imagine how government could function" if it were subject to the restrictions that the First Amendment imposes on private speech. . . . " '[T]he First Amendment forbids the government to regulate speech in ways that favor some viewpoints or ideas at the expense of others,' " . . . but imposing a requirement of viewpoint-neutrality on government speech would be paralyzing. When a government entity embarks on a course of action, it necessarily takes a particular viewpoint and rejects others. The Free Speech Clause does not require government to maintain viewpoint neutrality when its officers and employees speak about that venture.

Here is a simple example. During the Second World War, the Federal Government produced and distributed millions of posters to promote the war effort. There were posters urging enlistment, the purchase of war bonds, and the conservation of scarce resources. These posters expressed a viewpoint, but the First Amendment did not demand that the Government balance the message of these posters by producing and distributing posters encouraging Americans to refrain from engaging in these activities.

But while the government-speech doctrine is important—indeed, essential—it is a doctrine that is susceptible to dangerous misuse. If private speech could be passed off as government speech by simply affixing a government seal of approval, government could silence or muffle the expression of disfavored viewpoints. For this reason, we must exercise great caution before extending our government-speech precedents.

At issue here is the content of trademarks that are registered by the PTO, an arm of the Federal Government. The Federal Government does not dream up these marks, and it does not edit marks submitted for registration. Except as required by the statute involved here, 15 U. S. C. § 1052(a), an examiner may not reject a mark based on the viewpoint that it appears to express. Thus, unless that section is thought to apply, an examiner does not inquire whether any viewpoint conveyed by a mark is consistent with Government policy or whether any such viewpoint is consistent with that expressed by other marks already on the principal register. Instead, if the mark meets the Lanham Act's viewpoint-neutral requirements, registration is mandatory. . . . And if an examiner finds that a mark is eligible for placement on the principal register, that decision is not reviewed by any higher official unless the registration is challenged. See §§ 1062(a), 1071; 37 CFR § 41.31(a) (2016). Moreover, once a mark is registered, the PTO is not authorized to remove it from the register unless a party moves for cancellation, the registration expires, or the Federal Trade Commission initiates proceedings based on certain grounds. See 15 U. S. C. §§ 1058(a), 1059, 1064; 37 CFR §§ 2.111(b), 2.160.

In light of all this, it is far-fetched to suggest that the content of a registered mark is government speech. If the federal registration of a trademark makes the mark government speech, the Federal Government is babbling prodigiously and incoherently. It is saying many unseemly things. . . . It is expressing contradictory views. It is unashamedly endorsing a vast array of commercial products and services. And it is providing Delphic advice to the consuming public.

For example, if trademarks represent government speech, what does the Government have in mind when it advises Americans to "make.believe" (Sony), "Think different" (Apple), "Just do it" (Nike), or "Have it your way" (Burger King)? Was the Government warning about a coming disaster when it registered the mark "EndTime Ministries"?

The PTO has made it clear that registration does not constitute approval of a mark. See In re Old Glory Condom Corp., 26 USPQ 2d 1216, 1220, n. 3 (TTAB 1993) ("[I]ssuance of a trademark registration . . . is not a government imprimatur"). And it is unlikely that more than a tiny fraction of the public has any idea what federal registration of a trademark means. . . .

None of our government speech cases even remotely supports the idea that registered trademarks are government speech. In *Johanns* [v. *Livestock Marketing Assn.*, 544 U.S. 550 (2005)], we considered advertisements promoting the sale of beef products. A federal statute called for the creation of a program of paid advertising " 'to advance the image and desirability of beef and beef products.' " . . . Congress and the Secretary of Agriculture provided guidelines for the content of the ads, Department of Agriculture officials attended the meetings at which the content of specific ads was discussed, and the Secretary could edit or reject any proposed ad. . . . Noting that "[t]he message set out in the beef promotions [was] from beginning to end the message established by the Federal Government," we held that the ads were government speech. . . . The Government's involvement in the creation of these beef ads bears no resemblance to anything that occurs when a trademark is registered.

Our decision in [*Pleasant Grove* v.] *Summum* [, 555 U.S. 460 (2009)] is similarly far afield. A small city park contained 15 monuments. . . . Eleven had been donated by private groups, and one of these displayed the Ten Commandments. . . . A religious group claimed that the city, by accepting donated monuments, had created a limited public forum for private speech and was therefore obligated to place in the park a monument expressing the group's religious beliefs.

Holding that the monuments in the park represented government speech, we cited many factors. Governments have used monuments to speak to the public since ancient times; parks have traditionally been selective in accepting and displaying donated monuments; parks would be overrun if they were obligated to accept all monuments offered by private groups; "[p]ublic parks are often closely identified in the public mind with the government unit that owns the land"; and "[t]he monuments that are accepted . . . are meant to convey and have the effect of conveying a government message." . . .

Trademarks share none of these characteristics. Trademarks have not traditionally been used to convey a Government message. With the exception of the enforcement of 15 U. S. C. § 1052(a), the viewpoint expressed by a mark has not played a role in the decision whether to place it on the principal register. And there is no evidence that the public associates the contents of trademarks with the Federal Government.

This brings us to the case on which the Government relies most heavily, Walker [v. Texas Div., Sons of Confederate Veterans, Inc., 576 U.S. ___ (2015)] which likely marks the outer bounds of the government-speech doctrine. Holding that the messages on Texas specialty license plates are government speech, the *Walker* Court cited three factors distilled from *Summum*. . . . First, license plates have long been used by the States to convey state messages. . . . Second, license plates "are often closely identified in the public mind" with the State, since they are manufactured and owned by the State, generally designed by the State, and serve as a form of "government ID." . . . Third, Texas "maintain[ed] direct control over the messages conveyed on its specialty plates." . . . As explained above, none of these factors are present in this case.

In sum, the federal registration of trademarks is vastly different from the beef ads in *Johanns*, the monuments in *Summum*, and even the specialty license plates in *Walker*. Holding that the registration of a trademark converts the mark into government speech would constitute a huge and dangerous extension of the government-speech doctrine. For if the registration of trademarks constituted government speech, other systems of government registration could easily be characterized in the same way.

Perhaps the most worrisome implication of the Government's argument concerns the system of copyright registration. If federal registration makes a trademark government speech and thus eliminates all First Amendment protection, would the registration of the copyright for a book produce a similar transformation? . . .

The Government attempts to distinguish copyright on the ground that it is " 'the engine of free expression,' " Brief for Petitioner 47 . . . , but as this case illustrates, trademarks often have an expressive content. Companies spend huge amounts to create and publicize trademarks that convey a message. It is true that the necessary brevity of trademarks limits what they can say. But powerful messages can sometimes be conveyed in just a few words.

Trademarks are private, not government, speech.

B

We next address the Government's argument that this case is governed by cases in which this Court has upheld the constitutionality of government programs that subsidized speech expressing a particular viewpoint. These cases implicate a notoriously tricky question of constitutional law. "[W]e have held that the Government 'may not deny a benefit to a person on a basis that infringes his constitutionally protected . . . freedom of speech even if he has no entitlement to that benefit.' ". . . But at the same time, government is not required to subsidize activities that it does not wish to promote. . . . Determining which of these principles applies in a particular case "is not always self-evident," . . . but no difficult question is presented here.

Unlike the present case, the decisions on which the Government relies all involved cash subsidies or their equivalent. In Rust v. Sullivan, 500 U. S. 173 (1991), a federal law provided funds to private parties for family planning services. In National Endowment for Arts v. Finley, 524 U. S. 569 (1998), cash grants were awarded to artists. And federal funding for public libraries was at issue in United States v. American Library Assn., Inc., 539 U.S. 194 (2003). In other cases, we have regarded tax benefits as comparable to cash subsidies. See Regan v. Taxation With Representation of Wash., 461 U. S. 540 (1983); Cammarano v. United States, 358 U. S 498 (1959).

The federal registration of a trademark is nothing like the programs at issue in these cases. The PTO does not pay money to parties seeking registration of a mark. Quite the contrary is true: An applicant for registration must pay the PTO a filing fee of $225–$600. 37 CFR § 2.6(a)(1). . . . And to maintain federal registration, the holder of a mark must pay a fee of $300–$500 every 10 years. § 2.6(a)(5); see also 15 U. S. C. § 1059(a). The Federal Circuit concluded that these fees have fully supported the registration system for the past 27 years. . . .

The Government responds that registration provides valuable non-monetary benefits that "are directly traceable to the resources devoted by the federal government to examining, publishing, and issuing certificates of registration for those marks." . . . . But just about every government service requires the expenditure of government funds. This is true of services that benefit everyone, like police and fire protection, as well as services that are utilized by only some, *e.g.*, the adjudication of private lawsuits and the use of public parks and highways.

Trademark registration is not the only government registration scheme. For example, the Federal Government registers copyrights and patents. State governments and their subdivisions register the title to real property and security interests; they issue driver's licenses, motor vehicle registrations, and hunting, fishing, and boating licenses or permits.

Cases like *Rust* and *Finley* are not instructive in analyzing the constitutionality of restrictions on speech imposed in connection with such services.

C

Finally, the Government urges us to sustain the disparagement clause under a new doctrine that would apply to "government-program" cases. For the most part, this argument simply merges our government-speech cases and the previously discussed subsidy cases in an attempt to construct a broader doctrine that can be applied to the registration of trademarks. The only new element in this construct consists of two cases involving a public employer's collection of union dues from its employees. But those cases occupy a special area of First Amendment case law, and they are far removed from the registration of trademarks. In Davenport v. Washington Ed. Assn., 551 U. S. 177, 181–182 (2007), a Washington law permitted a public employer automatically to deduct from the wages of employees who chose not to join the union the portion of union dues used for activities related to collective bargaining. But unless these employees affirmatively consented, the law did not allow the employer to collect the portion of union dues that would be used in election activities. . . . A public employee union argued that this law unconstitutionally restricted its speech based on its content; that is, the law permitted the employer to assist union speech on matters relating to collective bargaining but made it harder for the union to collect money to support its election activities. . . . Upholding this law, we characterized it as imposing a "modest limitation" on an "extraordinary benefit," namely, taking money from the wages of non-union members and turning it over to the union free of charge. . . . Refusing to confer an even greater benefit, we held, did not upset the marketplace of ideas and did not abridge the union's free speech rights. . . .

Ysursa v. Pocatello Ed. Assn., 555 U. S. 353 (2009), is similar. There, we considered an Idaho law that allowed public employees to elect to have union dues deducted from their wages but did not allow such a deduction for money remitted to the union's political action committee. . . . We reasoned that "the government . . . [was] not required to assist others in funding the expression of particular ideas." . . .

Davenport and *Ysursa* are akin to our subsidy cases. Although the laws at issue in *Davenport* and *Ysursa* did not provide cash subsidies to the unions, they conferred a very valuable benefit—the right to negotiate a collective-bargaining agreement under which non-members would be obligated to pay an agency fee that the public employer would collect and turn over to the union free of charge. As in the cash subsidy cases, the laws conferred this benefit because it was thought that this arrangement served important government interests. See Abood v. Detroit Bd. of Ed., 431 U. S. 209, 224–226 (1977). But the challenged laws did not go further and provide convenient collection mechanisms for money to be used in political activities. In essence, the Washington and Idaho lawmakers chose to confer a substantial non-cash benefit for the purpose of furthering activities that they particularly desired to promote but not to provide a similar benefit for the purpose of furthering other activities. Thus, *Davenport* and *Ysursa* are no more relevant for present purposes than the subsidy cases previously discussed.

Potentially more analogous are cases in which a unit of government creates a limited public forum for private speech. . . . However, even in such cases, what we have termed "viewpoint discrimination" is forbidden. . . .

Our cases use the term "viewpoint" discrimination in a broad sense, . . . and in that sense, the disparagement clause discriminates on the bases of "viewpoint." To be sure, the clause evenhandedly prohibits disparagement of all groups. It applies equally to marks that damn Democrats and Republicans, capitalists and socialists, and those arrayed on both sides of every possible issue. It denies registration to any mark that is offensive to a substantial percentage of the members of any group. But in the sense relevant here, that is viewpoint discrimination: Giving offense is a viewpoint.

We have said time and again that "the public expression of ideas may not be prohibited merely because the ideas are themselves offensive to some of their hearers." Street v. New York, 394 U. S. 576, 592 (1969). See also Texas v. Johnson, 491 U. S. 397, 414 (1989) ("If there is a bedrock principle underlying the First Amendment, it is that the government may not prohibit the expression of an idea simply because society finds the idea itself offensive or disagreeable"); Hustler Magazine, Inc. v. Falwell, 485 U. S. 46, 55–56 (1988); Coates v. Cincinnati, 402 U. S. 611, 615 (1971); Bachellar v. Maryland, 397 U. S. 564, 567 (1970); Tinker v. Des Moines Independent Community School Dist., 393 U. S. 503, 509–514 (1969); Cox v. Louisiana, 379 U. S. 536, 551 (1965); Edwards v. South Carolina, 372 U. S. 229, 237–238 (1963); Terminiello v. Chicago, 337 U. S. 1, 4–5 (1949); Cantwell v. Connecticut, 310 U. S. 296, 311 (1940); Schneider v. State (Town of Irvington), 308 U. S. 147, 161 (1939); De Jonge v. Oregon, 299 U. S. 353, 365 (1937).

For this reason, the disparagement clause cannot be saved by analyzing it as a type of government program in which some content- and speaker-based restrictions are permitted.

IV

Having concluded that the disparagement clause cannot be sustained under our government-speech or subsidy cases or under the Government's proposed "government program" doctrine, we must confront a dispute between the parties on the question whether trademarks are commercial speech and are thus subject to the relaxed scrutiny outlined in Central Hudson Gas & Elec. Corp. v. Public Serv. Comm'n of N. Y., 447 U. S. 557 (1980). The Government and *amici* supporting its position argue that all trademarks are commercial speech. They note that the central purposes of trademarks are commercial and that federal law regulates trademarks to promote fair and orderly interstate commerce. Tam and his *amici*, on the other hand, contend that many, if not all, trademarks have an expressive component. In other words, these trademarks do not simply identify the source of a product or service but go on to say something more, either about the product or service or some broader issue. The trademark in this case illustrates this point. The name "The Slants" not only identifies the band but expresses a view about social issues.

We need not resolve this debate between the parties because the disparagement clause cannot withstand even *Central Hudson* review. Under *Central Hudson*, a restriction of speech must serve "a substantial interest," and it must be "narrowly drawn." . . . This means, among other things, that "[t]he regulatory technique may extend only as far as the interest it serves." . . . The disparagement clause fails this requirement.

It is claimed that the disparagement clause serves two interests. The first is phrased in a variety of ways in the briefs. Echoing language in one of the opinions below, the Government asserts an interest in preventing " 'underrepresented groups' " from being " 'bombarded with demeaning messages in commercial advertising.' " . . . . But no matter how the point is phrased, its unmistakable thrust is this: The Government has an interest in preventing speech expressing ideas that offend. And, as we have explained, that idea strikes at the heart of the First Amendment. Speech that demeans on the basis of race, ethnicity, gender, religion, age, disability, or any other similar ground is hateful; but the proudest boast of our free speech jurisprudence is that we protect the freedom to express "the thought that we hate." United States v. Schwimmer, 279 U. S. 644, 655 (1929) (Holmes, J., dissenting).

The second interest asserted is protecting the orderly flow of commerce. . . . Commerce, we are told, is disrupted by trademarks that "involv[e] disparagement of race, gender, ethnicity, national origin, religion, sexual orientation, and similar demographic classification." . . . Such trademarks are analogized to discriminatory conduct, which has been recognized to have an adverse effect on commerce. . . .

A simple answer to this argument is that the disparagement clause is not "narrowly drawn" to drive out trademarks that support invidious discrimination. The clause reaches any trademark that disparages *any person, group, or institution*. It applies to trademarks like the following: "Down with racists," "Down with sexists," "Down with homophobes." It is not an anti-discrimination clause; it is a happy-talk clause. In this way, it goes much further than is necessary to serve the interest asserted.

The clause is far too broad in other ways as well. The clause protects every person living or dead as well as every institution. Is it conceivable that commerce would be disrupted by a trademark saying: "James Buchanan was a disastrous president" or "Slavery is an evil institution"?

There is also a deeper problem with the argument that commercial speech may be cleansed of any expression likely to cause offense. The commercial market is well stocked with merchandise that disparages prominent figures and groups, and the line between commercial and non-commercial speech is not always clear, as this case illustrates. If affixing the commercial label permits the suppression of any speech that may lead to political or social "volatility," free speech would be endangered.

* * *

For these reasons, we hold that the disparagement clause violates the Free Speech Clause of the First Amendment. The judgment of the Federal Circuit is affirmed.

■ JUSTICE KENNEDY, with whom JUSTICE GINSBURG, JUSTICE SOTOMAYOR, and JUSTICE KAGAN join, concurring in part and concurring in the judgment.

. . .

As the Court is correct to hold, § 1052(a) constitutes viewpoint discrimination—a form of speech suppression so potent that it must be subject to rigorous constitutional scrutiny. The Government's action and the statute on which it is based cannot survive this scrutiny.

The Court is correct in its judgment, and I join Parts I, II, and III–A of its opinion. This separate writing explains in greater detail why the First Amendment's protections against viewpoint discrimination apply to the trademark here [and why] the viewpoint discrimination rationale renders unnecessary any extended treatment of other questions raised by the parties.

I

Those few categories of speech that the government can regulate or punish—for instance, fraud, defamation, or incitement—are well established within our constitutional tradition. . . . Aside from these and a few other narrow exceptions, it is a fundamental principle of the First Amendment that the government may not punish or suppress speech based on disapproval of the ideas or perspectives the speech conveys. . . .

The First Amendment guards against laws "targeted at specific subject matter," a form of speech suppression known as content based discrimination. . . . This category includes a subtype of laws that go further, aimed at the suppression of "particular views . . . on a subject." . . . . A law found to discriminate based on viewpoint is an "egregious form of content discrimination," which is "presumptively unconstitutional." . . .

At its most basic, the test for viewpoint discrimination is whether—within the relevant subject category—the government has singled out a subset of messages for disfavor based on the views expressed. . . . In the instant case, the disparagement clause the Government now seeks to implement and enforce identifies the relevant subject as "persons, living or dead, institutions, beliefs, or national symbols." 15 U. S. C. § 1052(a). Within that category, an applicant may register a positive or benign mark but not a derogatory one. The law thus reflects the Government's disapproval of a subset of messages it finds offensive. This is the essence of viewpoint discrimination.

The Government disputes this conclusion. It argues, to begin with, that the law is viewpoint neutral because it applies in equal measure to any trademark that demeans or offends. This misses the point. A subject that is first defined by content and then regulated or censored by mandating only one sort of comment is not viewpoint neutral. To prohibit all sides from criticizing their opponents makes a law more viewpoint based, not less so. . . . The logic of the Government's rule is that a law would be viewpoint neutral even if it provided that public officials could be praised but not condemned. The First Amendment's viewpoint neutrality principle protects more than the right to identify with a particular side. It protects the right to create and present arguments for particular positions in particular ways, as the speaker chooses. By mandating positivity, the law here might silence dissent and distort the marketplace of ideas.

The Government next suggests that the statute is viewpoint neutral because the disparagement clause applies to trademarks regardless of the applicant's personal views or reasons for using the mark. Instead, registration is denied based on the expected reaction of the applicant's audience. In this way, the argument goes, it cannot be said that Government is acting with hostility toward a particular point of view. For example, the Government does not dispute that respondent seeks to use his mark in a positive way. . . .

The Government may not insulate a law from charges of viewpoint discrimination by tying censorship to the reaction of the speaker's audience. The Court has suggested that viewpoint discrimination occurs when the government intends to suppress a speaker's beliefs, . . . but viewpoint discrimination need not take that form in every instance. The danger of viewpoint discrimination is that the government is attempting to remove certain ideas or perspectives from a broader debate. That danger is all the greater if the ideas or perspectives are ones a particular audience might think offensive, at least at first hearing. An initial reaction may prompt further reflection, leading to a more reasoned, more tolerant position. . . .

. . .

II

The parties dispute whether trademarks are commercial speech and whether trademark registration should be considered a federal subsidy. The former issue may turn on whether certain commercial concerns for the protection of trademarks might, as a general matter, be the basis for regulation. However that issue is resolved, the viewpoint based discrimination at issue here necessarily invokes heightened scrutiny.

"Commercial speech is no exception," the Court has explained, to the principle that the First Amendment "requires heightened scrutiny whenever the government creates a regulation of speech because of disagreement with the message it conveys." . . . Unlike content based discrimination, discrimination based on viewpoint, including a regulation that targets speech for its offensiveness, remains of serious concern in the commercial context. . . .

To the extent trademarks qualify as commercial speech, they are an example of why that term or category does not serve as a blanket exemption from the First Amendment's requirement of viewpoint neutrality. Justice Holmes' reference to the "free trade in ideas" and the "power of . . . thought to get itself accepted in the competition of the market," . . . was a metaphor. In the realm of trademarks, the metaphorical marketplace of ideas becomes a tangible, powerful reality. Here that real marketplace exists as a matter of state law and our common-law tradition, quite without regard to the Federal Government. . . . These marks make up part of the expression of everyday life, as with the names of entertainment groups, broadcast networks, designer clothing, newspapers, automobiles, candy bars, toys, and so on. . . . Nonprofit organizations—ranging from medical-research charities and other humanitarian causes to political advocacy groups—also have trademarks, which they use to compete in a real economic sense for funding and other resources as they seek to persuade others to join their cause. . . . To permit viewpoint discrimination in this context is to permit Government censorship.

This case does not present the question of how other provisions of the Lanham Act should be analyzed under the First Amendment. It is well settled, for instance, that to the extent a trademark is confusing or misleading the law can protect consumers and trademark owners. . . . This case also does not involve laws related to product labeling or otherwise designed to protect consumers. . . . These considerations, however, do not alter the speech principles that bar the viewpoint discrimination embodied in the statutory provision at issue here.

It is telling that the Court's precedents have recognized just one narrow situation in which viewpoint discrimination is permissible: where the government itself is speaking or recruiting others to communicate a message on its behalf. . . . The exception is necessary to allow the government to stake out positions and pursue policies. . . . But it is also narrow, to prevent the government from claiming that every government program is exempt from the First Amendment. These cases have identified a number of factors that, if present, suggest the government is speaking on its own behalf; but none are present here. . . .

. . .

* * *

A law that can be directed against speech found offensive to some portion of the public can be turned against minority and dissenting views to the detriment of all. The First Amendment does not entrust that power to the government's benevolence. Instead, our reliance must be on the substantial safeguards of free and open discussion in a democratic society.

For these reasons, I join the Court's opinion in part and concur in the judgment.

[Justice Thomas wrote separately, concurring in part and concurring in the judgment, to explain his failure to join Part II of Justice Alito's opinion (which involved a statutory interpretation argument Justice Thomas thought the Court should not address) and to reiterate his view that "when the government seeks to restrict truthful speech in order to suppress the ideas it conveys, strict scrutiny is appropriate, whether or not the speech in question may be characterized as 'commercial.' " . . .]

■ JUSTICE GORSUCH took no part in the consideration or decision of this case.

D. REGULATION OF COMMERCIAL SPEECH

Page 1355. Add after Note, "Overbreadth and Commercial Speech":

National Institute of Family and Life Advocates v. Becerra

585 U.S. ___, 138 S.Ct. 2361, ___ L.Ed.2d ___ (2018).

■ JUSTICE THOMAS delivered the opinion of the Court.

The California Reproductive Freedom, Accountability, Comprehensive Care, and Transparency Act (FACT Act) requires clinics that primarily serve pregnant women to provide certain notices. Cal. Health & Safety Code Ann. § 123470 *et seq.* (West 2018). Licensed clinics must notify women that California provides free or low-cost services, including abortions, and give them a phone number to call. Unlicensed clinics must notify women that California has not licensed the clinics to provide medical services. The question in this case is whether these notice requirements violate the First Amendment.

I

A

The California State Legislature enacted the FACT Act to regulate crisis pregnancy centers. Crisis pregnancy centers—according to a report commissioned by the California State Assembly . . .—are "pro-life (largely Christian belief-based) organizations that offer a limited range of free pregnancy options, counseling, and other services to individuals that visit a center." . . . "[U]nfortunately," the author of the FACT Act stated, "there are nearly 200 licensed and unlicensed" crisis pregnancy centers in California. . . . These centers "aim to discourage and prevent women from seeking abortions." . . . The author of the FACT Act observed that crisis pregnancy centers "are commonly affiliated with, or run by organizations whose stated goal" is to oppose abortion—including "the National Institute of Family and Life Advocates," one of the petitioners here. . . . To address this perceived problem, the FACT Act imposes two notice requirements on facilities that provide pregnancy-related services—one for licensed facilities and one for unlicensed facilities.

1

The first notice requirement applies to "licensed covered facilit[ies,]" [defined as] licensed primary care or specialty clinic[s] or [those that] qualify as an intermittent clinic. [The covered clinics] also must have the "primary purpose" of "providing family planning or pregnancy-related services" [a]nd . . . must satisfy at least two of the[se] six requirements:

"(1) The facility offers obstetric ultrasounds, obstetric sonograms, or prenatal care to pregnant women.

"(2) The facility provides, or offers counseling about, contraception or contraceptive methods.

"(3) The facility offers pregnancy testing or pregnancy diagnosis.

"(4) The facility advertises or solicits patrons with offers to provide prenatal sonography, pregnancy tests, or pregnancy options counseling.

"(5) The facility offers abortion services.

"(6) The facility has staff or volunteers who collect health information from clients." . . .

The FACT Act exempts . . . [c]linics operated by the United States or a federal agency . . ., [and] clinics that are "enrolled as a Medi-Cal provider" and participate in "the Family Planning, Access, Care, and Treatment Program" (Family PACT program)[, which requires] provid[ing] "the full scope of family planning . . . services specified for the program," . . . including sterilization and emergency contraceptive pills . . . .

If a clinic is a licensed covered facility, the FACT Act requires it to disseminate a government-drafted notice on site. . . . The notice states that "California has public programs that provide immediate free or low-cost access to comprehensive family planning services (including all FDA-approved methods of contraception), prenatal care, and abortion for eligible women. To determine whether you qualify, contact the county social services office at [insert the telephone number]." . . . This notice must be posted in the waiting room, printed and distributed to all clients, or provided digitally at check-in. . . . The notice must be in English and any additional languages identified by state law. . . . In some counties, that means the notice must be spelled out in 13 different languages. . . .

The stated purpose of the FACT Act . . . is to "ensure that California residents make their personal reproductive health care decisions knowing their rights and the health care services available to them." . . . The Legislature posited that "thousands of women remain unaware of the public programs available to provide them with contraception, health education and counseling, family planning, prenatal care, abortion, or delivery." . . . Citing the "time sensitive" nature of pregnancy-related decisions, . . . the Legislature concluded that requiring licensed facilities to inform patients themselves would be "[t]he most effective" way to convey this information . . . .

2

The second notice requirement . . . applies to "unlicensed covered facilit[ies," which are those without State licenses or licensed medical providers and which] have the "primary purpose" of "providing pregnancy-related services." . . . [They] also must satisfy at least two of the[se] four requirements:

"(1) The facility offers obstetric ultrasounds, obstetric sonograms, or prenatal care to pregnant women.

"(2) The facility offers pregnancy testing or pregnancy diagnosis.

"(3) The facility advertises or solicits patrons with offers to provide prenatal sonography, pregnancy tests, or pregnancy options counseling.

"(4) The facility has staff or volunteers who collect health information from clients." . . .

Clinics operated by the United States and licensed primary care clinics enrolled in Medi-Cal and Family PACT are excluded.

Unlicensed covered facilities must provide a government-drafted notice stating that "[t]his facility is not licensed as a medical facility by the State of California and has no licensed medical provider who provides or directly supervises the provision of services." . . . This notice must be provided on site and in all advertising materials. . . . Onsite, the notice must be posted "conspicuously" at the entrance of the facility and in at least one waiting area. . . . It must be "at least 8.5 inches by 11 inches and written in no less than 48-point type." . . . In advertisements, the notice must be in the same size or larger font than the surrounding text, or otherwise set off in a way that draws attention to it. . . . Like the licensed notice, the unlicensed notice must be in English and any additional languages specified by state law. . . . Its stated purpose is to ensure "that pregnant women in California know when they are getting medical care from licensed professionals." . . .

B

. . . [A] pregnancy center, an unlicensed pregnancy center, and an organization composed of crisis pregnancy centers [sued,] alleg[ing] that the [required] notices abridge the freedom of speech protected by the First Amendment. The District Court denied their motion for a preliminary injunction. [The Ninth Circuit affirmed,] conclud[ing] that the licensed notice survives the "lower level of scrutiny" that applies to regulations of "professional speech[,]" . . . [and] that the unlicensed notice satisfies any level of scrutiny.

We reverse with respect to both notice requirements.

II

A

. . .

The licensed notice is a content-based regulation of speech. By compelling individuals to speak a particular message, such notices "alte[r] the content of [their] speech." Riley v. National Federation of Blind of N. C., Inc., 487 U.S. 781, 795 (1988); . . . . Here, . . . licensed clinics must provide a government-drafted script about the availability of state-sponsored services, as well as contact information for how to obtain them. One of those services is abortion—the very practice that petitioners are devoted to opposing. By requiring petitioners to inform women how they can obtain state-subsidized abortions—at the same time petitioners try to dissuade women from choosing that option—the licensed notice plainly "alters the content" of petitioners' speech. . . .

B

Although the licensed notice is content based, the Ninth Circuit did not apply strict scrutiny because it concluded that the notice regulates "professional speech." . . . Some Courts of Appeals have recognized "professional speech" as a separate category of speech that is subject to different rules. . . . These courts define "professionals" as individuals who provide personalized services to clients and who are subject to "a generally applicable licensing and regulatory regime." . . . "Professional speech" is then defined as any speech by these individuals that is based on "[their] expert knowledge and judgment," . . . or that is "within the confines of [the] professional relationship," . . . . So defined, these courts except professional speech from the rule that content-based regulations of speech are subject to strict scrutiny. . . .

But this Court has not recognized "professional speech" as a separate category of speech. Speech is not unprotected merely because it is uttered by "professionals." This Court has "been reluctant to mark off new categories of speech for diminished constitutional protection." Denver Area Ed.

Telecommunications Consortium, Inc. v. FCC, 518 U.S. 727, 804 (1996) (Kennedy, J., concurring in part, concurring in judgment in part, and dissenting in part). And it has been especially reluctant to "exemp[t] a category of speech from the normal prohibition on content-based restrictions." United States v. Alvarez, 567 U.S. 709, 722 (2012) (plurality opinion). This Court's precedents do not permit governments to impose content-based restrictions on speech without " 'persuasive evidence . . . of a long (if heretofore unrecognized) tradition' " to that effect. . . .

This Court's precedents do not recognize such a tradition for a category called "professional speech." This Court has afforded less protection for professional speech in two circumstances—neither of which turned on the fact that professionals were speaking. First, our precedents have applied more deferential review to some laws that require professionals to disclose factual, noncontroversial information in their "commercial speech." See, e.g., Zauderer v. Office of Disciplinary Counsel of Supreme Court of Ohio, 471 U.S. 626, 651 (1985); Milavetz, Gallop & Milavetz, P. A. v. United States, 559 U.S. 229, 250 (2010); Ohralik v. Ohio State Bar Assn., 436 U.S. 447, 455–456 (1978). Second, under our precedents, States may regulate professional conduct, even though that conduct incidentally involves speech. See, e.g., id., at 456; Planned Parenthood of Southeastern Pa. v. Casey, 505 U.S. 833, 884 (1992) (opinion of O'Connor, Kennedy, and Souter, JJ.). But neither line of precedents is implicated here.

1

This Court's precedents have applied a lower level of scrutiny to laws that compel disclosures in certain contexts. In Zauderer, for example, this Court upheld a rule requiring lawyers who advertised their services on a contingency-fee basis to disclose that clients might be required to pay some fees and costs. . . . Noting that the disclosure requirement governed only "commercial advertising" and required the disclosure of "purely factual and uncontroversial information about the terms under which . . . services will be available," the Court explained that such requirements should be upheld unless they are "unjustified or unduly burdensome." . . .

The Zauderer standard does not apply here. Most obviously, the licensed notice is not limited to "purely factual and uncontroversial information about the terms under which . . . services will be available." 471 U.S., at 651; see also Hurley v. Irish-American Gay, Lesbian and Bisexual Group of Boston, Inc., 515 U.S. 557, 573 (1995) (explaining that Zauderer does not apply outside of these circumstances). The notice in no way relates to the services that licensed clinics provide. Instead, it requires these clinics to disclose information about state-sponsored services—including abortion, anything but an "uncontroversial" topic. Accordingly, Zauderer has no application here.

2

In addition to disclosure requirements under Zauderer, this Court has upheld regulations of professional conduct that incidentally burden speech. "[T]he First Amendment does not prevent restrictions directed at commerce or conduct from imposing incidental burdens on speech," Sorrell v. IMS Health Inc., 564 U.S. 552, 567 (2011), and professionals are no exception to this rule, see Ohralik . . . .

In Planned Parenthood of Southeastern Pa. v. Casey, . . . this Court upheld a law requiring physicians to obtain informed consent before they could perform an abortion. 505 U.S., at 884 (joint opinion of O'Connor, Kennedy, and Souter, JJ.). Pennsylvania law required physicians to inform their patients of "the nature of the procedure, the health risks of the abortion and childbirth, and the 'probable gestational age of the unborn child.' " . . . The law also required physicians to inform patients of the availability of printed materials from the State, which provided information about the child and various forms of assistance.

The joint opinion in *Casey* rejected a free-speech challenge to this informed-consent requirement. . . . The joint opinion explained that the law regulated speech only "as part of the *practice* of medicine, subject to reasonable licensing and regulation by the State." . . .

The licensed notice at issue here is not an informed-consent requirement or any other regulation of professional conduct. The notice does not facilitate informed consent to a medical procedure. In fact, it is not tied to a procedure at all. It applies to all interactions between a covered facility and its clients, regardless of whether a medical procedure is ever sought, offered, or performed. If a covered facility does provide medical procedures, the notice provides no information about the risks or benefits of those procedures. Tellingly, many facilities that provide the exact same services as covered facilities—such as general practice clinics . . .—are not required to provide the licensed notice. The licensed notice regulates speech as speech.

3

Outside of the two contexts discussed above—disclosures under *Zauderer* and professional conduct—this Court's precedents have long protected the First Amendment rights of professionals. For example, this Court has applied strict scrutiny to content-based laws that regulate the noncommercial speech of lawyers, see . . . In re Primus, 436 U.S. 412, 432 (1978); professional fundraisers, see *Riley*, 487 U.S., at 798; and organizations that provided specialized advice about international law, see Holder v. Humanitarian Law Project, 561 U.S. 1, 27–28 (2010). And the Court emphasized that the lawyer's statements in *Zauderer* would have been "fully protected" if they were made in a context other than advertising. 471 U.S., at 637, n. 7. Moreover, this Court has stressed the danger of content-based regulations "in the fields of medicine and public health, where information can save lives." . . .

The dangers associated with content-based regulations of speech are also present in the context of professional speech. As with other kinds of speech, regulating the content of professionals' speech "pose[s] the inherent risk that the Government seeks not to advance a legitimate regulatory goal, but to suppress unpopular ideas or information." . . . Throughout history, governments have "manipulat[ed] the content of doctor-patient discourse" to increase state power and suppress minorities . . . .

Further, when the government polices the content of professional speech, it can fail to " 'preserve an uninhibited marketplace of ideas in which truth will ultimately prevail.' " McCullen v. Coakley, ...

"Professional speech" is also a difficult category to define with precision. . . . As defined by the courts of appeals, the professional-speech doctrine would cover a wide array of individuals—doctors, lawyers, nurses, physical therapists, truck drivers, bartenders, barbers, and many others. . . . All that is required to make something a "profession," according to these courts, is that it involves personalized services and requires a professional license from the State. But that gives the States unfettered power to reduce a group's First Amendment rights by simply imposing a licensing requirement. . . .

C

In sum, neither California nor the Ninth Circuit has identified a persuasive reason for treating professional speech as a unique category that is exempt from ordinary First Amendment principles. We do not foreclose the possibility that some such reason exists. We need not do so because the licensed notice cannot survive even intermediate scrutiny. California asserts a single interest to justify the licensed notice: providing low-income women with information about state-sponsored services. Assuming that this is a substantial state interest, the licensed notice is not sufficiently drawn to achieve it.

If California's goal is to educate low-income women about the services it provides, then the licensed notice is "wildly underinclusive." . . . The notice applies only to clinics that have a "primary purpose" of "providing family planning or pregnancy-related services" and that provide two of six categories of specific services. . . . Other clinics that have another primary purpose, or that provide only one category of those services, also serve low-income women and could educate them about the State's services. According to the legislative record, California has "nearly 1,000 community clinics"—including "federally designated community health centers, migrant health centers, rural health centers, and frontier health centers"—that "serv[e] more than 5.6 million patients . . . annually through over 17 million patient encounters." . . . But most of those clinics are excluded from the licensed notice requirement without explanation. Such "[u]nderinclusiveness raises serious doubts about whether the government is in fact pursuing the interest it invokes, rather than disfavoring a particular speaker or viewpoint." . . .

The FACT Act also excludes, without explanation, federal clinics and Family PACT providers from the licensed-notice requirement. California notes that those clinics can enroll women in California's programs themselves, but California's stated interest is informing women that these services exist in the first place. California has identified no evidence that the exempted clinics are more likely to provide this information than the covered clinics. In fact, the exempted clinics have long been able to enroll women in California's programs, but the FACT Act was premised on the notion that "thousands of women remain unaware of [them]." . . . If the goal is to maximize women's awareness of these programs, then it would seem that California would ensure that the places that can immediately enroll women also provide this information. . . .

Further, California could inform low-income women about its services "without burdening a speaker with unwanted speech." . . . Most obviously, it could inform the women itself with a public-information campaign. . . . California could even post the information on public property near crisis pregnancy centers. California argues that it has already tried an advertising campaign, and that many women who are eligible for publicly-funded healthcare have not enrolled. But California has identified no evidence to that effect. And regardless, a "tepid response" does not prove that an advertising campaign is not a sufficient alternative. United States v. Playboy Entertainment Group, Inc., 529 U.S. 803, 816 (2000). . . .

In short, petitioners are likely to succeed on the merits of their challenge to the licensed notice. Contrary to the suggestion in the dissent, we do not question the legality of health and safety warnings long considered permissible, or purely factual and uncontroversial disclosures about commercial products.

III

. . . The parties dispute whether the unlicensed notice is subject to deferential review under *Zauderer*. We need not decide [because e]ven under *Zauderer*, a disclosure requirement cannot be "unjustified or unduly burdensome." . . . Our precedents require disclosures to remedy a harm that is "potentially real not purely hypothetical," Ibanez v. Florida Dept. of Business and Professional Regulation, Bd. of Accountancy, 512 U.S. 136, 146 (1994), and to extend "no broader than reasonably necessary," . . . . Otherwise, they risk "chilling" protected speech." . . . Importantly, California has the burden to prove that the unlicensed notice is neither unjustified nor unduly burdensome. . . . It has not met its burden.

. . . California has not demonstrated any justification for the unlicensed notice that is more than "purely hypothetical." . . . The only justification that the California Legislature put forward was ensuring that "pregnant women in California know when they are getting medical care from licensed professionals." . . . At oral argument, however, California denied that the justification for the FACT Act was that women "go into [crisis pregnancy centers] and they don't realize what they are." . . . Indeed, California points to nothing suggesting that pregnant women do not already know that the covered facilities are staffed by unlicensed medical professionals. The services that trigger the unlicensed notice—such as having "volunteers who collect health information from clients," "advertis[ing] . . . pregnancy options counseling," and offering over-the-counter "pregnancy testing," . . .—do not require a medical license. And California already makes it a crime for individuals without a medical license to practice medicine. . . . At this preliminary stage of the litigation, we agree that petitioners are likely to prevail on the question whether California has proved a justification for the unlicensed notice.

Even if California had presented a nonhypothetical justification for the unlicensed notice, the FACT Act unduly burdens protected speech. The unlicensed notice imposes a government-scripted, speaker-based disclosure requirement that is wholly disconnected from California's informational interest. It requires covered facilities to post California's precise notice, no matter what the facilities say on site or in their advertisements. And it covers a curiously narrow subset of speakers. While the licensed notice applies to facilities that provide "family planning" services and "contraception or contraceptive methods," . . . the California Legislature dropped these triggering conditions for the unlicensed notice. The unlicensed notice applies only to facilities that primarily provide "pregnancy-related" services. . . . Thus, a facility that advertises and provides pregnancy tests is covered by the unlicensed notice, but a facility across the street that advertises and provides nonprescription contraceptives is excluded—even though the latter is no less likely to make women think it is licensed. This Court's precedents are deeply skeptical of laws that "distinguis[h] among different speakers, allowing speech by some but not others." Citizens United v. Federal Election Comm'n, 558 U.S. 310, 340 (2010). Speaker-based laws run the risk that "the State has left unburdened those speakers whose messages are in accord with its own views." . . .

The application of the unlicensed notice to advertisements demonstrates just how burdensome it is. . . . As California conceded at oral argument, a billboard for an unlicensed facility that says "Choose Life" would have to surround that two-word statement with a 29-word statement from the government, in as many as 13 different languages. In this way, the unlicensed notice drowns out the facility's own message. . . .

For all these reasons, the unlicensed notice does not satisfy *Zauderer*, assuming that standard applies. California has offered no justification that the notice plausibly furthers. It targets speakers, not speech, and imposes an unduly burdensome disclosure requirement that will chill their protected speech. Taking all these circumstances together, we conclude that the unlicensed notice is unjustified and unduly burdensome under *Zauderer*. We express no view on the legality of a similar disclosure requirement that is better supported or less burdensome.

. . . We reverse . . . and remand . . . for further proceedings consistent with this opinion.

■ JUSTICE KENNEDY, with whom THE CHIEF JUSTICE, JUSTICE ALITO, and JUSTICE GORSUCH join, concurring.

I join the Court's opinion in all respects.

This separate writing seeks to underscore that the apparent viewpoint discrimination here is a matter of serious constitutional concern. The Court . . . is correct not to reach this question. It was not sufficiently developed, and the rationale for the Court's decision today suffices to resolve the case. And had the Court's analysis been confined to viewpoint discrimination, some legislators might have inferred that if the law were reenacted with a broader base and broader coverage it then would be upheld.

It does appear that viewpoint discrimination is inherent in the design and structure of this Act. This law is a paradigmatic example of the serious threat presented when government seeks to impose its own message in the place of individual speech, thought, and expression. For here the State requires primarily pro-life pregnancy centers to promote the State's own preferred message advertising abortions. This compels individuals to contradict their most deeply held beliefs, beliefs grounded in basic philosophical, ethical, or religious precepts, or all of these. And the history of the Act's passage and its underinclusive application suggest a real possibility that these individuals were targeted because of their beliefs.

The California Legislature included in its official history the congratulatory statement that the Act was part of California's legacy of "forward thinking." . . . But it is not forward thinking to force individuals to "be an instrument for fostering public adherence to an ideological point of view [they] fin[d] unacceptable." Wooley v. Maynard, 430 U.S. 705, 715 (1977). . . . Governments must not be allowed to force persons to express a message contrary to their deepest convictions. . . .

■ JUSTICE BREYER, with whom JUSTICE GINSBURG, JUSTICE SOTOMAYOR, and JUSTICE KAGAN join, dissenting.

. . .

[The majority's] constitutional approach threatens to create serious problems. Because much, perhaps most, human behavior takes place through speech and because much, perhaps most, law regulates that speech in terms of its content, the majority's approach at the least threatens considerable litigation over the constitutional validity of much, perhaps most, government regulation. Virtually every disclosure law could be considered "content based," for virtually every disclosure law requires individuals "to speak a particular message." See Reed v. Town of Gilbert, 576 U.S. ___, ___ (2015) (Breyer, J., concurring in judgment) (slip op., at 3) (listing regulations that inevitably involve content discrimination, ranging from securities disclosures to signs at petting zoos). Thus, the majority's view, if taken literally, could radically change prior law, perhaps placing much securities law or consumer protection law at constitutional risk, depending on how broadly its exceptions are interpreted.

Many ordinary disclosure laws would fall outside the majority's exceptions for disclosures related to the professional's own services or conduct. These include numerous commonly found disclosure requirements relating to the medical profession. . . .

The majority . . . , perhaps recognizing this problem, . . . says that it does not "question the legality of health and safety warnings long considered permissible, or purely factual and uncontroversial disclosures about commercial products." But this generally phrased disclaimer would seem more likely to invite litigation than to provide needed limitation and clarification. The majority, for example, does not explain why the Act here, which is justified in part by health and safety considerations, does not fall within its "health" category. . . . [S]ee also Planned Parenthood of Southeastern Pa. v. Casey, 505 U.S. 833, 882–884 (1992) (joint opinion of O'Connor, Kennedy, and Souter, JJ.) (reasoning that disclosures related to fetal development and childbirth are related to the health of a woman seeking an abortion). Nor does the majority opinion offer any reasoned basis that might help apply its disclaimer for distinguishing lawful from unlawful disclosures. In the absence of a reasoned explanation of the disclaimer's meaning and rationale, the disclaimer is unlikely to withdraw the invitation to litigation that the majority's general broad "content-based" test issues. That test invites courts around the Nation to apply an unpredictable First Amendment to ordinary social and economic regulation, striking down disclosure laws that judges may disfavor, while upholding others, all without grounding their decisions in reasoned principle.

Notably, the majority says nothing about limiting its language to the kind of instance where the Court has traditionally found the First Amendment wary of content-based laws, namely, in cases of viewpoint discrimination. . . . But the mine run of disclosure requirements . . . simply alert the public about child seat belt laws, the location of stairways, and the process to have their garbage collected, among other things.

Precedent does not require a test such as the majority's. . . . Historically, the Court has been wary of claims that regulation of business activity, particularly health-related activity, violates the Constitution. . . .

The Court has taken this same respectful approach to economic and social legislation when a First Amendment claim like the claim present here is at issue. See, *e.g.,* Zauderer v. Office of Disciplinary Counsel of Supreme Court of Ohio, 471 U.S. 626, 651 (1985) (upholding reasonable disclosure requirements for attorneys); Milavetz, Gallop & Milavetz, P.A. v. United States, 559 U.S. 229, 252–253 (2010) (same); . . . .

Even during the *Lochner* era, when this Court struck down numerous economic regulations concerning industry, this Court was careful to defer to state legislative judgments concerning the medical profession. . . . In the name of the First Amendment, the majority today treads into territory where the pre-New Deal, as well as the post-New Deal, Court refused to go.

. . . [T]he majority pays . . . First Amendment goals a serious disservice through dilution. Using the First Amendment to strike down economic and social laws that legislatures long would have thought themselves free to enact will, for the American public, obscure, not clarify, the true value of protecting freedom of speech.

B

Still, what about this specific case? The disclosure at issue here concerns speech related to abortion. It involves health, differing moral values, and differing points of view. [R]ather than set forth broad, new, First Amendment principles, I believe that we should focus more directly upon precedent . . . [regarding] disclosure laws relating to reproductive health. Though those rules or holdings have changed over time, they should govern our disposition of this case.

. . .

[After reviewing earlier cases holding otherwise, and referring to the information requirement addressed in Planned Parenthood of Southeastern Pa. v. Casey, 505 U.S. 833 (1992), Justice Breyer observed that t]his time a joint opinion of the Court, in judging whether the State could impose these informational requirements, asked whether doing so imposed an "undue burden" upon women seeking an abortion [and] held that it did not. [And he observed that in] overruling the earlier cases, it wrote:

> "To the extent *Akron I* and *Thornburgh* find a constitutional violation when the government requires, as it does here, the giving of truthful, nonmisleading information about the nature of the procedure, the attendant health risks and those of childbirth, and the 'probable gestational age' of the fetus, those cases go too far, are inconsistent with *Roe*'s acknowledgment of an important interest in potential life, and are overruled." . . .

The joint opinion . . . [also] concluded that the statute did not violate the First Amendment. It wrote:

> "All that is left of petitioners' argument is an asserted First Amendment right of a physician not to provide information about the risks of abortion, and childbirth, in a manner mandated by the State. To be sure, the physician's First Amendment rights not to speak are implicated, see Wooley v. Maynard, 430 U.S. 705 (1977), but only as part of the practice of medicine, subject to reasonable licensing and regulation by the State, cf. Whalen v. Roe, 429 U.S. 589, 603 (1977). We see no constitutional infirmity in the requirement that the physician provide the information mandated by the State here." *Casey*, 505 U.S., at 884.

Thus, the Court considered the State's statutory requirements, including the requirement that the doctor must inform his patient about where she could learn how to have the newborn child adopted (if carried to term) and how she could find related financial assistance. . . . To repeat the point, the Court then held that the State's requirements did *not* violate either the Constitution's protection of free speech or its protection of a woman's right to choose to have an abortion.

C

Taking *Casey* as controlling, the law's demand for evenhandedness requires a different answer than that perhaps suggested by *Akron* and *Thornburgh*. If a State can lawfully require a doctor to tell a woman seeking an abortion about adoption services, why should it not be able, as here, to require a medical counselor to tell a woman seeking prenatal care or other reproductive healthcare about childbirth and abortion services? As the question suggests, there is no convincing reason to distinguish between information about adoption and information about abortion in this context. . . .

1

The majority tries to distinguish *Casey* as concerning a regulation of professional conduct that only incidentally burdened speech. *Casey*, in its view, applies only when obtaining "informed consent" to a medical procedure is directly at issue.

This distinction, however, lacks moral, practical, and legal force. The individuals at issue here are all medical personnel engaging in activities that directly affect a woman's health—not significantly different from the doctors at issue in *Casey*. After all, the statute here applies only to "primary care clinics," which provide "services for the care and treatment of patients for whom the clinic accepts responsibility." . . . And the persons responsible for patients at those clinics are all persons "licensed, certified or registered to provide" pregnancy-related medical services. . . . The petitioners have not . . . provided any example of a covered clinic that is not operated by licensed doctors or what the statute specifies are equivalent professionals. . . .

The Act requires these medical professionals to disclose information about the possibility of abortion (including potential financial help) that is as likely helpful to granting "informed consent" as is information about the possibility of adoption and childbirth (including potential financial help). That is why I find it impossible to drive any meaningful legal wedge between the law, as interpreted in *Casey*, and the law as it should be applied in this case. If the law in *Casey* regulated speech "only 'as part of the *practice* of medicine,' " . . . so too here.

The majority contends that the disclosure here is unrelated to a "medical procedure," unlike that in *Casey*, and so the State has no reason to inform a woman about alternatives to childbirth (or, presumably, the health risks of childbirth). . . . Really? No one doubts that choosing an abortion is a medical procedure that involves certain health risks. . . . But the same is true of carrying a child to term and giving birth. . . . Indeed, nationwide "childbirth is 14 times more likely than abortion to result in" the woman's death. . . . Health considerations do not favor disclosure of alternatives and risks associated with the latter but not those associated with the former.

In any case, informed consent principles apply more broadly than only to discrete "medical procedures." Prescription drug labels warn patients of risks even though taking prescription drugs may not be considered a "medical procedure." 21 CFR § 201.56 (2017). In California, clinics that screen for breast cancer must post a sign in their offices notifying patients that, if they are diagnosed with breast cancer, their doctor must provide "a written summary of alternative efficacious methods of treatment," a notification that does not relate to the *screening* procedure at issue. . . . If even these disclosures fall outside the majority's cramped view of *Casey* and informed consent, it undoubtedly would invalidate the many other disclosures that are routine in the medical context as well.

The majority also finds it "[t]ellin[g]" that general practice clinics—*i.e.*, paid clinics—are not required to provide the licensed notice. But the lack-of-information problem that the statute seeks to ameliorate is a problem that the State explains is commonly found among low-income women. . . . That those with low income might lack the time to become fully informed and that this circumstance might prove disproportionately correlated with income is not intuitively surprising. Nor is it surprising that those with low income, whatever they choose in respect to pregnancy, might find information about financial assistance particularly useful. . . .

2

Separately, finding no First Amendment infirmity in the licensed notice is consistent with earlier Court rulings. [I]n *Zauderer* we . . . refused to apply heightened scrutiny, instead asking whether the disclosure requirements were "reasonably related to the State's interest in preventing deception of consumers." . . .

The majority concludes that *Zauderer* does not apply because the disclosure "in no way relates to the services that licensed clinics provide." But information about state resources for family planning, prenatal care, and abortion *is* related to the services that licensed clinics provide. These clinics provide counseling about contraception (which is a family-planning service), ultrasounds or pregnancy testing (which is prenatal care), or abortion. . . . The required disclosure is related to the clinic's services because it provides information about state resources for the very same services. A patient who knows that she can receive free prenatal care from the State may well prefer to forgo the prenatal care offered at one of the clinics here. And for those interested in family planning and abortion services, information about such alternatives is relevant information to patients offered prenatal care, just as *Casey* considered information about adoption to be relevant to the abortion decision.

Regardless, *Zauderer* is not so limited. *Zauderer* turned on the "material differences between disclosure requirements and outright prohibitions on speech." . . . A disclosure requirement does not prevent speakers "from conveying information to the public," but "only require[s] them to provide somewhat more information than they might otherwise be inclined to present." . . . Where a State's requirement to speak "purely factual and uncontroversial information" does not attempt "to 'prescribe what shall be orthodox in politics, nationalism, religion, or other matters of opinion or force citizens to confess by word or act their faith therein,' " it does not warrant heightened scrutiny. . . .

In *Zauderer*, the Court emphasized the reason that the First Amendment protects commercial speech at all: "the value to consumers of the information such speech provides." . . . For that reason, a professional's "constitutionally protected interest in *not* providing any particular factual information in his advertising is minimal." . . . But this rationale is not in any way tied to advertisements about a professional's own services. For instance, it applies equally to a law that requires doctors, when discharging a child under eight years of age, to "provide to and discuss with the parents . . . information on the current law requiring child passenger restraint systems, safety belts, and the transportation of children in rear seats." Cal. Veh. Code . . . . Even though child seat belt laws do not directly relate to the doctor's own services, telling parents about such laws does nothing to undermine the flow of factual information. Whether the context is advertising the professional's own services or other commercial speech, a doctor's First Amendment interest in not providing factual information to patients is the same: minimal, because his professional speech is protected precisely because of its informational value to patients. There is no reason to subject such laws to heightened scrutiny.

Accordingly, the majority's reliance on cases that prohibit rather than require speech is misplaced. I agree that " 'in the fields of medicine and public heath, . . . information can save lives,' " but the licensed disclosure *serves* that informational interest by requiring clinics to notify patients of the availability of state resources for family planning services, prenatal care, and abortion, which—unlike the majority's examples of normative statements—is truthful and nonmisleading information. Abortion is a controversial topic and a source of normative debate, but the availability of state resources is not a normative statement or a fact of debatable truth. The disclosure . . . expresses no official preference for one choice over the other. Similarly, . . . the marketplace of ideas . . . is fostered, not hindered, by providing information to patients to enable them to make fully informed medical decisions in respect to their pregnancies.

Of course, one might take the majority's decision to mean that speech about abortion is special, that it involves in this case not only professional medical matters, but also views based on deeply held religious and moral beliefs about the nature of the practice. To that extent, arguably, the speech here is different from that at issue in *Zauderer*. But . . . the need for evenhandedness . . . should prove particularly weighty in a case involving abortion rights[,] because Americans hold strong, and differing, views about the matter. . . . [I]t is particularly important to interpret the First Amendment so that it applies evenhandedly as between those who disagree so strongly. For this reason too a Constitution that allows States to insist that medical providers tell women about the possibility of adoption should also allow States similarly to insist that medical providers tell women about the possibility of abortion.

D

It is particularly unfortunate that the majority . . . declines to reach . . . arguments that the Act discriminates on the basis of viewpoint. The petitioners argue that . . . the statute unnecessarily imposes a disproportionate burden upon facilities with pro-life views, the very facilities most likely to find the statute's references to abortion morally abhorrent. . . .

. . . [T]he majority . . . conclude[es] that the Act is underinclusive. But the key question is whether . . . exempt clinics are significantly more likely than are the pro-life clinics to tell or to have told their pregnant patients about the existence of these programs—in the absence of any statutory compulsion. If so, it may make sense—in terms of the statute's informational objective—to exempt them, namely if there is no need to cover them. . . . But, if there are not good reasons to exempt these clinics from coverage, *i.e.*, if, for example, they too frequently do not tell their patients about the availability of abortion services, the petitioners' claim of viewpoint discrimination becomes much stronger.

The petitioners, however, did not develop this point in the record below. . . . Given the absence of evidence in the record before the lower courts, the "viewpoint discrimination" claim could not justify the issuance of a preliminary injunction.

II

. . .

[With respect to the notice provision requiring facilities not licensed as medical facilities to say so,] the majority . . . applies a searching standard of review based on our precedents that deal with speech *restrictions*, not *disclosures*. . . . This approach is incompatible with *Zauderer*. . . .

There is no basis for finding the State's interest "hypothetical." The legislature heard that information-related delays in qualified healthcare negatively affect women seeking to terminate their pregnancies as well as women carrying their pregnancies to term, with delays in qualified prenatal care causing life-long health problems for infants. . . . Even without such testimony, it is "self-evident" that patients might think they are receiving qualified medical care when they enter facilities that collect health information, perform obstetric ultrasounds or sonograms, diagnose pregnancy, and provide counseling about pregnancy options or other prenatal care. . . . The State's conclusion to that effect is certainly reasonable.

The majority also suggests that the Act applies too broadly . . . . But the Court has long held that a law is not unreasonable merely because it is overinclusive. . . .

Relatedly, the majority suggests that the Act is suspect because it covers some speakers but not others. I agree that a law's exemptions can reveal viewpoint discrimination (although the majority does not reach this point). . . . Accordingly, where a law's exemptions "facilitate speech on only one side of the abortion debate," there is a "clear form of viewpoint discrimination." *McCullen* . . . .

There is no cause for such concern here. The Act does not, on its face, distinguish between facilities that favor pro-life and those that favor pro-choice points of view. Nor is there any convincing evidence before us or in the courts below that discrimination was the purpose or the effect of the statute. Notably, California does not single out pregnancy-related facilities for this type of disclosure requirement. . . . And it is unremarkable that the State excluded the provision of family planning and contraceptive services as triggering conditions. After all, the State was seeking to ensure that "pregnant women in California know when they are getting medical care from licensed professionals," and pregnant women generally do not need contraceptive services.

Finally, . . . I agree that "unduly burdensome disclosure requirements might offend the First Amendment." *Zauderer*, ... But these and similar claims are claims that the statute could be applied unconstitutionally, not that it is unconstitutional on its face. . . . And it will be open to the petitioners to make these claims if and when the State threatens to enforce the statute in this way. But facial relief is inappropriate here . . . .

For instance, . . . I understand the Act [to] require disclosure in no more than two languages—English and Spanish—in the vast majority of California's 58 counties. The exception is Los Angeles County, where, given the large number of different-language speaking groups, expression in many languages may prove necessary to communicate the message to those whom that message will help. Whether the requirement of 13 different languages goes too far and is unnecessarily burdensome in light of the need to secure the statutory objectives is a matter that concerns Los Angeles County alone, and it is a proper subject for a Los Angeles-based as applied challenge in light of whatever facts a plaintiff finds relevant. At most, such facts might show a need for fewer languages, not invalidation of the statute.

. . .

Page 1376. Add at the end of the section:

Matal v. Tam

582 U.S. ___, 137 S.Ct. 1744, 198 L.Ed.2d 366 (2017).

[The report of this case appears supra, at p. 71.]

CHAPTER 14

RESTRICTIONS ON TIME, PLACE, OR MANNER OF EXPRESSION

2. THE NON-TRADITIONAL FORUM: SPEECH ACTIVITIES IN PUBLIC PROPERTY OTHER THAN PARKS AND STREETS

Page 1422. Add after Lee v. International Society for Krishna Consciousness, Inc.:

Minnesota Voters Alliance v. Mansky, 585 U.S. ___, 138 S.Ct. 1876 (2018). The Court held that a Minnesota statute banning the wearing of a "political badge, political button, or other political insignia" inside a polling place on Election Day—in this case applied to the wearing of Tea Party shirts and "Please I.D. Me" buttons—"violates the Free Speech Clause of the First Amendment." Because the ban applied only to "the interior of a polling place" on Election Day, Chief Justice Roberts, in his opinion for the Court, stated that nonpublic forum analysis was appropriate, There being no claim of viewpoint discrimination, the question was therefore whether Minnesota's ban was " 'reasonable in light of the purpose served by the forum': voting."

The Court had upheld "a Tennessee law imposing a 100-foot campaign-free zone around polling place entrances" in Burson v. Freeman, 504 U.S. 191 (1992), and Chief Justice Roberts reaffirmed that a "State may reasonably take steps to ensure that partisan discord not follow the voter up to the voting booth, and distract from a sense of shared civic obligation at the moment it counts the most[—an] interest [that] may be thwarted by displays that do not raise significant concerns in other situations." Still, despite the objective being permissible, Minnesota failed to "draw a reasonable line" concerning what "political" items were prohibited and what were not, and "the unmoored use of the term 'political' in the Minnesota law, combined with haphazard interpretations the State has provided in official guidance and representations to this Court, cause Minnesota's restriction to fail even this forgiving test."

The Court determined that the "indeterminate scope of the political apparel provision" was not sufficiently clarified by the State's Election Day Policy, which was offered "as authoritative guidance regarding implementation of the statute." That guidance included as banned items " '[i]ssue oriented material designed to influence or impact voting,' [which] raises more questions than it answers." A "rule whose fair enforcement requires an election judge to maintain a mental index of the platforms and positions of every candidate and party on the ballot is not reasonable."

Another part of the Policy, which banned "any item 'promoting a group with recognizable political views,' . . . makes matters worse." It did not help that the "State construes the category as limited to groups with 'views' about 'the issues confronting voters in a given election[,]' " for "[a]ny number of associations, educational institutions, businesses, and religious organizations could have an opinion on an 'issue[ ] confronting voters in a given election.' " Nor did the State's suggestion that "the ban covers only apparel promoting groups whose political positions are sufficiently 'well-known[,]' " which "only increases the potential for erratic application."

Chief Justice Roberts further elaborated what would and would not suffice in these paragraphs:

"It is 'self-evident' that an indeterminate prohibition carries with it '[t]he opportunity for abuse, especially where [it] has received a virtually open-ended interpretation.' *Jews for Jesus*, 482 U. S., at 576; see Heffron v. International Soc. for Krishna Consciousness, Inc., 452 U. S. 640, 649 (1981) (warning of the 'more covert forms of discrimination that may result when arbitrary discretion is vested in some governmental authority'). . . . We do not doubt that the vast majority of election judges strive to enforce the statute in an evenhanded manner, nor that some degree of discretion in this setting is necessary. But that discretion must be guided by objective, workable standards. Without them, an election judge's own politics may shape his views on what counts as 'political.' And if voters experience or witness episodes of unfair or inconsistent enforcement of the ban, the State's interest in maintaining a polling place free of distraction and disruption would be undermined by the very measure intended to further it.

"That is not to say that Minnesota has set upon an impossible task. Other States have laws proscribing displays (including apparel) in more lucid terms. See, *e.g.,* Cal. Elec. Code Ann. § 319.5 (West Cum. Supp. 2018) (prohibiting 'the visible display . . . of information that advocates for or against any candidate or measure,' including the 'display of a candidate's name, likeness, or logo,' the 'display of a ballot measure's number, title, subject, or logo,' and '[b]uttons, hats,' or 'shirts' containing such information); Tex. Elec. Code Ann. § 61.010(a) . . . . We do not suggest that such provisions set the outer limit of what a State may proscribe, and do not pass on the constitutionality of laws that are not before us. But we do hold that if a State wishes to set its polling places apart as areas free of partisan discord, it must employ a more discernible approach than the one Minnesota has offered here.

". . . Minnesota has not supported its good intentions with a law capable of reasoned application."

A dissent by Justice Sotomayor, joined by Justice Breyer, contended that the Court should have "certif[ied] this case to the Minnesota Supreme Court for a definitive interpretation of the political apparel ban . . . , which likely would obviate the hypothetical line-drawing problems that form the basis of the Court's decision today." In her view, "[e]specially where there are undisputedly many constitutional applications of a state law that further weighty state interests, the Court should be wary of invalidating a law without giving the State's highest court an opportunity to pass upon it."

3. SPEECH ON PRIVATE PREMISES

Page 1447. Add at end of section:

Packingham v. North Carolina, 582 U.S. ___, 137 S.Ct. 1730 (2017). A North Carolina law made it a felony for a registered sex offender "to gain access to a number of websites, including commonplace social media websites like Facebook and Twitter." A unanimous Court (with Justice Gorsuch not participating) held the law to be a violation of the First Amendment's Free Speech Clause, although three Justices concurred only in the judgment. Justice Kennedy's majority opinion observed that the statute "applies to about 20,000 people in North Carolina and the State has prosecuted over 1,000 people for violating it." As a 21-year-old college student, Packingham had sex with a 13-year-old girl and later pled guilty to a sex crime, which required him to register as a sex offender—a "status that can endure for 30 years or more." Eight years later, happy that a court had dismissed a traffic ticket, he posted a celebratory message on his Facebook profile, which led to his indictment for violating the statute. Though convicted, the Court noted that "[a]t no point during trial or sentencing did the State allege that petitioner contacted a minor—or committed any other illicit act—on the Internet." The Court of Appeals of North Carolina agreed with his First Amendment defense, but a divided North Carolina Supreme Court reversed, rejecting the constitutional claim. Justice Kennedy's opinion reversing that judgment included the following:

II

"A fundamental principle of the First Amendment is that all persons have access to places where they can speak and listen, and then, after reflection, speak and listen once more. The Court has sought to protect the right to speak in this spatial context. A basic rule, for example, is that a street or a park is a quintessential forum for the exercise of First Amendment rights. See Ward v. Rock Against Racism, 491 U. S. 781, 796 (1989). Even in the modern era, these places are still essential venues for public gatherings to celebrate some views, to protest others, or simply to learn and inquire. While in the past there may have been difficulty in identifying the most important places (in a spatial sense) for the exchange of views, today the answer is clear. It is cyberspace—the "vast democratic forums of the Internet" in general, Reno v. American Civil Liberties Union, 521 U. S. 844, 868 (1997), and social media in particular. Seven in ten American adults use at least one Internet social networking service. . . . One of the most popular of these sites is Facebook, the site used by petitioner leading to his conviction in this case. According to sources cited to the Court in this case, Facebook has 1.79 billion active users. . . . This is about three times the population of North America.

"Social media offers 'relatively unlimited, low-cost capacity for communication of all kinds.' . . . On Facebook, for example, users can debate religion and politics with their friends and neighbors or share vacation photos. On LinkedIn, users can look for work, advertise for employees, or review tips on entrepreneurship. And on Twitter, users can petition their elected representatives and otherwise engage with them in a direct manner. Indeed, Governors in all 50 States and almost every Member of Congress have set up accounts for this purpose. . . . In short, social media users employ these websites to engage in a wide array of protected First Amendment activity on topics 'as diverse as human thought.' *Reno*, ...

". . . While we now may be coming to the realization that the Cyber Age is a revolution of historic proportions, we cannot appreciate yet its full dimensions and vast potential to alter how we think, express ourselves, and define who we want to be. The forces and directions of the Internet are so new, so protean, and so far reaching that courts must be conscious that what they say today might be obsolete tomorrow.

"This case is one of the first this Court has taken to address the relationship between the First Amendment and the modern Internet. As a result, the Court must exercise extreme caution before suggesting that the First Amendment provides scant protection for access to vast networks in that medium.

III

"This background informs [our] analysis . . . . Even making the assumption that the statute is content neutral and thus subject to intermediate scrutiny, the provision cannot stand. In order to survive intermediate scrutiny, a law must be 'narrowly tailored to serve a significant governmental interest.' McCullen v. Coakley, ... In other words, the law must not 'burden substantially more speech than is necessary to further the government's legitimate interests.' "

[After reaffirming that "it is clear that a legislature 'may pass valid laws to protect children' and other victims of sexual assault 'from abuse[,]' " Justice Kennedy found it "necessary to make two assumptions to resolve this case. First, given the broad wording of the North Carolina statute at issue, it might well bar access not only to commonplace social media websites but also to websites as varied as Amazon.com, Washingtonpost.com, and Webmd.com."]

"Second, this opinion should not be interpreted as barring a State from enacting more specific laws than the one at issue. . . . Though the issue is not before the Court, it can be assumed that the First Amendment permits a State to enact specific, narrowly tailored laws that prohibit a sex offender from engaging in conduct that often presages a sexual crime, like contacting a minor or using a website to gather information about a minor. . . . Specific laws of that type must be the State's first resort to ward off the serious harm that sexual crimes inflict. (Of importance, the troubling fact that the law imposes severe restrictions on persons who already have served their sentence and are no longer subject to the supervision of the criminal justice system is also not an issue before the Court.)

"Even with these assumptions about the scope of the law and the State's interest, the statute here enacts a prohibition unprecedented in the scope of First Amendment speech it burdens. Social media allows users to gain access to information and communicate with one another about it on any subject that might come to mind. . . . By prohibiting sex offenders from using those websites, North Carolina with one broad stroke bars access to what for many are the principal sources for knowing current events, checking ads for employment, speaking and listening in the modern public square, and otherwise exploring the vast realms of human thought and knowledge. These websites can provide perhaps the most powerful mechanisms available to a private citizen to make his or her voice heard. . . .

"In sum, to foreclose access to social media altogether is to prevent the user from engaging in the legitimate exercise of First Amendment rights. It is unsettling to suggest that only a limited set of websites can be used even by persons who have completed their sentences. Even convicted criminals—and in some instances especially convicted criminals—might receive legitimate benefits from these means for access to the world of ideas, in particular if they seek to reform and to pursue lawful and rewarding lives."

As for the State's contention "that the law must be this broad to serve its preventative purpose of keeping convicted sex offenders away from vulnerable victims[,]" the State "has not . . . met its burden to show that this sweeping law is necessary or legitimate to serve that purpose." Justice Kennedy said that "no case or holding of this Court has approved of a statute as broad in its reach[,]" and he drew an analogy to "Board of Airport Comm'rs of Los Angeles v. Jews for Jesus, Inc., 482 U. S. 569 (1987), where the Court struck down an ordinance prohibiting any 'First Amendment activities' at Los Angeles International Airport because the ordinance covered all manner of protected, nondisruptive behavior including 'talking and reading, or the wearing of campaign buttons or symbolic clothing,' . . . . If a law prohibiting 'all protected expression' at a single airport is not constitutional . . ., it follows with even greater force that the State may not enact this complete bar to the exercise of First Amendment rights on websites integral to the fabric of our modern society and culture." He concluded the majority opinion this way:

"It is well established that, as a general rule, the Government 'may not suppress lawful speech as the means to suppress unlawful speech.' Ashcroft v. Free Speech Coalition, 535 U. S., at 255. That is what North Carolina has done here. Its law must be held invalid."

Justice Alito, joined by Chief Justice Roberts and Justice Thomas, concurred in the judgment "[b]ecause of the law's extraordinary breadth," but he objected to the majority's "undisciplined dicta." In particular, the "Court is unable to resist musings that seem to equate the entirety of the internet with public streets and parks. And this language is bound to be interpreted by some to mean that the States are largely powerless to restrict even the most dangerous sexual predators from visiting any internet sites, including, for example, teenage dating sites and sites designed to permit minors to discuss personal problems with their peers." His opinion emphasized the following:

"The State's interest in protecting children from recidivist sex offenders plainly applies to internet use. Several factors make the internet a powerful tool for the would-be child abuser. First, children often use the internet in a way that gives offenders easy access to their personal information—by, for example, communicating with strangers and allowing sites to disclose their location. Second, the internet provides previously unavailable ways of communicating with, stalking, and ultimately abusing children. An abuser can create a false profile that misrepresents the abuser's age and gender. The abuser can lure the minor into engaging in sexual conversations, sending explicit photos, or even meeting in person. And an abuser can use a child's location posts on the internet to determine the pattern of the child's day-to-day activities—and even the child's location at a given moment. . . .

"Because protecting children from abuse is a compelling state interest and sex offenders can (and do) use the internet to engage in such abuse, it is legitimate and entirely reasonable for States to try to stop abuse from occurring before it happens."

Nonetheless, the statute's "fatal problem . . . is that its wide sweep precludes access to a large number of websites that are most unlikely to facilitate the commission of a sex crime against a child." Taking as examples of the statute's coverage Amazon.com, Washingtonpost.com, and WebMD, Justice Alito concluded:

"As these examples illustrate, the North Carolina law has a very broad reach and covers websites that are ill suited for use in stalking or abusing children. The focus of the discussion on these sites—shopping, news, health—does not provide a convenient jumping off point for conversations that may lead to abuse. In addition, the social exchanges facilitated by these websites occur in the open, and this reduces the possibility of a child being secretly lured into an abusive situation. These websites also give sex offenders little opportunity to gather personal details about a child; the information that can be listed in a profile is limited, and the profiles are brief. What is more, none of these websites make it easy to determine a child's precise location at a given moment. For example, they do not permit photo streams (at most, a child could upload a single profile photograph), and they do not include up-to-the minute location services. Such websites would provide essentially no aid to a would-be child abuser.

"Placing this set of websites categorically off limits from registered sex offenders prohibits them from receiving or engaging in speech that the First Amendment protects and does not appreciably advance the State's goal of protecting children from recidivist sex offenders. I am therefore compelled to conclude that, while the law before us addresses a critical problem, it sweeps far too broadly to satisfy the demands of the Free Speech Clause.

II

"While I thus agree with the Court that the particular law at issue in this case violates the First Amendment, I am troubled by the Court's loose rhetoric. . . . [I]f the entirety of the internet or even just 'social media' sites are the 21st century equivalent of public streets and parks, then States may have little ability to restrict the sites that may be visited by even the most dangerous sex offenders. May a State preclude an adult previously convicted of molesting children from visiting a dating site for teenagers? Or a site where minors communicate with each other about personal problems? The Court should be more attentive to the implications of its rhetoric for, contrary to the Court's suggestion, there are important differences between cyberspace and the physical world.

"I will mention a few that are relevant to internet use by sex offenders. First, it is easier for parents to monitor the physical locations that their children visit and the individuals with whom they speak in person than it is to monitor their internet use. Second, if a sex offender is seen approaching children or loitering in a place frequented by children, this conduct may be observed by parents, teachers, or others. Third, the internet offers an unprecedented degree of anonymity and easily permits a would-be molester to assume a false identity."

5. GOVERNMENT SUBSIDIES TO SPEECH

Page 1498. Add after Walker v. Texas Division, Sons of Confederate Veterans:

Matal v. Tam

582 U.S. ___, 137 S.Ct. 1744, 198 L.Ed.2d 366 (2017).

[The report of this case appears *supra*, at p. 71]

CHAPTER 15

PROTECTION OF PENUMBRAL FIRST AMENDMENT RIGHTS

2. COMPELLED AFFIRMATION OF BELIEF

Page 1525. Add after Rumsfeld v. Forum for Academic and Institutional Rights, Inc.:

National Institute of Family and Life Advocates v. Becerra

585 U.S. ___, 138 S.Ct. 2361, ___ L.Ed.2d ___ (2018).

[The report of this case appears supra, at p. 84.]

3. FREEDOM OF ASSOCIATION

D. COMPULSORY MEMBERSHIP AND FUNDING FOR ASSOCIATION SPEECH

Page 1539. Replace Davenport v. Washington Education Association, Ysursa v. Pocatello Education Association, Knox v. Service Employees International Union and Harris v. Quinn with the following:

Janus v. American Federation of State, County and Municipal Employees, Council 31

585 U.S. ___, 138 S.Ct. 2448, ___ L.Ed.2d ___ (2018).

■ JUSTICE ALITO delivered the opinion of the Court.

Under Illinois law, public employees are forced to subsidize a union, even if they choose not to join and strongly object to the positions the union takes in collective bargaining and related activities. We conclude that this arrangement violates the free speech rights of nonmembers by compelling them to subsidize private speech on matters of substantial public concern.

We upheld a similar law in Abood v. Detroit Bd. of Ed., 431 U.S. 209 (1977), and we recognize the importance of following precedent unless there are strong reasons for not doing so. But there are very strong reasons in this case.

Fundamental free speech rights are at stake. *Abood* was poorly reasoned. It has led to practical problems and abuse. It is inconsistent with other First Amendment cases and has been undermined by more recent decisions.

Developments since *Abood* was handed down have shed new light on the issue of agency fees, and no reliance interests on the part of public-sector unions are sufficient to justify the perpetuation of the free speech violations that *Abood* has countenanced for the past 41 years. *Abood* is therefore overruled.

I

A

Under the Illinois Public Labor Relations Act (IPLRA), employees of the State and its political subdivisions are permitted to unionize. If a majority of the employees in a bargaining unit vote to be represented by a union, that union is designated as the exclusive representative of all the employees. Employees in the unit are not obligated to join the union selected by their co-workers, but whether they join or not, that union is deemed to be their sole permitted representative.

Once a union is so designated, it is vested with broad authority. Only the union may negotiate with the employer on matters relating to "pay, wages, hours[,] and other conditions of employment." . . . And this authority extends to the negotiation of what the IPLRA calls "policy matters," such as merit pay, the size of the work force, layoffs, privatization, promotion methods, and non-discrimination policies. . . .

Designating a union as the employees' exclusive representative substantially restricts the rights of individual employees. Among other things, this designation means that individual employees may not be represented by any agent other than the designated union; nor may individual employees negotiate directly with their employer. Protection of the employees' interests is placed in the hands of the union, and therefore the union is required by law to provide fair representation for all employees in the unit, members and nonmembers alike.

Employees who decline to join the union are not assessed full union dues but must instead pay what is generally called an "agency fee," which amounts to a percentage of the union dues. Under *Abood*, nonmembers may be charged for the portion of union dues attributable to activities that are "germane to [the union's] duties as collective-bargaining representative,". . . but nonmembers may not be required to fund the union's political and ideological projects. In labor-law parlance, the outlays in the first category are known as "chargeable" expenditures, while those in the latter are labeled "nonchargeable." . . .

Illinois law does not specify in detail which expenditures are chargeable and which are not. The IPLRA provides that an agency fee may compensate a union for the costs incurred in "the collective bargaining process, contract administration[,] and pursuing matters affecting wages, hours[,] and conditions of employment." . . . Excluded from the agency-fee calculation are union expenditures "related to the election or support of any candidate for political office." . . .

Applying this standard, a union categorizes its expenditures as chargeable or nonchargeable and thus determines a nonmember's "proportionate share," . . . this determination is then audited; the amount of the "proportionate share" is certified to the employer; and the employer automatically deducts that amount from the nonmembers' wages. Nonmembers need not be asked, and they are not required to consent before the fees are deducted.

After the amount of the agency fee is fixed each year, the union must send nonmembers what is known as a *Hudson* notice. See Teachers v. Hudson, 475 U.S. 292 (1986). This notice is supposed to provide nonmembers with "an adequate explanation of the basis for the [agency] fee." . . . If nonmembers "suspect that a union has improperly put certain expenses in the [chargeable] category," they may challenge that determination. . . .

As illustrated by the record in this case, unions charge nonmembers, not just for the cost of collective bargaining per se, but also for many other supposedly connected activities. See App. to Pet. for Cert. 28a–39a. Here, the nonmembers were told that they had to pay for "[l]obbying," "[s]ocial and recreational activities," "advertising," "[m]embership meetings and conventions," and "litigation," as well as other unspecified "[s]ervices" that "may ultimately inure to the benefit of the members of the local bargaining unit." . . . The total chargeable amount for nonmembers was 78.06% of full union dues.

B

Petitioner Mark Janus is employed by the Illinois Department of Healthcare and Family Services as a child support specialist. The employees in his unit are among the 35,000 public employees in Illinois who are represented by respondent American Federation of State, County, and Municipal Employees, Council 31 (Union). Janus refused to join the Union because he opposes "many of the public policy positions that [it] advocates," including the positions it takes in collective bargaining. Janus believes that the Union's "behavior in bargaining does not appreciate the current fiscal crises in Illinois and does not reflect his best interests or the interests of Illinois citizens." . . . Therefore, if he had the choice, he "would not pay any fees or otherwise subsidize [the Union]." . . . Under his unit's collective-bargaining agreement, however, he was required to pay an agency fee of $44.58 per month—which would amount to about $535 per year.

. . .

[The] amended complaint [Janus filed] claims that all "nonmember fee deductions are coerced political speech" and that "the First Amendment forbids coercing any money from the nonmembers." . . . Respondents moved to dismiss the amended complaint, correctly recognizing that the claim it asserted was foreclosed by *Abood*. The District Court granted the motion and the Court of Appeals for the Seventh Circuit affirmed. . . .

Janus then sought review in this Court, asking us to overrule *Abood* and hold that public-sector agency-fee arrangements are unconstitutional. We granted certiorari to consider this important question.

. . .

III

In *Abood*, the Court upheld the constitutionality of an agency-shop arrangement like the one now before us, but in more recent cases we have recognized that this holding is "something of an anomaly," Knox v. Service Employees, 567 U.S. 298, 311 (2012), and that *Abood*'s "analysis is questionable on several grounds," Harris v. Quinn, 573 U.S., at ___ (2014); see id. at ___ (discussing flaws in *Abood*'s reasoning). We have therefore refused to extend *Abood* to situations where it does not squarely control, see *Harris, supra*, at ___, while leaving for another day the question whether *Abood* should be overruled, *Harris, supra*, at ___, n. 19; see *Knox, supra*, at 310–311.

We now address that question. We first consider whether *Abood*'s holding is consistent with standard First Amendment principles.

A

The First Amendment, made applicable to the States by the Fourteenth Amendment, forbids abridgment of the freedom of speech. We have held time and again that freedom of speech "includes both the right to speak freely and the right to refrain from speaking at all." Wooley v. Maynard, 430 U.S. 705 (1977); see Riley v. National Federation of Blind of N. C., Inc., 487 U.S. 781, 796–797 (1988); Harper & Row, Publishers, Inc. v. Nation Enterprises, 471 U.S. 539, 559 (1985); Miami Herald Publishing Co. v. Tornillo, 418 U.S. 241, 256–257 (1974); accord, Pacific Gas & Elec. Co. v. Public Util. Comm'n of Cal., 475 U.S. 1, 9 (1986) (plurality opinion). The right to eschew association for expressive purposes is likewise protected. Roberts v. United States Jaycees, 468 U.S. 609, 623 (1984) ("Freedom of association . . . plainly presupposes a freedom not to associate"); see Pacific Gas & Elec., *supra*, at 12 ("[F]orced associations that burden protected speech are impermissible"). As Justice Jackson memorably put it: "If there is any fixed star in our constitutional constellation, it is that no official, high or petty, can prescribe what shall be orthodox in politics, nationalism, religion, or other matters of opinion or force citizens to confess by word or act their faith therein." West Virginia Bd. of Ed. v. Barnette, 319 U.S. 624, 642 (1943) (emphasis added).

Compelling individuals to mouth support for views they find objectionable violates that cardinal constitutional command, and in most contexts, any such effort would be universally condemned. Suppose, for example, that the State of Illinois required all residents to sign a document expressing support for a particular set of positions on controversial public issues—say, the platform of one of the major political parties. No one, we trust, would seriously argue that the First Amendment permits this.

Perhaps because such compulsion so plainly violates the Constitution, most of our free speech cases have involved restrictions on what can be said, rather than laws compelling speech. But measures compelling speech are at least as threatening.

Free speech serves many ends. It is essential to our democratic form of government, see, e.g., Garrison v. Louisiana, 379 U.S. 64, 74–75 (1964), and it furthers the search for truth, see, e.g., Thornhill v. Alabama, 310 U.S. 88, 95 (1940). Whenever the Federal Government or a State prevents individuals from saying what they think on important matters or compels them to voice ideas with which they disagree, it undermines these ends.

When speech is compelled, however, additional damage is done. In that situation, individuals are coerced into betraying their convictions. Forcing free and independent individuals to endorse ideas they find objectionable is always demeaning, and for this reason, one of our landmark free speech cases said that a law commanding "involuntary affirmation" of objected-to beliefs would require "even more immediate and urgent grounds" than a law demanding silence. *Barnette*, *supra*, at 633; see also *Riley*, *supra*, at 796–797 (rejecting "deferential test" for compelled speech claims).

Compelling a person to subsidize the speech of other private speakers raises similar First Amendment concerns. *Knox*, *supra*, at 309; United States v. United Foods, Inc., 533 U.S. 405, 410 (2001); *Abood*, *supra*, at 222, 234–235. As Jefferson famously put it, "to compel a man to furnish contributions of money for the propagation of opinions which he disbelieves and abhor[s] is sinful and tyrannical." A Bill for Establishing Religious Freedom, in 2 Papers of Thomas

Jefferson 545 (J. Boyd ed. 1950) (emphasis deleted and footnote omitted); see also *Hudson*, 475 U.S., at 305, n. 15. We have therefore recognized that a " 'significant impingement on First Amendment rights' " occurs when public employees are required to provide financial support for a union that "takes many positions during collective bargaining that have powerful political and civic consequences." *Knox, supra*, at 310–311 (quoting Ellis v. Railway Clerks, 466 U.S. 435, 455 (1984)).

Because the compelled subsidization of private speech seriously impinges on First Amendment rights, it cannot be casually allowed. Our free speech cases have identified "levels of scrutiny" to be applied in different contexts, and in three recent cases, we have considered the standard that should be used in judging the constitutionality of agency fees. See *Knox, supra; Harris, supra*; Friedrichs v. California Teachers Assn., 578 U.S. ___ (2016) (per curiam) (affirming decision below by equally divided Court).

In *Knox*, the first of these cases, we found it sufficient to hold that the conduct in question was unconstitutional under even the test used for the compulsory subsidization of commercial speech. Even though commercial speech has been thought to enjoy a lesser degree of protection, prior precedent in that area, specifically *United Foods, supra*, had applied what we characterized as "exacting" scrutiny, . . . a less demanding test than the "strict" scrutiny that might be thought to apply outside the commercial sphere. Under "exacting" scrutiny, we noted, a compelled subsidy must "serve a compelling state interest that cannot be achieved through means significantly less restrictive of associational freedoms."

In *Harris*, the second of these cases, we again found that an agency-fee requirement failed "exacting scrutiny." . . . But we questioned whether that test provides sufficient protection for free speech rights, since "it is apparent that the speech compelled" in agency-fee cases "is not commercial speech." . . .

Picking up that cue, petitioner in the present case contends that the Illinois law at issue should be subjected to "strict scrutiny." The dissent, on the other hand, proposes that we apply what amounts to rational-basis review, that is, that we ask only whether a government employer could reasonably believe that the exaction of agency fees serves its interests. See post, at ___ (KAGAN, J., dissenting) ("A government entity could reasonably conclude that such a clause was needed"). This form of minimal scrutiny is foreign to our free-speech jurisprudence, and we reject it here. At the same time, we again find it unnecessary to decide the issue of strict scrutiny because the Illinois scheme cannot survive under even the more permissive standard applied in *Knox* and *Harris*.

. . .

B

In *Abood*, the main defense of the agency-fee arrangement was that it served the State's interest in "labor peace." . . . By "labor peace," the *Abood* Court meant avoidance of the conflict and disruption that it envisioned would occur if the employees in a unit were represented by more than one union. In such a situation, the Court predicted, "inter-union rivalries" would foster "dissension within the work force," and the employer could face "conflicting demands from different unions." . . . Confusion would ensue if the employer entered into and attempted to "enforce two or more agreements specifying different terms and conditions of employment." And a settlement with one union would be "subject to attack from [a] rival labor organizatio[n]." . . .

We assume that "labor peace," in this sense of the term, is a compelling state interest, but *Abood* cited no evidence that the pandemonium it imagined would result if agency fees were not allowed, and it is now clear that *Abood*'s fears were unfounded. The *Abood* Court assumed that designation of a union as the exclusive representative of all the employees in a unit and the exaction of agency fees are inextricably linked, but that is simply not true. . . .

The federal employment experience is illustrative. Under federal law, a union chosen by majority vote is designated as the exclusive representative of all the employees, but federal law does not permit agency fees. See 5 U.S.C. §§ 7102, 7111(a), 7114(a). Nevertheless, nearly a million federal employees—about 27% of the federal work force—are union members. The situation in the Postal Service is similar. Although permitted to choose an exclusive representative, Postal Service employees are not required to pay an agency fee, 39 U.S.C. §§ 1203(a), 1209(c), and about 400,000 are union members. Likewise, millions of public employees in the 28 States that have laws generally prohibiting agency fees are represented by unions that serve as the exclusive representatives of all the employees. Whatever may have been the case 41 years ago when *Abood* was handed down, it is now undeniable that "labor peace" can readily be achieved "through means significantly less restrictive of associational freedoms" than the assessment of agency fees. . . .

C

In addition to the promotion of "labor peace," *Abood* cited "the risk of 'free riders' " as justification for agency fees. . . . Respondents and some of their amici endorse this reasoning, contending that agency fees are needed to prevent nonmembers from enjoying the benefits of union representation without shouldering the costs.

Petitioner strenuously objects to this free-rider label. He argues that he is not a free rider on a bus headed for a destination that he wishes to reach but is more like a person shanghaied for an unwanted voyage.

Whichever description fits the majority of public employees who would not subsidize a union if given the option, avoiding free riders is not a compelling interest. As we have noted, "free-rider arguments . . . are generally insufficient to overcome First Amendment objections." *Knox*, 567 U.S., at 311. To hold otherwise across the board would have startling consequences. Many private groups speak out with the objective of obtaining government action that will have the effect of benefiting nonmembers. May all those who are thought to benefit from such efforts be compelled to subsidize this speech?

Suppose that a particular group lobbies or speaks out on behalf of what it thinks are the needs of senior citizens or veterans or physicians, to take just a few examples. Could the government require that all seniors, veterans, or doctors pay for that service even if they object? It has never been thought that this is permissible. . . . In simple terms, the First Amendment does not permit the government to compel a person to pay for another party's speech just because the government thinks that the speech furthers the interests of the person who does not want to pay.

Those supporting agency fees contend that the situation here is different because unions are statutorily required to "represen[t] the interests of all public employees in the unit," whether or not they are union members. . . . Why might this matter?

We can think of two possible arguments. It might be argued that a State has a compelling interest in requiring the payment of agency fees because (1) unions would otherwise be unwilling to represent nonmembers or (2) it would be fundamentally unfair to require unions to provide fair representation for nonmembers if nonmembers were not required to pay. Neither of these arguments is sound.

First, it is simply not true that unions will refuse to serve as the exclusive representative of all employees in the unit if they are not given agency fees. As noted, unions represent millions of public employees in jurisdictions that do not permit agency fees. No union is ever compelled to seek that designation. On the contrary, designation as exclusive representative is avidly sought. Why is this so?

Even without agency fees, designation as the exclusive representative confers many benefits. As noted, that status gives the union a privileged place in negotiations over wages, benefits, and working conditions. . . . Not only is the union given the exclusive right to speak for all the employees in collective bargaining, but the employer is required by state law to listen to and to bargain in good faith with only that union. . . . Designation as exclusive representative thus "results in a tremendous increase in the power" of the union.

In addition, a union designated as exclusive representative is often granted special privileges, such as obtaining information about employees . . . and having dues and fees deducted directly from employee wages . . . . The collective-bargaining agreement in this case guarantees a long list of additional privileges.

These benefits greatly outweigh any extra burden imposed by the duty of providing fair representation for nonmembers. What this duty entails, in simple terms, is an obligation not to "act solely in the interests of [the union's] own members." . . .

What does this mean when it comes to the negotiation of a contract? The union may not negotiate a collective-bargaining agreement that discriminates against nonmembers, but the union's bargaining latitude would be little different if state law simply prohibited public employers from entering into agreements that discriminate in that way. And for that matter, it is questionable whether the Constitution would permit a public-sector employer to adopt a collective-bargaining agreement that discriminates against nonmembers. . . . It is noteworthy that neither respondents nor any of the 39 amicus briefs supporting them—nor the dissent—has explained why the duty of fair representation causes public-sector unions to incur significantly greater expenses than they would otherwise bear in negotiating collective-bargaining agreements.

What about the representation of nonmembers in grievance proceedings? Unions do not undertake this activity solely for the benefit of nonmembers— which is why Illinois law gives a public-sector union the right to send a representative to such proceedings even if the employee declines union representation. . . . Representation of nonmembers furthers the union's interest in keeping control of the administration of the collective-bargaining agreement, since the resolution of one employee's grievance can affect others. And when a union controls the grievance process, it may, as a practical matter, effectively subordinate "the interests of [an] individual employee. . .to the collective interests of all employees in the bargaining unit." . . .

In any event, whatever unwanted burden is imposed by the representation of nonmembers in disciplinary matters can be eliminated "through means significantly less restrictive of associational freedoms" than the imposition of agency fees. Individual nonmembers could be required to pay for that service or could be denied union representation altogether. Thus, agency fees cannot be sustained on the ground that unions would otherwise be unwilling to represent nonmembers.

Nor can such fees be justified on the ground that it would otherwise be unfair to require a union to bear the duty of fair representation. That duty is a necessary concomitant of the authority that a union seeks when it chooses to serve as the exclusive representative of all the employees in a unit. As explained, designating a union as the exclusive representative of nonmembers substantially restricts the nonmembers' rights. Protection of their interests is placed in the hands of the union, and if the union were free to disregard or even work against those interests, these employees would be wholly unprotected. That is why we said many years ago that serious "constitutional questions [would] arise" if the union were not subject to the duty to represent all employees fairly.

In sum, we do not see any reason to treat the free-rider interest any differently in the agency-fee context than in any other First Amendment context. We therefore hold that agency fees cannot be upheld on free-rider grounds.

IV

Implicitly acknowledging the weakness of *Abood*'s own reasoning, proponents of agency fees have come forward with alternative justifications for the decision, and we now address these arguments.

A

The most surprising of these new arguments is the Union respondent's originalist defense of *Abood*. According to this argument, *Abood* was correctly decided because the First Amendment was not originally understood to provide any protection for the free speech rights of public employees.

As an initial matter, we doubt that the Union—or its members—actually want us to hold that public employees have "*no* [free speech] rights." . . .

It is particularly discordant to find this argument in a brief that trumpets the importance of *stare decisis*. See Brief for Union Respondent 47–57. Taking away free speech protection for public employees would mean overturning decades of landmark precedent. Under the Union's theory, Pickering v. Board of Ed. of Township High School Dist. 205, Will Cty., 391 U.S. 563 (1968), and its progeny would fall. Yet *Pickering*, as we will discuss, is now the foundation for respondents' chief defense of *Abood*. And indeed, *Abood* itself would have to go if public employees have no free speech rights, since *Abood* holds that the First Amendment prohibits the exaction of agency fees for political or ideological purposes. Our political patronage cases would be doomed. See, e.g., Rutan v. Republican Party of Ill., 497 U.S. 62 (1990); Branti v. Finkel, 445 U.S. 507 (1980); Elrod v. Burns, 427 U.S. 347 (1976). Also imperiled would be older precedents like Wieman v. Updegraff, 344 U.S. 183 (1952) (loyalty oaths), Shelton v. Tucker, 364 U.S. 479 (1960) (disclosure of memberships and contributions), and Keyishian v. Board of Regents of Univ. of State of N. Y., 385 U.S. 589 (1967) (subversive speech). Respondents presumably want none of this, desiring instead that we apply the Constitution's supposed original meaning only when it suits them—to retain the part of *Abood* that they like. See Tr. of Oral Arg. 56–57. We will not engage in this halfway originalism.

Nor, in any event, does the First Amendment's original meaning support the Union's claim. The Union offers no persuasive founding-era evidence that public employees were understood to lack free speech protections. While it observes that restrictions on federal employees' activities have existed since the First Congress, most of its historical examples involved limitations on public officials' outside business dealings, not on their speech. The only early speech restrictions the Union identifies are an 1806 statute prohibiting military personnel from using " 'contemptuous or disrespectful words against the President' " and other officials, and an 1801 directive limiting electioneering by top government employees. . . . But those examples at most show that the government was understood to have power to limit employee speech that threatened important governmental interests (such as maintaining military discipline and preventing corruption)—not that public employees' speech was entirely unprotected. Indeed, more recently this Court has upheld similar restrictions even while recognizing that government employees possess First Amendment rights. . . .

Ultimately, the Union relies, not on founding-era evidence, but on dictum from a 1983 opinion of this Court stating that, "[f]or most of th[e 20th] century, the unchallenged dogma was that a public employee had no right to object to conditions placed upon the terms of employment—including those which restricted the exercise of constitutional rights." Connick v. Myers, 461 U.S. 138, 143. Even on its own terms, this dictum about 20th-century views does not purport to describe how the First Amendment was understood in 1791. And a careful examination of the decisions by this Court that *Connick* cited to support its dictum reveals that none of them rested on the facile premise that public employees are unprotected by the First Amendment. Instead, they considered (much as we do today) whether particular speech restrictions were "necessary to protect" fundamental government interests. . . .

. . . We can safely say that, at the time of the adoption of the First Amendment, no one gave any thought to whether public-sector unions could charge nonmembers agency fees. Entities resembling labor unions did not exist at the founding, and public-sector unions did not emerge until the mid-20th century. The idea of public-sector unionization and agency fees would astound those who framed and ratified the Bill of Rights. Thus, the Union cannot point to any accepted founding-era practice that even remotely resembles the compulsory assessment of agency fees from public-sector employees. We do know, however, that prominent members of the founding generation condemned laws requiring public employees to affirm or support beliefs with which they disagreed. As noted, Jefferson denounced compelled support for such beliefs as "sinful and tyrannical," and others expressed similar views. . . .

    . . .

B

The principal defense of *Abood* advanced by respondents and the dissent is based on our decision in *Pickering*, 391 U.S. 563, which held that a school district violated the First Amendment by firing a teacher for writing a letter critical of the school administration. Under *Pickering* and later cases in the same line, employee speech is largely unprotected if it is part of what the employee is paid to do, see Garcetti v. Ceballos, 547 U.S. 410, 421–422 (2006), or if it involved a matter of only private concern, see *Connick*. On the other hand, when a public employee speaks as a citizen on a matter of public concern, the employee's speech is protected unless " 'the interest of the state, as an employer, in promoting the efficiency of the public services it performs through its employees' outweighs 'the interests of the [employee], as a citizen, in commenting upon matters of public concern.' " *Pickering* was the centerpiece of the defense of *Abood* in *Harris*, see 573 U.S., at ___ (Kagan, J., dissenting), and we found the argument unpersuasive. . . . The intervening years have not improved its appeal.

As we pointed out in *Harris*, *Abood* was not based on *Pickering*. . . . And we have previously taken a dim view of similar attempts to recast problematic First Amendment decisions. . . . We see no good reason, at this late date, to try to shoehorn *Abood* into the *Pickering* framework.

Even if that were attempted, the shoe would be a painful fit for at least three reasons.

First, the *Pickering* framework was developed for use in a very different context—in cases that involve "one employee's speech and its impact on that employee's public responsibilities." . . . This case, by contrast, involves a blanket requirement that all employees subsidize speech with which they may not agree. While we have sometimes looked to *Pickering* in considering general rules that affect broad categories of employees, we have acknowledged that the standard *Pickering* analysis requires modification in that situation. A speech-restrictive law with "widespread impact," we have said, "gives rise to far more serious concerns than could any single supervisory decision." . . . Therefore, when such a law is at issue, the government must shoulder a correspondingly "heav[ier]" burden, and is entitled to considerably less deference in its assessment that a predicted harm justifies a particular impingement on First Amendment rights. . . . The end product of those adjustments is a test that more closely resembles exacting scrutiny than the traditional *Pickering* analysis.

The core collective-bargaining issue of wages and benefits illustrates this point. Suppose that a single employee complains that he or she should have received a 5% raise. This individual complaint would likely constitute a matter of only private concern and would therefore be unprotected under *Pickering*. But a public-sector union's demand for a 5% raise for the many thousands of employees it represents would be another matter entirely. Granting such a raise could have a serious impact on the budget of the government unit in question, and by the same token, denying a raise might have a significant effect on the performance of government services. When a large number of employees speak through their union, the category of speech that is of public concern is greatly enlarged, and the category of speech that is of only private concern is substantially shrunk. By disputing this, the dissent denies the obvious.

Second, the *Pickering* framework fits much less well where the government compels speech or speech subsidies in support of third parties. *Pickering* is based on the insight that the speech of a public-sector employee may interfere with the effective operation of a government office. When a public employer does not simply restrict potentially disruptive speech but commands that its employees mouth a message on its own behalf, the calculus is very different. Of course, if the speech in question is part of an employee's official duties, the employer may insist that the employee deliver any lawful message. Otherwise, however, it is not easy to imagine a situation in which a public employer has a legitimate need to demand that its employees recite words with which they disagree. And we have never applied *Pickering* in such a case.

. . .

Third, although both *Pickering* and *Abood* divided speech into two categories, the cases' categorization schemes do not line up. Superimposing the *Pickering* scheme on *Abood* would significantly change the *Abood* regime.

Let us first look at speech that is not germane to collective bargaining but instead concerns political or ideological issues. Under *Abood*, a public employer is flatly prohibited from permitting nonmembers to be charged for this speech, but under *Pickering*, the employees' free speech interests could be overcome if a court found that the employer's interests outweighed the employees'.

A similar problem arises with respect to speech that is germane to collective bargaining. The parties dispute how much of this speech is of public concern, but respondents concede that much of it falls squarely into that category. Under *Abood*, nonmembers may be required to pay for all this speech, but *Pickering* would permit that practice only if the employer's interests outweighed those of the employees. Thus, recasting *Abood* as an application of Pickering would substantially alter the *Abood* scheme.

For all these reasons, *Pickering* is a poor fit indeed.

. . .

VI

For the reasons given above, we conclude that public-sector agency-shop arrangements violate the First Amendment, and *Abood* erred in concluding otherwise. There remains the question whether *stare decisis* nonetheless counsels against overruling *Abood*. It does not.

"*Stare decisis* is the preferred course because it promotes the evenhanded, predictable, and consistent development of legal principles, fosters reliance on judicial decisions, and contributes to the actual and perceived integrity of the judicial process." . . . We will not overturn a past decision unless there are strong grounds for doing so. But as we have often recognized, *stare decisis* is " 'not an inexorable command.' " . . .

The doctrine "is at its weakest when we interpret the Constitution because our interpretation can be altered only by constitutional amendment or by overruling our prior decisions." . . . And *stare decisis* applies with perhaps least force of all to decisions that wrongly denied First Amendment rights: "This Court has not hesitated to overrule decisions offensive to the First Amendment (a fixed star in our constitutional constellation, if there is one)." . . .

Our cases identify factors that should be taken into account in deciding whether to overrule a past decision. Five of these are most important here: the quality of *Abood*'s reasoning, the workability of the rule it established, its consistency with other related decisions, developments since the decision was handed down, and reliance on the decision. After analyzing these factors, we conclude that *stare decisis* does not require us to retain *Abood*.

A

. . .

Abood went wrong at the start when it concluded that two prior decisions, Railway Employes v. Hanson, 351 U.S. 225 (1956), and Machinists v. Street, 367 U.S. 740 (1961), "appear[ed] to require validation of the agency-shop agreement before [the Court]." . . . Properly understood, those decisions did no such thing. Both cases involved Congress's "bare authorization" of private-sector union shops under the Railway Labor Act.[24] *Abood* failed to appreciate that a very different First Amendment question arises when a State requires its employees to pay agency fees.

Moreover, neither *Hanson* nor *Street* gave careful consideration to the First Amendment. . . . *Abood* nevertheless took the view that *Hanson* and *Street* "all but decided" the important free speech issue that was before the Court. . . .

Abood's unwarranted reliance on *Hanson* and *Street* appears to have contributed to another mistake: *Abood* judged the constitutionality of public-sector agency fees under a deferential standard that finds no support in our free speech cases. . . .

. . .

In sum . . . *Abood* was not well reasoned.

B

Another relevant consideration in the *stare decisis* calculus is the workability of the precedent in question, and that factor also weighs against *Abood*.

1

Abood's line between chargeable and nonchargeable union expenditures has proved to be impossible to draw with precision. . . .

In *Knox*, for example, we confronted a union's claim that the costs of lobbying the legislature and the electorate about a ballot measure were chargeable expenses. . . . The Court rejected this claim out of hand, 567 U.S., at 320–321, but the dissent refused to do so, id., at 336 (opinion of Breyer, J.). And in the present case, nonmembers are required to pay for unspecified "[l]obbying" expenses and for "[s]ervices" that "may ultimately inure to the benefit of the members of the local bargaining unit." App. to Pet. for Cert. 31a–32a. That formulation is broad enough to encompass just about anything that the union might choose to do.

Respondents agree that *Abood*'s chargeable-nonchargeable line suffers from "a vagueness problem," that it sometimes "allows what it shouldn't allow," and that "a firm[er] line c[ould] be drawn." Tr. of Oral Arg. 47–48. They therefore

---

[24] No First Amendment issue could have properly arisen in those cases unless Congress's enactment of a provision allowing, but not requiring, private parties to enter into union-shop arrangements was sufficient to establish governmental action. That proposition was debatable when Abood was decided, and is even more questionable today. See American Mfrs. Mut. Ins. Co. v. Sullivan, 526 U.S. 40, 53 (1999); Jackson v. Metropolitan Edison Co., 419 U.S. 345, 357 (1974). Compare, e.g., White v. Communications Workers of Am., AFL-CIO, Local 1300, 370 F.3d 346, 350 (C.A.3 2004) (no state action), and Kolinske v. Lubbers, 712 F.2d 471, 477–478 (C.A.D.C.1983) (same), with Beck v. Communications Workers of Am., 776 F.2d 1187, 1207 (C.A.4 1985) (state action), and Linscott v. Millers Falls Co., 440 F.2d 14, 16, and n. 2 (C.A.1 1971) (same). We reserved decision on this question in Communications Workers v. Beck, 487 U.S. 735, 761 (1988), and do not resolve it here.

argue that we should "consider revisiting" this part of *Abood*. Tr. of Oral Arg. 66; see Brief for Union Respondent 46–47; Brief for State Respondents 30. This concession only underscores the reality that *Abood* has proved unworkable: Not even the parties defending agency fees support the line that it has taken this Court over 40 years to draw.

. . .

C

Developments since *Abood*, both factual and legal, have also "eroded" the decision's "underpinnings" and left it an outlier among our First Amendment cases.

1

Abood pinned its result on the "unsupported empirical assumption" that "the principle of exclusive representation in the public sector is dependent on a union or agency shop." But, as already noted, experience has shown otherwise.

It is also significant that the Court decided *Abood* against a very different legal and economic backdrop. Public-sector unionism was a relatively new phenomenon in 1977. . . . Since then, public-sector union membership has come to surpass private-sector union membership, even though there are nearly four times as many total private-sector employees as public-sector employees.

This ascendance of public-sector unions has been marked by a parallel increase in public spending. In 1970, total state and local government expenditures amounted to $646 per capita in nominal terms, or about $4,000 per capita in 2014 dollars. See Dept. of Commerce, Statistical Abstract of the United States: 1972, p. 419 . . . . By 2014, that figure had ballooned to approximately $10,238 per capita. ProQuest, Statistical Abstract of the United States: 2018, pp. 17, Table 14, 300, Table 469. Not all that increase can be attributed to public-sector unions, of course, but the mounting costs of public-employee wages, benefits, and pensions undoubtedly played a substantial role. We are told, for example, that Illinois' pension funds are underfunded by $129 billion as a result of generous public-employee retirement packages. . . . Unsustainable collective-bargaining agreements have also been blamed for multiple municipal bankruptcies. See Brief for State of Michigan et al. as Amici Curiae 10–19. These developments, and the political debate over public spending and debt they have spurred, have given collective-bargaining issues a political valence that *Abood* did not fully appreciate.

Abood is also an "anomaly" in our First Amendment jurisprudence, as we recognized in *Harris* and *Knox* . . .

. . .

D

In some cases, reliance provides a strong reason for adhering to established law, and this is the factor that is stressed most strongly by respondents, their amici, and the dissent. They contend that collective-bargaining agreements now in effect were negotiated with agency fees in mind and that unions may have given up other benefits in exchange for provisions granting them such fees. In this case, however, reliance does not carry decisive weight.

For one thing, it would be unconscionable to permit free speech rights to be abridged in perpetuity in order to preserve contract provisions that will expire on their own in a few years' time. "The fact that [public-sector unions] may view [agency fees] as an entitlement does not establish the sort of reliance interest that could outweigh the countervailing interest that [nonmembers] share in having their constitutional rights fully protected." Arizona v. Gant, 556 U.S. 332, 349 (2009).

For another, *Abood* does not provide "a clear or easily applicable standard, so arguments for reliance based on its clarity are misplaced." South Dakota v. Wayfair, Inc., 585 U.S. ___, ___ (2018).

. . .

We recognize that the loss of payments from nonmembers may cause unions to experience unpleasant transition costs in the short term, and may require unions to make adjustments in order to attract and retain members. But we must weigh these disadvantages against the considerable windfall that unions have received under *Abood* for the past 41 years. It is hard to estimate how many billions of dollars have been taken from nonmembers and transferred to public-sector unions in violation of the First Amendment. Those unconstitutional exactions cannot be allowed to continue indefinitely.

. . .

VII

For these reasons, States and public-sector unions may no longer extract agency fees from nonconsenting employees. Under Illinois law, if a public-sector collective-bargaining agreement includes an agency-fee provision and the union certifies to the employer the amount of the fee, that amount is automatically deducted from the nonmember's wages. . . . No form of employee consent is required.

This procedure violates the First Amendment and cannot continue. Neither an agency fee nor any other payment to the union may be deducted from a nonmember's wages, nor may any other attempt be made to collect such a payment, unless the employee affirmatively consents to pay. By agreeing to pay, nonmembers are waiving their First Amendment rights, and such a waiver cannot be presumed. Rather, to be effective, the waiver must be freely given and shown by "clear and compelling" evidence. Unless employees clearly and affirmatively consent before any money is taken from them, this standard cannot be met.

Abood was wrongly decided and is now overruled. The judgment of the United States Court of Appeals for the Seventh Circuit is reversed, and the case is remanded for further proceedings consistent with this opinion.

. . .

■ JUSTICE SOTOMAYOR, dissenting.

I join Justice Kagan's dissent in full. Although I joined the majority in Sorrell v. IMS Health Inc., 564 U.S. 552 (2011), I disagree with the way that this Court has since interpreted and applied that opinion. . . . Having seen the troubling development in First Amendment jurisprudence over the years, both in this Court and in lower courts, I agree fully with Justice Kagan that *Sorrell*—in the way it has been read by this Court—has allowed courts to "wiel[d] the First Amendment in . . . an aggressive way" just as the majority does today. . . .

■ JUSTICE KAGAN, with whom JUSTICE GINSBURG, JUSTICE BREYER, and JUSTICE SOTOMAYOR join, dissenting.

For over 40 years, [*Abood*] struck a stable balance between public employees' First Amendment rights and government entities' interests in running their workforces as they thought proper. Under that decision, a government entity could require public employees to pay a fair share of the cost that a union incurs when negotiating on their behalf over terms of employment. But no part of that fair-share payment could go to any of the union's political or ideological activities.

That holding fit comfortably with this Court's general framework for evaluating claims that a condition of public employment violates the First Amendment. The Court's decisions have long made plain that government entities have substantial latitude to regulate their employees' speech—especially about terms of employment—in the interest of operating their workplaces effectively. *Abood* allowed governments to do just that. While protecting public employees' expression about non-workplace matters, the decision enabled a government to advance important managerial interests—by ensuring the presence of an exclusive employee representative to bargain with. Far from an "anomaly," the *Abood* regime was a paradigmatic example of how the government can regulate speech in its capacity as an employer.

Not any longer. Today, the Court succeeds in its 6-year campaign to reverse *Abood*. See Friedrichs v. California Teachers Assn., 578 U.S. ___ (2016) (per curiam); Harris v. Quinn, 573 U.S. ___ (2014); Knox v. Service Employees, 567 U.S. 298 (2012). Its decision will have large-scale consequences. Public employee unions will lose a secure source of financial support. State and local governments that thought fair-share provisions furthered their interests will need to find new ways of managing their workforces. Across the country, the relationships of public employees and employers will alter in both predictable and wholly unexpected ways.

Rarely if ever has the Court overruled a decision—let alone one of this import—with so little regard for the usual principles of *stare decisis*. There are no special justifications for reversing *Abood*. It has proved workable. No recent developments have eroded its underpinnings. And it is deeply entrenched, in both the law and the real world. More than 20 States have statutory schemes built on the decision. Those laws underpin thousands of ongoing contracts involving millions of employees. Reliance interests do not come any stronger than those surrounding *Abood*. And likewise, judicial disruption does not get any greater than what the Court does today. I respectfully dissent.

I

I begin with *Abood*, the 41-year-old precedent the majority overrules. That case involved a union that had been certified as the exclusive representative of Detroit's public school teachers. The union's collective-bargaining agreement with the city included an "agency shop" clause, which required teachers who had not joined the union to pay it "a service charge equal to the regular dues required of [u]nion members." . . . A group of non-union members sued over that clause, arguing that it violated the First Amendment.

In considering their challenge, the Court canvassed the purposes of the "agency shop" clause. It was rooted, the Court understood, in the "principle of exclusive union representation"—a "central element" in "industrial relations" since the New Deal. Significant benefits, the Court explained, could derive from the "designation of a single [union] representative" for all similarly situated employees in a workplace. . . . In particular, such arrangements: "avoid[ ] the confusion that would result from attempting to enforce two or more agreements specifying different terms and conditions of employment"; "prevent[ ] inter-union rivalries from creating dissension within the work force"; "free[ ] the employer from the possibility of facing conflicting demands from different unions"; and "permit[ ] the employer and a single union to reach agreements and settlements that are not subject to attack from rival labor organizations." . . . As proof, the Court pointed to the example of exclusive-representation arrangements in the private-employment sphere: There, Congress had long thought that such schemes would promote "peaceful labor relations" and "labor stability." . . . A public employer like Detroit, the Court believed, could reasonably make the same calculation.

But for an exclusive-bargaining arrangement to work, such an employer often thought, the union needed adequate funding. . . . "The tasks of negotiating and administering a collective-bargaining agreement and representing the interests of employees in settling disputes and processing grievances are continuing and difficult ones." . . . Those activities, the Court noted, require the "expenditure of much time and money"—for example, payment for the "services of lawyers, expert negotiators, economists, and a research staff." . . . And there is no way to confine the union's services to union members alone (and thus to trim costs) because unions must by law fairly represent all employees in a given bargaining unit—union members and non-members alike. . . .

But the Court acknowledged as well the "First Amendment interests" of dissenting employees. . . . It recognized that some workers might oppose positions the union takes in collective bargaining, or even "unionism itself." . . . And still more, it understood that unions often advance "political and ideological" views outside the collective-bargaining context—as when they "contribute to political candidates." . . . Employees might well object to the use of their money to support such "ideological causes." . . .

So the Court struck a balance, which has governed this area ever since. On the one hand, employees could be required to pay fees to support the union in "collective bargaining, contract administration, and grievance adjustment." . . . There, the Court held, the "important government interests" in having a stably funded bargaining partner justify "the impingement upon" public employees' expression. . . . But on the other hand, employees could not be compelled to fund the union's political and ideological activities. Outside the collective-bargaining sphere, the Court determined, an employee's First Amendment rights defeated any conflicting government interest.

II

Unlike the majority, I see nothing "questionable" about *Abood*'s analysis. . . .

A

Abood's reasoning about governmental interests has three connected parts. First, exclusive representation arrangements benefit some government entities because they can facilitate stable labor relations. . . . Second, the government may be unable to avail itself of those benefits unless the single union has a secure source of funding. . . . And third, agency fees are often needed to ensure such stable funding. That is because without those fees, employees have every incentive to free ride on the union dues paid by others.

The majority does not take issue with the first point. . . . The majority claims that the second point never appears in *Abood*, but is willing to assume it for the sake of argument. So the majority stakes everything on the third point—the conclusion that maintaining an effective system of exclusive representation often entails agency fees.

But basic economic theory shows why a government would think that agency fees are necessary for exclusive representation to work. What ties the two together, as *Abood* recognized, is the likelihood of free-riding when fees are absent. Remember that once a union achieves exclusive-representation status, the law compels it to fairly represent all workers in the bargaining unit, whether or not they join or contribute to the union. Because of that legal duty, the union cannot give special advantages to its own members. And that in turn creates a collective action problem of nightmarish proportions. Everyone—not just those who oppose the union, but also those who back it—has an economic incentive to withhold dues; only altruism or loyalty—as against financial self-interest—can explain why an employee would pay the union for its services. . . .

The majority's initial response to this reasoning is simply to dismiss it. "[F]ree rider arguments,". . . the majority pronounces, "are generally insufficient to overcome First Amendment objections." . . . "To hold otherwise," it continues, "would have startling consequences" because "[m]any private groups speak out" in ways that will "benefit[ ] nonmembers." . . . But that disregards the defining characteristic of this free-rider argument—that unions, unlike those many other private groups, must serve members and non-members alike. Groups advocating for "senior citizens or veterans" (to use the majority's examples) have no legal duty to provide benefits to all those individuals: They can spur people to pay dues by conferring all kinds of special advantages on their dues-paying members. Unions are—by law—in a different position, as this Court has long recognized. . . . That special feature was what justified *Abood*: "Where the state imposes upon the union a duty to deliver services, it may permit the union to demand reimbursement for them." . . .

The majority's fallback argument purports to respond to the distinctive position of unions, but still misses *Abood*'s economic insight. Here, the majority delivers a four-page exegesis on why unions will seek to serve as an exclusive bargaining representative even "if they are not given agency fees." . . . The gist of the account is that "designation as the exclusive representative confers many benefits,". . . which outweigh the costs of providing services to non-members. But that response avoids the key question, which is whether unions without agency fees will be able to (not whether they will want to) carry on as an effective exclusive representative. And as to that question, the majority again fails to reckon with how economically rational actors behave—in public as well as private workplaces. Without a fair-share agreement, the class of union non-members spirals upward. Employees (including those who love the union) realize that they can get the same benefits even if they let their memberships expire. And as more and more stop paying dues, those left must take up the financial slack (and anyway, begin to feel like suckers)—so they too quit the union. And when the vicious cycle finally ends, chances are that the union will lack the resources to effectively perform the responsibilities of an exclusive representative—or, in the worst case, to perform them at all. The result is to frustrate the interests of every government entity that thinks a strong exclusive-representation scheme will promote stable labor relations.

Of course, not all public employers will share that view. Some would rather not bargain with an exclusive representative. Others would prefer that representative to be poorly funded—to serve more as a front than an effectual bargaining partner. But as reflected in the number of fair-share statutes and contracts across the Nation, many government entities think that effective exclusive representation makes for good labor relations—and recognize, just as *Abood* did, that representation of that kind often depends on agency fees. . . .

B

1

In many cases over many decades, this Court has addressed how the First Amendment applies when the government, acting not as sovereign but as employer, limits its workers' speech. Those decisions have granted substantial latitude to the government, in recognition of its significant interests in managing its workforce so as to best serve the public. *Abood* fit neatly with that caselaw, in both reasoning and result. Indeed, its reversal today creates a significant anomaly—an exception, applying to union fees alone, from the usual rules governing public employees' speech.

. . .

In striking the proper balance between employee speech rights and managerial interests, the Court has long applied a test originating in [*Pickering*]. . . .

Abood coheres with that framework. The point here is not, as the majority suggests, that *Abood* is an overt, one-to-one "application of *Pickering*." It is not. *Abood* related to a municipality's labor policy, and so the Court looked to prior cases about unions, not to *Pickering*'s analysis of an employee's dismissal. (And truth be told, *Pickering* was not at that time much to look at: What the Court now thinks of as the two-step *Pickering* test, as the majority's own citations show, really emerged from *Garcetti* and *Connick*—two cases post-dating *Abood*). But *Abood* and *Pickering* raised variants of the same basic issue: the extent of the government's authority to make employment decisions affecting expression. And in both, the Court struck the same basic balance, enabling the government to curb speech when—but only when—the regulation was designed to protect its managerial interests. . . .

. . .

Abood thus dovetailed with the Court's usual attitude in First Amendment cases toward the regulation of public employees' speech. That attitude is one of respect—even solicitude—for the government's prerogatives as an employer. So long as the government is acting as an employer—rather than exploiting the employment relationship for other ends—it has a wide berth, comparable to that of a private employer. And when the regulated expression concerns the terms and conditions of employment—the very stuff of the employment relationship—the government really cannot lose. There, managerial interests are obvious and strong. And so government employees are . . . just employees, even though they work for the government. Except that today the government does lose, in a first for the law. Now, the government can constitutionally adopt all policies regulating core workplace speech in pursuit of managerial goals—save this single one.

. . .

2

The majority claims it is not making a special and unjustified exception. It offers two main reasons for declining to apply here our usual deferential approach, as exemplified in *Pickering*, to the regulation of public employee speech. First, the majority says, this case involves a "blanket" policy rather than an individualized employment decision, so *Pickering* is a "painful fit." Second, the majority asserts, the regulation here involves compelling rather than restricting speech, so the pain gets sharper still. . . .

First, this Court has applied the same basic approach whether a public employee challenges a general policy or an individualized decision. . . .

Second, the majority's distinction between compelling and restricting speech also lacks force. The majority posits that compelling speech always works a greater injury, and so always requires a greater justification. . . . But the only case the majority cites for that reading of our precedent is possibly (thankfully) the most exceptional in our First Amendment annals: It involved the state forcing children to swear an oath contrary to their religious beliefs. . . . Regulations challenged as compelling expression do not usually look anything like that—and for that reason, the standard First Amendment rule is that the "difference between compelled speech and compelled silence" is "without constitutional significance." . . . And if anything, the First Amendment scales tip the opposite way when (as here) the government is not compelling actual speech, but instead compelling a subsidy that others will use for expression. See Brief for Eugene Volokh et al. as *Amici Curiae* 4–5 (offering many examples to show that the First Amendment "simply do[es] not guarantee that one's hard-earned dollars will never be spent on speech one disapproves of "). So when a government mandates a speech subsidy from a public employee—here, we might think of it as levying a tax to support collective bargaining—it should get at least as much deference as when it restricts the employee's speech. As this case shows, the former may advance a managerial interest as well as the latter—in which case the government's "freer hand" in dealing with its employees should apply with equal (if not greater) force.

. . .

III

But the worse part of today's opinion is where the majority subverts all known principles of *stare decisis*. The majority makes plain, in the first 33 pages of its decision, that it believes *Abood* was wrong. But even if that were true (which it is not), it is not enough. "Respecting *stare decisis* means sticking to some wrong decisions." Kimble v. Marvel Entertainment, LLC, 576 U.S. ___ (2015). Any departure from settled precedent (so the Court has often stated) demands a "special justification—over and above the belief that the precedent was wrongly decided." Id., at ___ . . .; see, e.g., Arizona v. Rumsey, 467 U.S. 203, 212 (1984). And the majority does not have anything close. To the contrary: all that is "special" in this case—especially the massive reliance interests at stake— demands retaining *Abood*, beyond even the normal precedent.

Consider first why these principles about precedent are so important. *Stare decisis*—"the idea that today's Court should stand by yesterday's decisions"—is "a foundation stone of the rule of law." . . . It "promotes the evenhanded, predictable, and consistent development" of legal doctrine. . . . It fosters respect for and reliance on judicial decisions. And it "contributes to the actual and perceived integrity of the judicial process," by ensuring that decisions are "founded in the law rather than in the proclivities of individuals." . . .

And *Abood* is not just any precedent: It is embedded in the law (not to mention . . . in the world) in a way not many decisions are. Over four decades, this Court has cited *Abood* favorably many times, and has affirmed and applied its central distinction between the costs of collective bargaining (which the government can charge to all employees) and those of political activities (which it cannot). . . .

Ignoring our repeated validation of *Abood*, the majority claims it has become "an outlier among our First Amendment cases." . . . That claim fails most spectacularly for reasons already discussed: *Abood* coheres with the *Pickering* approach to reviewing regulation of public employees' speech. . . . Dicta in . . . recent decisions indeed began the assault on *Abood* that has culminated today. But neither actually addressed the extent to which a public employer may regulate its own employees' speech. Relying on them is bootstrapping—and mocking *stare decisis*. Don't like a decision? Just throw some gratuitous criticisms into a couple of opinions and a few years later point to them as "special justifications."

The majority is likewise wrong to invoke "workability" as a reason for overruling *Abood*. Does *Abood* require drawing a line? Yes, between a union's collective-bargaining activities and its political activities. Is that line perfectly and pristinely "precis[e]," as the majority demands? . . . Well, not quite that—but as exercises of constitutional linedrawing go, *Abood* stands well above average. In the 40 years since *Abood*, this Court has had to resolve only a handful of cases raising questions about the distinction. To my knowledge, the circuit courts are not divided on any classification issue; neither are they issuing distress signals of the kind that sometimes prompt the Court to reverse a decision. And that tranquility is unsurprising: There may be some gray areas (there always are), but in the mine run of cases, everyone knows the difference between politicking and collective bargaining. The majority cites some disagreement in two of the classification cases this Court decided—as if non-unanimity among Justices were something startling. . . . As I wrote in *Harris* a few Terms ago: "If the kind of hand-wringing about blurry lines that the majority offers were enough to justify breaking with precedent, we might have to discard whole volumes of the United States Reports. . . .

And in any event, one *stare decisis* factor—reliance—dominates all others here and demands keeping *Abood*. *Stare decisis*, this Court has held, "has added force when the legislature, in the public sphere, and citizens, in the private realm, have acted in reliance on a previous decision." . . . That is because overruling a decision would then "require an extensive legislative response" or "dislodge settled rights and expectations." . . . Both will happen here: The Court today wreaks havoc on entrenched legislative and contractual arrangements.

Over 20 States have by now enacted statutes authorizing fair-share provisions. To be precise, 22 States, the District of Columbia, and Puerto Rico—plus another two States for police and firefighter unions. Many of those States have multiple statutory provisions, with variations for different categories of public employees. See, e.g., Brief for State of California as Amicus Curiae 24–25. Every one of them will now need to come up with new ways—elaborated in new statutes—to structure relations between government employers and their workers. The majority responds . . . that this is of no proper concern to the Court. But in fact, we have weighed heavily against "abandon[ing] our settled jurisprudence" that "[s]tate legislatures have relied upon" it and would have to "reexamine [and amend] their statutes" if it were overruled. . . .

. . .

The majority asserts that no one should care much because the canceled agreements are "of rather short duration" . . . and would "expire on their own in a few years' time." . . . But to begin with, that response ignores the substantial time and effort that state legislatures will have to devote to revamping their statutory schemes. And anyway, it misunderstands the nature of contract negotiations when the parties have a continuing relationship. The parties, in renewing an old collective-bargaining agreement, don't start on an empty page. Instead, various "long-settled" terms—like fair-share provisions—are taken as a given. So the majority's ruling does more than advance by a few years a future renegotiation (though even that would be significant). In most cases, it commands new bargaining over how to replace a term that the parties never expected to change. And not just new bargaining; given the interests at stake, complicated and possibly contentious bargaining as well.

The majority, though, offers another reason for not worrying about reliance: . . . Here, the majority proudly lays claim to its 6-year crusade to ban agency fees [and the notice that provided to public-sector unions.] . . .

But that argument reflects a radically wrong understanding of how *stare decisis* operates. Justice Scalia once confronted a similar argument for "disregard[ing] reliance interests" and showed how antithetical it was to rule-of-law principles. Quill Corp. v. North Dakota, 504 U.S. 298, 320 (1992) (concurring opinion). He noted first what we always tell lower courts: "If a precedent of this Court has direct application in a case, yet appears to rest on reasons rejected in some other line of decisions, [they] should follow the case which directly controls, leaving to this Court the prerogative of overruling its own decisions." . . . That instruction, Justice Scalia explained, was "incompatible" with an expectation that "private parties anticipate our overrulings." 504 U.S., at 320. He concluded: "[R]eliance upon a square, unabandoned holding of the Supreme Court is always justifiable reliance." . . . *Abood*'s holding was square. It was unabandoned before today. It was, in other words, the law—however much some were working overtime to make it not. Parties, both unions and governments, were thus justified in relying on it. And they did rely, to an extent rare among our decisions. To dismiss the overthrowing of their settled expectations as entailing no more than some "adjustments" and "unpleasant transition costs," . . . is to trivialize *stare decisis*.

IV

There is no sugarcoating today's opinion. The majority overthrows a decision entrenched in this Nation's law—and in its economic life—for over 40 years. As a result, it prevents the American people, acting through their state and local officials, from making important choices about workplace governance.

And it does so by weaponizing the First Amendment, in a way that unleashes judges, now and in the future, to intervene in economic and regulatory policy.

. . . The majority has overruled *Abood* for no exceptional or special reason, but because it never liked the decision. It has overruled *Abood* because it wanted to.

Because, that is, it wanted to pick the winning side in what should be—and until now, has been—an energetic policy debate. Some state and local governments (and the constituents they serve) think that stable unions promote healthy labor relations and thereby improve the provision of services to the public. Other state and local governments (and their constituents) think, to the contrary, that strong unions impose excessive costs and impair those services. Americans have debated the pros and cons for many decades—in large part, by deciding whether to use fair-share arrangements. Yesterday, 22 States were on one side, 28 on the other (ignoring a couple of in-betweeners). Today, that healthy—that democratic—debate ends. The majority has adjudged who should prevail. Indeed, the majority is bursting with pride over what it has accomplished: Now those 22 States, it crows, "can follow the model of the federal government and 28 other States." . . .

And maybe most alarming, the majority has chosen the winners by turning the First Amendment into a sword, and using it against workaday economic and regulatory policy. Today is not the first time the Court has wielded the First Amendment in such an aggressive way. See, e.g., National Institute of Family and Life Advocates v. Becerra, ___ U.S. ___ (2018) (invalidating a law requiring medical and counseling facilities to provide relevant information to users); Sorrell v. IMS Health Inc., 564 U.S. 552 (2011) (striking down a law that restricted pharmacies from selling various data). And it threatens not to be the last. Speech is everywhere—a part of every human activity (employment, health care, securities trading, you name it). For that reason, almost all economic and regulatory policy affects or touches speech. So the majority's road runs long. And at every stop are black-robed rulers overriding citizens' choices. The First Amendment was meant for better things. It was meant not to undermine but to protect democratic governance—including over the role of public-sector unions.

CHAPTER 17

RELIGION AND THE CONSTITUTION

1. THE ESTABLISHMENT CLAUSE

A. INTRODUCTION

Page 1697. Add after Note, "Denominational Preferences":

Trump v. Hawaii

585 U.S. ___, 138 S.Ct. 2392, ___ L.Ed.2d ___ (2018).

■ CHIEF JUSTICE ROBERTS delivered the opinion of the Court.

Under the Immigration and Nationality Act, foreign nationals seeking entry into the United States undergo a vetting process to ensure that they satisfy the numerous requirements for admission. The Act also vests the President with authority to restrict the entry of aliens whenever he finds that their entry "would be detrimental to the interests of the United States." 8 U.S.C. § 1182(f). Relying on that delegation, the President concluded that it was necessary to impose entry restrictions on nationals of countries that do not share adequate information for an informed entry determination, or that otherwise present national security risks. Presidential Proclamation No. 9645, 82 Fed. Reg. 45161 (2017) (Proclamation). The plaintiffs . . . challenged the application of those entry restrictions to certain aliens abroad. We now decide whether the President had authority under the Act to issue the Proclamation, and whether the entry policy violates the Establishment Clause of the First Amendment.

I

A

Shortly after taking office, President Trump signed [Executive Order 13769 (EO–1),] direct[ing] the Secretary of Homeland Security to conduct a review to examine the adequacy of information provided by foreign governments about their nationals seeking to enter the United States . . . [and] suspend[ing] for 90 days the entry of foreign nationals from seven countries—Iran, Iraq, Libya, Somalia, Sudan, Syria, and Yemen—that had been previously identified by Congress or prior administrations as posing heightened terrorism risks. . . .

[The order was stayed by lower courts, and] the President revoked EO–1, replacing it with Executive Order No. 13780 [EO–2], which again directed a worldwide review. Citing investigative burdens on agencies and the need to diminish the risk that dangerous individuals would enter without adequate vetting, EO–2 also temporarily restricted [for 90 days] the entry (with case-by-case waivers) of foreign nationals from six of the countries covered by EO–1: Iran, Libya, Somalia, Sudan, Syria, and Yemen. The order explained that those countries had been selected because each "is a state sponsor of terrorism, has been significantly compromised by terrorist organizations, or contains active conflict zones." . . .

. . . District Courts for . . . Maryland and Hawaii entered nationwide preliminary injunctions barring enforcement of the entry suspension, [which] the respective Courts of Appeals upheld . . . . This Court . . . stayed the injunctions—allowing the entry suspension to go into effect—with respect to foreign nationals who lacked a "credible claim of a bona fide relationship" with a person or entity in the United States. Trump v. IRAP, 582 U.S. ___, ___ (2017) (*per curiam*) . . . . The temporary restrictions in EO–2 expired before this Court took any action, and we vacated the lower court decisions as moot. . . .

On September 24, 2017, after completion of the worldwide review, the President issued the Proclamation before us—Proclamation No. 9645, Enhancing Vetting Capabilities and Processes for Detecting Attempted Entry Into the United States by Terrorists or Other Public-Safety Threats. 82 Fed. Reg. 45161. The Proclamation (as its title indicates) sought to improve vetting procedures by identifying ongoing deficiencies in the information needed to assess whether nationals of particular countries present "public safety threats." § 1(a). To further that purpose, the Proclamation placed entry restrictions on the nationals of eight foreign states whose systems for managing and sharing information about their nationals the President deemed inadequate.

The Proclamation described how foreign states were selected for inclusion based on the review undertaken pursuant to EO–2. As part of that review, the Department of Homeland Security (DHS), in consultation with the State Department and several intelligence agencies, developed a "baseline" for the information required from foreign governments to confirm the identity of individuals seeking entry into the United States, and to determine whether those individuals pose a security threat. § 1(c). The baseline included three components. The first, "identity-management information," focused on whether a foreign government ensures the integrity of travel documents by issuing electronic passports, reporting lost or stolen passports, and making available additional identity-related information. Second, the agencies considered the extent to which the country discloses information on criminal history and suspected terrorist links, provides travel document exemplars, and facilitates the U.S. Government's receipt of information about airline passengers and crews traveling to the United States. Finally, the agencies weighed various indicators of national security risk, including whether the foreign state is a known or potential terrorist safe haven and whether it regularly declines to receive returning nationals following final orders of removal from the United States. *Ibid.*

DHS collected and evaluated data regarding all foreign governments. § 1(d). It identified 16 countries as having deficient information-sharing practices and presenting national security concerns, and another 31 countries as "at risk" of similarly failing to meet the baseline. § 1(e). The State Department then undertook diplomatic efforts over a 50-day period to encourage all foreign governments to improve their practices. § 1(f). As a result of that effort, numerous countries provided DHS with travel document exemplars and agreed to share information on known or suspected terrorists. *Ibid.*

Following the 50-day period, the Acting Secretary of Homeland Security concluded that eight countries—Chad, Iran, Iraq, Libya, North Korea, Syria, Venezuela, and Yemen—remained deficient in terms of their risk profile and willingness to provide requested information. The Acting Secretary recommended that the President impose entry restrictions on certain nationals from all of those countries except Iraq. . . . She also concluded that although Somalia generally satisfied the information-sharing component of the baseline standards, its "identity-management deficiencies" and "significant terrorist presence" presented special circumstances justifying additional limitations. She therefore recommended entry limitations for certain nationals of that country. . . . As for Iraq, the Acting Secretary found that entry limitations on its nationals were not warranted given the close cooperative relationship between the U.S. and Iraqi Governments and Iraq's commitment to combating ISIS. . . .

After consulting with multiple Cabinet members and other officials, the President adopted the Acting Secretary's recommendations and issued the Proclamation. Invoking his authority under 8 U.S.C. § 1182(f) and 1185(a), the President determined that certain entry restrictions were necessary to "prevent the entry of those foreign nationals about whom the United States Government lacks sufficient information"; "elicit improved identity-management and information-sharing protocols and practices from foreign governments"; and otherwise "advance [the] foreign policy, national security, and counterterrorism objectives" of the United States. Proclamation § 1(h). The President explained that these restrictions would be the "most likely to encourage cooperation" while "protect[ing] the United States until such time as improvements occur." *Ibid.*

The Proclamation imposed a range of restrictions that vary based on the "distinct circumstances" in each of the eight countries. . . . For countries that do not cooperate with the United States in identifying security risks (Iran, North Korea, and Syria), the Proclamation suspends entry of all nationals, except for Iranians seeking nonimmigrant student and exchange-visitor visas. . . . For countries that have information-sharing deficiencies but are nonetheless "valuable counterterrorism partner[s]" (Chad, Libya, and Yemen), it restricts entry of nationals seeking immigrant visas and nonimmigrant business or tourist visas. . . . Because Somalia generally satisfies the baseline standards but was found to present special risk factors, the Proclamation suspends entry of nationals seeking immigrant visas and requires additional scrutiny of nationals seeking nonimmigrant visas. . . . And for Venezuela, which refuses to cooperate in information sharing but for which alternative means are available to identify its nationals, the Proclamation limits entry only of certain government officials and their family members on nonimmigrant business or tourist visas. . . .

The Proclamation exempts lawful permanent residents and foreign nationals who have been granted asylum. § 3(b). It also provides for case-by-case waivers when a foreign national demonstrates undue hardship, and that his entry is in the national interest and would not pose a threat to public safety. § 3(c)(i); see also § 3(c)(iv) (listing examples of when a waiver might be appropriate, such as if the foreign national seeks to reside with a close family member, obtain urgent medical care, or pursue significant business obligations). The Proclamation further directs DHS to assess on a continuing basis whether entry restrictions should be modified or continued, and to report to the President every 180 days. § 4. Upon completion of the first such review period, the President, on the recommendation of the Secretary of Homeland Security, determined that Chad had sufficiently improved its practices, and he accordingly lifted restrictions on its nationals. Presidential Proclamation No. 9723 . . . (2018).

B

[The State of Hawaii, which operates its University, which in turn "recruits students and faculty from the designated countries," three individual "U.S. citizens or lawful permanent residents who have relatives from Iran, Syria, and Yemen applying for immigrant or nonimmigrant visas," and the Muslim Association of Hawaii, which "operates a mosque in Hawaii," "challenged the Proclamation—except as applied to North Korea and Venezuela" for contravening the Immigration and Nationality Act (INA), and for "violat[ing] the Establishment Clause of the First Amendment, because it was motivated not by concerns pertaining to national security but by animus toward Islam."]

The District Court granted a nationwide preliminary injunction barring enforcement of the entry restrictions [based on violations of the INA. After an intervening stay from the Supreme Court, the Ninth Circuit affirmed the District Court ruling, but "did not reach plaintiffs' Establishment Clause claim."]

. . .

III

. . .

By its plain language, § 1182(f) [which the Court also wrote "exudes deference to the President in every clause"] grants the President broad discretion to suspend the entry of aliens into the United States. The President lawfully exercised that discretion based on his findings—following a worldwide, multi-agency review—that entry of the covered aliens would be detrimental to the national interest. And plaintiffs' attempts to identify a conflict with other provisions in the INA, and their appeal to the statute's purposes and legislative history, fail to overcome the clear statutory language.

. . .

We may assume that § 1182(f) does not allow the President to expressly override particular provisions of the INA. But plaintiffs have not identified any conflict between the statute and the Proclamation that would implicitly bar the President from addressing deficiencies in the Nation's vetting system.

. . .

The Proclamation is squarely within the scope of Presidential authority under the INA. Indeed, neither dissent even attempts any serious argument to the contrary, despite the fact that plaintiffs' primary contention below and in their briefing before this Court was that the Proclamation violated the statute.

IV

A

We now turn to plaintiffs' claim that the Proclamation was issued for the unconstitutional purpose of excluding Muslims. . . .

. . .

. . . [T]he individual plaintiffs have Article III standing to challenge the exclusion of their relatives under the Establishment Clause.

B

. . . Our cases recognize that "[t]he clearest command of the Establishment Clause is that one religious denomination cannot be officially preferred over another." Larson v. Valente, 456 U.S. 228, 244 (1982). Plaintiffs believe that the

Proclamation violates this prohibition by singling out Muslims for disfavored treatment. The entry suspension, they contend, operates as a "religious gerrymander," in part because most of the countries covered by the Proclamation have Muslim-majority populations. And in their view, deviations from the information-sharing baseline criteria suggest that the results of the multi-agency review were "foreordained." Relying on Establishment Clause precedents concerning laws and policies applied domestically, plaintiffs allege that the primary purpose of the Proclamation was religious animus and that the President's stated concerns about vetting protocols and national security were but pretexts for discriminating against Muslims. . . .

At the heart of plaintiffs' case is a series of statements by the President and his advisers casting doubt on the official objective of the Proclamation. For example, while a candidate on the campaign trail, the President published a "Statement on Preventing Muslim Immigration" that called for a "total and complete shutdown of Muslims entering the United States until our country's representatives can figure out what is going on." . . . That statement remained on his campaign website until May 2017. . . . Then-candidate Trump also stated that "Islam hates us" and asserted that the United States was "having problems with Muslims coming into the country." . . . Shortly after being elected, when asked whether violence in Europe had affected his plans to "ban Muslim immigration," the President replied, "You know my plans. All along, I've been proven to be right." . . .

One week after his inauguration, the President issued EO–1. In a television interview, one of the President's campaign advisers explained that when the President "first announced it, he said, 'Muslim ban.' He called me up. He said, 'Put a commission together. Show me the right way to do it legally.' " . . . The adviser said he assembled a group of Members of Congress and lawyers that "focused on, instead of religion, danger. . . . [The order] is based on places where there [is] substantial evidence that people are sending terrorists into our country." . . .

Plaintiffs also note that after issuing EO–2 to replace EO–1, the President expressed regret that his prior order had been "watered down" and called for a "much tougher version" of his "Travel Ban." Shortly before the release of the Proclamation, he stated that the "travel ban . . . should be far larger, tougher, and more specific," but "stupidly that would not be politically correct." . . . More recently, on November 29, 2017, the President retweeted links to three anti-Muslim propaganda videos. In response to questions about those videos, the President's deputy press secretary denied that the President thinks Muslims are a threat to the United States, explaining that "the President has been talking about these security issues for years now, from the campaign trail to the White House" and "has addressed these issues with the travel order that he issued earlier this year and the companion proclamation." . . .

The President of the United States possesses an extraordinary power to speak to his fellow citizens and on their behalf. Our Presidents have frequently used that power to espouse the principles of religious freedom and tolerance on which this Nation was founded. In 1790 George Washington reassured the Hebrew Congregation of Newport, Rhode Island that "happily the Government of the United States . . . gives to bigotry no sanction, to persecution no assistance [and] requires only that they who live under its protection should demean themselves as good citizens." . . . President Eisenhower, at the opening of the

Islamic Center of Washington, similarly pledged to a Muslim audience that "America would fight with her whole strength for your right to have here your own church," declaring that "[t]his concept is indeed a part of America." . . . And just days after the attacks of September 11, 2001, President George W. Bush returned to the same Islamic Center to implore his fellow Americans—Muslims and non-Muslims alike—to remember during their time of grief that "[t]he face of terror is not the true faith of Islam," and that America is "a great country because we share the same values of respect and dignity and human worth." . . . Yet it cannot be denied that the Federal Government and the Presidents who have carried its laws into effect have—from the Nation's earliest days—performed unevenly in living up to those inspiring words.

Plaintiffs argue that this President's words strike at fundamental standards of respect and tolerance, in violation of our constitutional tradition. But the issue before us is not whether to denounce the statements. It is instead the significance of those statements in reviewing a Presidential directive, neutral on its face, addressing a matter within the core of executive responsibility. In doing so, we must consider not only the statements of a particular President, but also the authority of the Presidency itself.

The case before us differs in numerous respects from the conventional Establishment Clause claim. Unlike the typical suit involving religious displays or school prayer, plaintiffs seek to invalidate a national security directive regulating the entry of aliens abroad. Their claim accordingly raises a number of delicate issues regarding the scope of the constitutional right and the manner of proof. The Proclamation, moreover, is facially neutral toward religion. Plaintiffs therefore ask the Court to probe the sincerity of the stated justifications for the policy by reference to extrinsic statements—many of which were made before the President took the oath of office. These various aspects of plaintiffs' challenge inform our standard of review.

C

For more than a century, this Court has recognized that the admission and exclusion of foreign nationals is a "fundamental sovereign attribute exercised by the Government's political departments largely immune from judicial control." Fiallo v. Bell, 430 U.S. 787, 792 (1977) . . . . Because decisions in these matters may implicate "relations with foreign powers," or involve "classifications defined in the light of changing political and economic circumstances," such judgments "are frequently of a character more appropriate to either the Legislature or the Executive." Mathews v. Diaz, 426 U.S. 67, 81 (1976).

Nonetheless, although foreign nationals seeking admission have no constitutional right to entry, this Court has engaged in a circumscribed judicial inquiry when the denial of a visa allegedly burdens the constitutional rights of a U.S. citizen. In Kleindienst v. Mandel, the Attorney General denied admission to a Belgian journalist and self-described "revolutionary Marxist," . . . who had been invited to speak at a conference at Stanford University. . . . The professors who wished to hear Mandel speak challenged that decision under the First Amendment, and we acknowledged that their constitutional "right to receive information" was implicated. . . . But we limited our review to whether the Executive gave a "facially legitimate and bona fide" reason for its action. . . . Given the authority of the political branches over admission, we held that "when the Executive exercises this [delegated] power negatively on the basis of a facially legitimate and bona fide reason, the courts will neither look behind the exercise of that discretion, nor test it by balancing its justification" against the asserted constitutional interests of U.S. citizens. . . .

The principal dissent suggests that *Mandel* has no bearing on this case (opinion of Sotomayor, J.) . . ., but our opinions have reaffirmed and applied its deferential standard of review across different contexts and constitutional claims. . . .

Mandel's narrow standard of review "has particular force" in admission and immigration cases that overlap with "the area of national security." *Din*, 576 U.S., at ___ (Kennedy, J., concurring in judgment) . . . For one, "[j]udicial inquiry into the national-security realm raises concerns for the separation of powers" by intruding on the President's constitutional responsibilities in the area of foreign affairs. Ziglar v. Abbasi, 582 U.S. ___, ___ (2017). . . . For another, "when it comes to collecting evidence and drawing inferences" on questions of national security, "the lack of competence on the part of the courts is marked." *Humanitarian Law Project*, 561 U.S., at 34.

The upshot of our cases in this context is clear: "Any rule of constitutional law that would inhibit the flexibility" of the President "to respond to changing world conditions should be adopted only with the greatest caution," and our inquiry into matters of entry and national security is highly constrained. *Mathews*, ... We need not define the precise contours of that inquiry in this case. A conventional application of *Mandel*, asking only whether the policy is facially legitimate and bona fide, would put an end to our review. But the Government has suggested that it may be appropriate here for the inquiry to extend beyond the facial neutrality of the order. . . . For our purposes today, we assume that we may look behind the face of the Proclamation to the extent of applying rational basis review. That standard of review considers whether the entry policy is plausibly related to the Government's stated objective to protect the country and improve vetting processes. See Railroad Retirement Bd. v. Fritz, 449 U.S. 166, 179 (1980). As a result, we may consider plaintiffs' extrinsic evidence, but will uphold the policy so long as it can reasonably be understood to result from a justification independent of unconstitutional grounds.[5]

D

Given the standard of review, it should come as no surprise that the Court hardly ever strikes down a policy as illegitimate under rational basis scrutiny. On the few occasions where we have done so, a common thread has been that the laws at issue lack any purpose other than a "bare . . . desire to harm a politically unpopular group." Department of Agriculture v. Moreno, 413 U.S. 528, 534 (1973)[; . . .] Cleburne v. Cleburne Living Center, Inc.[; . . .] Romer v. Evans . . . .

The Proclamation does not fit this pattern. It cannot be said that it is impossible to "discern a relationship to legitimate state interests" or that the policy is "inexplicable by anything but animus." . . . [B]ecause there is persuasive evidence that the entry suspension has a legitimate grounding in national

---

[5]   The dissent finds "perplexing" the application of rational basis review in this context. But what is far more problematic is the dissent's assumption that courts should review immigration policies, diplomatic sanctions, and military actions under the *de novo* "reasonable observer" inquiry applicable to cases involving holiday displays and graduation ceremonies. . . . [A] circumscribed inquiry applies to any constitutional claim concerning the entry of foreign nationals. . . . The dissent can cite no authority for its proposition that the more free-ranging inquiry it proposes is appropriate in the national security and foreign affairs context.

security concerns, quite apart from any religious hostility, we must accept that independent justification.

The Proclamation is expressly premised on legitimate purposes: preventing entry of nationals who cannot be adequately vetted and inducing other nations to improve their practices. The text says nothing about religion. Plaintiffs and the dissent nonetheless emphasize that five of the seven nations currently included in the Proclamation have Muslim-majority populations. Yet that fact alone does not support an inference of religious hostility, given that the policy covers just 8% of the world's Muslim population and is limited to countries that were previously designated by Congress or prior administrations as posing national security risks. . . .

The Proclamation, moreover, reflects the results of a worldwide review process undertaken by multiple Cabinet officials and their agencies. Plaintiffs . . . point[ ] to deviations from the review's baseline criteria resulting in the inclusion of Somalia and omission of Iraq. But . . . Somalia . . . "stands apart . . . in the degree to which [it] lacks command and control of its territory." Proclamation § 2(h)(i). As for Iraq, the Secretary of Homeland Security determined that entry restrictions were not warranted in light of the close cooperative relationship between the U.S. and Iraqi Governments and the country's key role in combating terrorism in the region. § 1(g). It is, in any event, difficult to see how exempting one of the largest predominantly Muslim countries in the region from coverage under the Proclamation can be cited as evidence of animus toward Muslims.

. . .

More fundamentally, plaintiffs and the dissent challenge the entry suspension based on their perception of its effectiveness and wisdom. They suggest that the policy is overbroad and does little to serve national security interests. But we cannot substitute our own assessment for the Executive's predictive judgments on such matters . . . .

Three additional features of the entry policy support the Government's claim of a legitimate national security interest. First, since the President introduced entry restrictions in January 2017, three Muslim-majority countries—Iraq, Sudan, and Chad—have been removed from the list of covered countries. . . .

Second, for those countries that remain subject to entry restrictions, the Proclamation includes significant exceptions for various categories of foreign nationals. . . . The[ ] carveouts for nonimmigrant visas are substantial: Over the last three fiscal years—before the Proclamation was in effect—the majority of visas issued to nationals from the covered countries were nonimmigrant visas. . . . The Proclamation also exempts permanent residents and individuals who have been granted asylum. . . .

Third, the Proclamation creates a waiver program open to all covered foreign nationals seeking entry as immigrants or nonimmigrants. . . .[7]

Finally, the dissent invokes Korematsu v. United States, 323 U.S. 214 (1944). . . . *Korematsu* has nothing to do with this case. The forcible relocation of

---

[7]　. . . Justice Breyer suggests that not enough individuals are receiving waivers or exemptions. Yet even if such an inquiry were appropriate under rational basis review, the evidence he cites provides "but a piece of the picture" and does not affect our analysis.

U. S. citizens to concentration camps, solely and explicitly on the basis of race, is objectively unlawful and outside the scope of Presidential authority. But it is wholly inapt to liken that morally repugnant order to a facially neutral policy denying certain foreign nationals the privilege of admission. The entry suspension is an act that is well within executive authority and could have been taken by any other President—the only question is evaluating the actions of this particular President in promulgating an otherwise valid Proclamation.

The dissent's reference to *Korematsu*, however, affords this Court the opportunity to make express what is already obvious: *Korematsu* was gravely wrong the day it was decided, has been overruled in the court of history, and—to be clear—"has no place in law under the Constitution." 323 U.S., at 248 (Jackson, J., dissenting).

* * *

Under these circumstances, the Government has set forth a sufficient national security justification to survive rational basis review. We express no view on the soundness of the policy. We simply hold today that plaintiffs have not demonstrated a likelihood of success on the merits of their constitutional claim.

V

. . . [W]e reverse the grant of the preliminary injunction as an abuse of discretion. . . . The case now returns to the lower courts for such further proceedings as may be appropriate. . . .

. . .

■ JUSTICE KENNEDY, concurring.

I join the Court's opinion in full.

There may be some common ground between the opinions in this case, in that the Court does acknowledge that in some instances, governmental action may be subject to judicial review to determine whether or not it is "inexplicable by anything but animus," Romer v. Evans, 517 U.S. 620, 632 (1996), which in this case would be animosity to a religion. Whether judicial proceedings may properly continue in this case, in light of the substantial deference that is and must be accorded to the Executive in the conduct of foreign affairs, and in light of today's decision, is a matter to be addressed in the first instance on remand. And even if further proceedings are permitted, it would be necessary to determine that any discovery and other preliminary matters would not themselves intrude on the foreign affairs power of the Executive.

. . . There are numerous instances in which the statements and actions of Government officials are not subject to judicial scrutiny or intervention. That does not mean those officials are free to disregard the Constitution and the rights it proclaims and protects. . . . [T]he very fact that an official may have broad discretion, discretion free from judicial scrutiny, makes it all the more imperative for him or her to adhere to the Constitution and to its meaning and its promise.

The First Amendment prohibits the establishment of religion and promises the free exercise of religion. . . . It is an urgent necessity that officials adhere to these constitutional guarantees and mandates in all their actions, even in the sphere of foreign affairs. . . .

■ THOMAS, J., concurring.

I join the Court's opinion, which highlights just a few of the many problems with the plaintiffs' claims. There are several more. Section 1182(f) does not set forth any judicially enforceable limits that constrain the President. . . . Nor could it, since the President has *inherent* authority to exclude aliens from the country. . . . Further, the Establishment Clause does not create an individual right to be free from all laws that a "reasonable observer" views as religious or antireligious. See Town of Greece v. Galloway, 572 U.S. ___, ___ (2014) (Thomas, J., concurring in part and concurring in judgment) . . . . The plaintiffs cannot raise any other First Amendment claim, since the alleged religious discrimination in this case was directed at aliens abroad. . . . And, even on its own terms, the plaintiffs' proffered evidence of anti-Muslim discrimination is unpersuasive.

Merits aside, I write separately to address the ["universal" or "nationwide" injunction the District Court imposed] . . . that barred the Government from enforcing the President's Proclamation against anyone, not just the plaintiffs. . . .

I am skeptical that district courts have the authority to enter universal injunctions. . . .

. . .

■ JUSTICE BREYER, with whom JUSTICE KAGAN joins, dissenting.

. . . Members of the Court principally disagree . . . about whether or the extent to which religious animus played a significant role in the Proclamation's promulgation or content.

In my view, the Proclamation's elaborate system of exemptions and waivers can and should help us answer this question. . . .

On the one hand, if the Government is applying the exemption and waiver provisions as written, then its argument for the Proclamation's lawfulness is strengthened. For one thing, the Proclamation then resembles more closely the two important Presidential precedents on point, President Carter's Iran order and President Reagan's Cuba proclamation, both of which contained similar categories of persons authorized to obtain case-by-case exemptions. . . . For another thing, the Proclamation then follows more closely the basic statutory scheme, which provides for strict case-by-case scrutiny of applications. It would deviate from that system, not across the board, but where circumstances may require that deviation.

Further, since the case-by-case exemptions and waivers apply without regard to the individual's religion, application of that system would help make clear that the Proclamation does not deny visas to numerous Muslim individuals (from those countries) who do not pose a security threat. And that fact would help to rebut the First Amendment claim that the Proclamation rests upon anti-Muslim bias rather than security need. Finally, of course, the very fact that Muslims from those countries would enter the United States (under Proclamation-provided exemptions and waivers) would help to show the same thing.

On the other hand, if the Government is *not* applying the system of exemptions and waivers that the Proclamation contains, then its argument for the Proclamation's lawfulness becomes significantly weaker. . . .

. . .

. . . [I]f the Government is not applying the Proclamation's exemption and waiver system, the claim that the Proclamation is a "Muslim ban," rather than a "security-based" ban, becomes much stronger. How could the Government successfully claim that the Proclamation rests on security needs if it is excluding Muslims who satisfy the Proclamation's own terms? At the same time, denying visas to Muslims who meet the Proclamation's own security terms would support the view that the Government excludes them for reasons based upon their religion.

Unfortunately there is evidence that supports the second possibility, *i.e.*, that the Government is not applying the Proclamation as written. The Proclamation provides that the Secretary of State and the Secretary of Homeland Security "shall coordinate to adopt guidance" for consular officers to follow when deciding whether to grant a waiver. . . . Yet, to my knowledge, no guidance has issued . . . for consular officers as to how they are to exercise their discretion. . . .

An examination of publicly available statistics also provides cause for concern. The State Department reported that during the Proclamation's first month, two waivers were approved out of 6,555 eligible applicants. . . . [T]he Government claims that number increased from 2 to 430 during the first four months of implementation. . . . That number, . . . however, when compared with the number of pre-Proclamation visitors, accounts for a miniscule percentage of those likely eligible for visas, in such categories as persons requiring medical treatment, academic visitors, students, family members, and others belonging to groups that, when considered as a group (rather than case by case), would not seem to pose security threats.

Amici have suggested that there are numerous applicants who could meet the waiver criteria[, such as 2100 scholars.] . . . [Separately, t]he Pars Equality Center identified 1,000 individuals—including parents and children of U.S. citizens—who sought and were denied entry under the Proclamation['s close family member waiver opportunity], hundreds of whom seem to meet the waiver criteria. . . .

Other data suggest the same. The Proclamation does not apply to asylum seekers or refugees. . . . Yet few refugees have been admitted since the Proclamation took effect. While more than 15,000 Syrian refugees arrived in the United States in 2016, only 13 have arrived since January 2018. . . . Similarly few refugees have been admitted since January from Iran (3), Libya (1), Yemen (0), and Somalia (122).

. . .

. . . [O]nly 258 student visas were issued to applicants from Iran (189), Libya (29), Yemen (40), and Somalia (0) in the first three months of 2018. . . . This is less than a quarter of the volume needed to be on track for 2016 student visa levels. And only 40 nonimmigrant visas have been issued to Somali nationals, a decrease of 65 percent from 2016. . . . While this is but a piece of the picture, it does not provide grounds for confidence.

. . .

[I]n a pending case in the Eastern District of New York, a consular official has filed a sworn affidavit asserting that he and other officials do not, in fact, have discretion to grant waivers. . . .

Declarations, anecdotal evidence, facts, and numbers taken from *amicus* briefs are not judicial factfindings. The Government has not had an opportunity to respond, and a court has not had an opportunity to decide. But, given the importance of the decision in this case, the need for assurance that the Proclamation does not rest upon a "Muslim ban," and the assistance in deciding the issue that answers to the "exemption and waiver" questions may provide, I would send this case back to the District Court for further proceedings. And, I would leave the injunction in effect while the matter is litigated. Regardless, the Court's decision today leaves the District Court free to explore these issues on remand.

If this Court must decide the question without this further litigation, I would, on balance, find the evidence of antireligious bias, including statements on a website taken down only after the President issued the two executive orders preceding the Proclamation, along with the other statements also set forth in Justice Sotomayor's opinion, a sufficient basis to set the Proclamation aside. And for these reasons, I respectfully dissent.

■ JUSTICE SOTOMAYOR, with whom JUSTICE GINSBURG joins, dissenting.

. . . The Court's decision today . . . leaves undisturbed a policy first advertised openly and unequivocally as a "total and complete shutdown of Muslims entering the United States" because the policy now masquerades behind a façade of national-security concerns. But this repackaging does little to cleanse Presidential Proclamation No. 9645 of the appearance of discrimination that the President's words have created. Based on the evidence in the record, a reasonable observer would conclude that the Proclamation was motivated by anti-Muslim animus. That alone suffices to show that plaintiffs are likely to succeed on the merits of their Establishment Clause claim. . . .

I

. . . Whatever the merits of plaintiffs' complex statutory claims, the Proclamation . . . runs afoul of the Establishment Clause's guarantee of religious neutrality.

A

. . . The "clearest command" of the Establishment Clause is that the Government cannot favor or disfavor one religion over another. . . . Consistent with that clear command, this Court has long acknowledged that governmental actions that favor one religion "inevitabl[y]" foster "the hatred, disrespect and even contempt of those who [hold] contrary beliefs." Engel v. Vitale, 370 U.S. 421, 431 (1962). That is so, this Court has held, because such acts send messages to members of minority faiths " 'that they are outsiders, not full members of the political community.' " Santa Fe Independent School Dist. v. Doe, 530 U.S. 290, 309 (2000). To guard against this serious harm, the Framers mandated a strict "principle of denominational neutrality." *Larson*, ...

"When the government acts with the ostensible and predominant purpose" of disfavoring a particular religion, "it violates that central Establishment Clause value of official religious neutrality, there being no neutrality when the government's ostensible object is to take sides." McCreary County v. American Civil Liberties Union of Ky., 545 U.S. 844, 860 (2005). To determine whether plaintiffs have proved an Establishment Clause violation, the Court asks whether a reasonable observer would view the government action as enacted for the purpose of disfavoring a religion. See *id.*, at 862, 866; accord, Town of Greece v. Galloway, 572 U.S. ___, ___ (2014) (plurality opinion) . . . .

In answering that question, this Court has generally considered the text of the government policy, its operation, and any available evidence regarding "the historical background of the decision under challenge, the specific series of events leading to the enactment or official policy in question, and the legislative or administrative history, including contemporaneous statements made by" the decisionmaker. . . . At the same time, however, courts must take care not to engage in "any judicial psychoanalysis of a drafter's heart of hearts." . . .

B

1

. . . The full record paints a . . . harrowing picture, from which a reasonable observer would readily conclude that the Proclamation was motivated by hostility and animus toward the Muslim faith.

. . . [President Trump's campaign] statement, which remained on his campaign website until May 2017 (several months into his Presidency), read in full:

> "Donald J. Trump is calling for a total and complete shutdown of Muslims entering the United States until our country's representatives can figure out what is going on. According to Pew Research, among others, there is great hatred towards Americans by large segments of the Muslim population. Most recently, a poll from the Center for Security Policy released data showing '25% of those polled agreed that violence against Americans here in the United States is justified as a part of the global jihad' and 51% of those polled 'agreed that Muslims in America should have the choice of being governed according to Shariah.' Shariah authorizes such atrocities as murder against nonbelievers who won't convert, beheadings and more unthinkable acts that pose great harm to Americans, especially women.

> "Mr. Trum[p] stated, 'Without looking at the various polling data, it is obvious to anybody the hatred is beyond comprehension. Where this hatred comes from and why we will have to determine. Until we are able to determine and understand this problem and the dangerous threat it poses, our country cannot be the victims of the horrendous attacks by people that believe only in Jihad, and have no sense of reason or respect of human life. If I win the election for President, we are going to Make America Great Again.'—Donald J. Trump." . . .

On December 8, 2015, Trump justified his proposal during a television interview by noting that President Franklin D. Roosevelt "did the same thing" with respect to the internment of Japanese Americans during World War II. . . . In January 2016, during a Republican primary debate, Trump was asked whether he wanted to "rethink [his] position" on "banning Muslims from entering the country." . . . He answered, "No." . . . A month later, at a rally in South Carolina, Trump told an apocryphal story about United States General John J. Pershing killing a large group of Muslim insurgents in the Philippines with bullets dipped in pigs' blood in the early 1900's. . . . In March 2016, he expressed his belief that "Islam hates us. . . . [W]e can't allow people coming into this country who have this hatred of the United States . . . [a]nd of people that are not Muslim." . . . That same month, Trump asserted that "[w]e're having problems with the Muslims, and we're having problems with Muslims coming into the country." . . . He therefore called for surveillance of mosques in the United States, blaming terrorist attacks on Muslims' lack of "assimilation" and their commitment to "sharia law." . . . A day later, he opined that Muslims "do not respect us at all" and "don't respect a lot of the things that are happening throughout not only our country, but they don't respect other things." . . .

As Trump's presidential campaign progressed, he began to describe his policy proposal in slightly different terms. . . . Asked in July 2016 whether he was "pull[ing] back from" his pledged Muslim ban, Trump responded, "I actually don't think it's a rollback. In fact, you could say it's an expansion." . . . He then explained that he used different terminology because "[p]eople were so upset when [he] used the word Muslim." . . .

. . .

[The day he signed EO–1,] President Trump explained to the media that, under EO–1, Christians would be given priority for entry as refugees into the United States. In particular, he bemoaned the fact that in the past, "[i]f you were a Muslim [refugee from Syria] you could come in, but if you were a Christian, it was almost impossible." . . . Considering that past policy "very unfair," President Trump explained that EO–1 was designed "to help" the Christians in Syria. . . . The following day, one of President Trump's key advisers candidly drew the connection between EO–1 and the "Muslim ban" that the President had pledged to implement if elected. . . . According to that adviser, "[W]hen [Donald Trump] first announced it, he said, 'Muslim ban.' He called me up. He said, 'Put a commission together. Show me the right way to do it legally.' " . . .

. . .

While litigation over EO–2 was ongoing, President Trump repeatedly made statements alluding to a desire to keep Muslims out of the country. . . . During a rally in April 2017, President Trump recited the lyrics to a song called "The Snake," a song about a woman who nurses a sick snake back to health but then is attacked by the snake, as a warning about Syrian refugees entering the country. . . . And in June 2017, the President stated on Twitter that the Justice Department had submitted a "watered down, politically correct version" of the "original Travel Ban" "to S[upreme] C[ourt]." . . . . The President went on to tweet: "People, the lawyers and the courts can call it whatever they want, but I am calling it what we need and what it is, a TRAVEL BAN!" . . . He added: "That's right, we need a TRAVEL BAN for certain DANGEROUS countries, not some politically correct term that won't help us protect our people!" . . . Then, on August 17, 2017, President Trump issued yet another tweet about Islam, once more referencing the story about General Pershing's massacre of Muslims in the Philippines: "Study what General Pershing . . . did to terrorists when caught. There was no more Radical Islamic Terror for 35 years!" . . .

In September 2017, President Trump tweeted that "[t]he travel ban into the United States should be far larger, tougher and more specific—but stupidly, that would not be politically correct!" . . . Later that month, on September 24, 2017, President Trump issued Presidential Proclamation No. 9645 . . . . On November 29, 2017, President Trump "retweeted" three anti-Muslim videos, entitled "Muslim Destroys a Statue of Virgin Mary!", "Islamist mob pushes teenage boy off roof and beats him to death!", and "Muslim migrant beats up Dutch boy on crutches!" . . .

2

As the majority correctly notes, "the issue before us is not whether to denounce" these offensive statements. Rather, the dispositive and narrow question here is whether a reasonable observer, presented with all "openly available data," the text and "historical context" of the Proclamation, and the "specific sequence of events" leading to it, would conclude that the primary purpose of the Proclamation is to disfavor Islam and its adherents by excluding them from the country. See *McCreary*, ... The answer is unquestionably yes.

. . .

. . . Given President Trump's failure to correct the reasonable perception of his apparent hostility toward the Islamic faith, it is unsurprising that the President's lawyers have, at every step in the lower courts, failed in their attempts to launder the Proclamation of its discriminatory taint. . . . Notably, the Court recently found less pervasive official expressions of hostility and the failure to disavow them to be constitutionally significant. Cf. Masterpiece Cakeshop, Ltd. v. Colorado Civil Rights Comm'n, 584 U.S. ___, ___ (2018) . . . . It should find the same here.

Ultimately, what began as a policy explicitly "calling for a total and complete shutdown of Muslims entering the United States" has since morphed into a "Proclamation" putatively based on national-security concerns. But this new window dressing cannot conceal an unassailable fact: the words of the President and his advisers create the strong perception that the Proclamation is contaminated by impermissible discriminatory animus against Islam and its followers.

II

. . . [T]he Government urges this Court to . . . defer to the President on issues related to immigration and national security. The majority accepts that invitation and incorrectly applies a watered-down legal standard in an effort to short circuit plaintiffs' Establishment Clause claim.

. . . The extent to which *Mandel* and *Din* apply at all to this case is unsettled, and there is good reason to think they do not.[5] Indeed, even the Government agreed at oral argument that where the Court confronts a situation involving "all kinds of denigrating comments about" a particular religion and a subsequent policy that is designed with the purpose of disfavoring that religion but that

---

[5]   *Mandel* and *Din* are readily distinguishable from this case for a number of reasons. First, *Mandel* and *Din* each involved a constitutional challenge to an Executive Branch decision to exclude a single foreign national under a specific statutory ground of inadmissibility. . . . Here, by contrast, President Trump . . . promulgated an executive order affecting millions of individuals on a categorical basis. Second, *Mandel* and *Din* did not purport to establish the framework for adjudicating cases (like this one) involving claims that the Executive Branch violated the Establishment Clause by acting pursuant to an unconstitutional purpose. Applying *Mandel*'s narrow standard of review to such a claim would run contrary to this Court's repeated admonition that "[f]acial neutrality is not determinative" in the Establishment Clause context. . . . Likewise, the majority's passing invocation of Fiallo v. Bell, 430 U.S. 787 (1977), is misplaced. *Fiallo*, unlike this case, addressed a constitutional challenge to a statute enacted by Congress, not an order of the President. . . . Finally, even assuming that *Mandel* and *Din* apply here, they would not preclude us from looking behind the face of the Proclamation because plaintiffs have made "an affirmative showing of bad faith," *Din*, . . . by the President who, among other things, instructed his subordinates to find a "lega[l]" way to enact a Muslim ban . . . .

"dot[s] all the i's and . . . cross[es] all the t's," *Mandel* would not "pu[t] an end to judicial review of that set of facts." . . .

. . . [T]he Court, without explanation or precedential support, limits its review of the Proclamation to rational-basis scrutiny. . . . That approach is perplexing, given that in other Establishment Clause cases, including those involving claims of religious animus or discrimination, this Court has applied a more stringent standard of review. . . . As explained above, the Proclamation is plainly unconstitutional under that heightened standard.

But even under rational-basis review, the Proclamation must fall . . . because the Proclamation is " 'divorced from any factual context from which we could discern a relationship to legitimate state interests,' and 'its sheer breadth [is] so discontinuous with the reasons offered for it' " that the policy is " 'inexplicable by anything but animus.' " . . . The President's statements, which the majority utterly fails to address in its legal analysis, strongly support the conclusion that the Proclamation was issued to express hostility toward Muslims and exclude them from the country. Given the overwhelming record evidence of anti-Muslim animus, it simply cannot be said that the Proclamation has a legitimate basis. . . .

. . . [E]ven a cursory review of the Government's asserted national-security rationale reveals that the Proclamation is nothing more than a " 'religious gerrymander.' " *Lukumi* . . . .

. . . [T]he Proclamation, just like its predecessors, overwhelmingly targets Muslim-majority nations. . . . [T]he inclusion of North Korea and Venezuela, and the removal of other countries, simply reflect subtle efforts to start "talking territory instead of Muslim," . . . precisely so the Executive Branch could evade criticism or legal consequences for the Proclamation's otherwise clear targeting of Muslims. The Proclamation's effect on North Korea and Venezuela, for example, is insubstantial, if not entirely symbolic. A prior sanctions order already restricts entry of North Korean nationals, . . . and the Proclamation targets only a handful of Venezuelan government officials and their immediate family members . . . . As such, the President's inclusion of North Korea and Venezuela does little to mitigate the anti-Muslim animus that permeates the Proclamation.

. . .

. . . [T]he worldwide review does little to break the clear connection between the Proclamation and the President's anti-Muslim statements. . . .

[T]he majority empowers the President to hide behind an administrative review process that the Government refuses to disclose to the public. . . . Furthermore, evidence of which we can take judicial notice indicates that the multiagency review process could not have been very thorough. . . . [T]he September 2017 report the Government produced after its review process was a mere 17 pages. . . . That the Government's analysis of the vetting practices of hundreds of countries boiled down to such a short document raises serious questions about the legitimacy of the President's proclaimed national-security rationale.

Beyond that, Congress has already addressed the national-security concerns supposedly undergirding the Proclamation through an "extensive and complex" framework governing "immigration and alien status." . . .

. . .

Put simply, Congress has already erected a statutory scheme that fulfills the putative national-security interests the Government now puts forth to justify the Proclamation. Tellingly, the Government remains wholly unable to articulate any credible national-security interest that would go unaddressed by the current statutory scheme absent the Proclamation. . . .

For many of these reasons, several former national-security officials from both political parties . . . have advised that the Proclamation and its predecessor orders "do not advance the national-security or foreign policy interests of the United States, and in fact do serious harm to those interests." . . . .

. . . In addition, the Proclamation permits certain nationals from the countries named in the Proclamation to obtain nonimmigrant visas, which undermines the Government's assertion that it does not already have the capacity and sufficient information to vet these individuals adequately. . . .

Equally unavailing is the majority's reliance on the Proclamation's waiver program[, as] there is reason to suspect that the Proclamation's waiver program is nothing more than a sham. . . . The remote possibility of obtaining a waiver pursuant to an ad hoc, discretionary, and seemingly arbitrary process scarcely demonstrates that the Proclamation is rooted in a genuine concern for national security. See (Breyer, J., dissenting) (outlining evidence suggesting "that the Government is not applying the Proclamation as written," that "waivers are not being processed in an ordinary way," and that consular and other officials "do not, in fact, have discretion to grant waivers").

In sum, none of the features of the Proclamation highlighted by the majority supports the Government's claim that the Proclamation is genuinely and primarily rooted in a legitimate national-security interest. What the unrebutted evidence actually shows is that a reasonable observer would conclude, quite easily, that the primary purpose and function of the Proclamation is to disfavor Islam by banning Muslims from entering our country.

III

As the foregoing analysis makes clear, plaintiffs are likely to succeed on the merits of their Establishment Clause claim. . . .

. . .

IV

The First Amendment stands as a bulwark against official religious prejudice and embodies our Nation's deep commitment to religious plurality and tolerance. . . . Instead of vindicating those principles, today's decision tosses them aside. . . .

. . .

Today's holding is all the more troubling given the stark parallels between the reasoning of this case and that of Korematsu v. United States, 323 U.S. 214 (1944). . . . As here, the Government invoked an ill-defined national-security threat to justify an exclusionary policy of sweeping proportion. . . . As here, the exclusion order was rooted in dangerous stereotypes about, *inter alia*, a particular group's supposed inability to assimilate and desire to harm the United States. . . . As here, the Government was unwilling to reveal its own intelligence agencies' views of the alleged security concerns to the very citizens it purported to protect. . . . And as here, there was strong evidence that impermissible hostility and animus motivated the Government's policy.

. . .

In the intervening years since *Korematsu*, our Nation has done much to leave its sordid legacy behind. . . . Today, the Court takes the important step of finally overruling *Korematsu*, denouncing it as "gravely wrong the day it was decided." . . . This formal repudiation of a shameful precedent is laudable and long overdue. But it does not make the majority's decision here acceptable or right. By blindly accepting the Government's misguided invitation to sanction a discriminatory policy motivated by animosity toward a disfavored group, all in the name of a superficial claim of national security, the Court redeploys the same dangerous logic underlying *Korematsu* and merely replaces one "gravely wrong" decision with another.

. . . [W]ith profound regret, I dissent.

2. THE FREE EXERCISE OF RELIGION

Page 1804. Add after Church of the Lukumi Babalu Aye, Inc. v. City of Hialeah:

Masterpiece Cakeshop, Ltd. v. Colorado Civil Rights Commission

584 U.S. ___, 138 S.Ct. 1719, ___ L.Ed. 2d ___ (2018).

■ JUSTICE KENNEDY delivered the opinion of the Court.

[In 2012, when same-sex marriage was not yet legal in Colorado, two gay men, who planned to wed in Massachusetts and later hold a reception in Denver, were rebuffed by a Colorado baker, Phillips, when they asked him to create a wedding cake for their celebration. Phillips cited his religious opposition to same-sex marriage as the reason, although he offered to make their birthday cakes and shower cakes and to sell them brownies or cookies.] The couple filed a charge with the Colorado Civil Rights Commission alleging discrimination on the basis of sexual orientation in violation of the Colorado Anti-Discrimination Act[—a charge the Commission upheld and whose enforcement the state courts affirmed.]

The case presents difficult questions as to the proper reconciliation of at least two principles. The first is the authority of a State and its governmental entities to protect the rights and dignity of gay persons who are, or wish to be, married but who face discrimination when they seek goods or services. The second is the right of all persons to exercise fundamental freedoms under the First Amendment[—here "both the freedom of speech and the free exercise of religion."]

. . . The free speech aspect of this case is difficult, for few persons who have seen a beautiful wedding cake might have thought of its creation as an exercise of protected speech. This is an instructive example, however, of the proposition that the application of constitutional freedoms in new contexts can deepen our understanding of their meaning.

One of the difficulties in this case is that the parties disagree as to the extent of the baker's refusal to provide service. If a baker refused to design a special cake with words or images celebrating the marriage—for instance, a cake showing words with religious meaning—that might be different from a refusal to sell any cake at all. In defining whether a baker's creation can be protected, these details might make a difference.

The same difficulties arise in determining whether a baker has a valid free exercise claim. A baker's refusal to attend the wedding to ensure that the cake is cut the right way, or a refusal to put certain religious words or decorations on the cake, or even a refusal to sell a cake that has been baked for the public generally but includes certain religious words or symbols on it are just three examples of possibilities that seem all but endless.

Whatever the confluence of speech and free exercise principles might be in some cases, the Colorado Civil Rights Commission's consideration of this case was inconsistent with the State's obligation of religious neutrality. The reason and motive for the baker's refusal were based on his sincere religious beliefs and convictions. The Court's precedents make clear that the baker, in his capacity as the owner of a business serving the public, might have his right to the free exercise of religion limited by generally applicable laws. Still, the delicate question of when the free exercise of his religion must yield to an otherwise valid exercise of state power needed to be determined in an adjudication in which religious hostility on the part of the State itself would not be a factor in the balance the State sought to reach. That requirement, however, was not met here. When the Colorado Civil Rights Commission considered this case, it did not do so with the religious neutrality that the Constitution requires.

. . . [W]hatever the outcome of some future controversy involving facts similar to these, the Commission's actions here violated the Free Exercise Clause
. . . .

I

. . .

[The Colorado Anti-Discrimination Act (CADA), amended in 2007 and 2008 to add sexual orientation to the list of prohibited discrimination in places of public accommodation (defined broadly to include any place of business that sells goods or services to the public), uses an administrative system to resolve discrimination claims. Complaints are investigated by the Colorado Civil Rights Division, which refers the matter to the Commission if probable cause that CADA has been violated is found.] The Commission, in turn, decides whether to initiate a formal hearing before a state Administrative Law Judge (ALJ), who will hear evidence and argument before issuing a written decision. . . . The decision of the ALJ may be appealed to the full Commission, a seven-member appointed body. The Commission holds a public hearing and deliberative session before voting on the case. If the Commission determines that the evidence proves a CADA violation, it may impose [certain] remedial measures [that do not include assessing money damages or fines.]

. . .

[In this case, the Civil Rights Division investigator] found that "on multiple occasions," Phillips "turned away potential customers on the basis of their sexual orientation, stating that he could not create a cake for a same-sex wedding ceremony or reception" because his religious beliefs prohibited it and because the potential customers "were doing something illegal" at that time. . . . The investigation found that Phillips had declined to sell custom wedding cakes to about six other same-sex couples on this basis. . . . [T]he Division found probable cause that Phillips violated CADA and referred the case to the . . . Commission.

The Commission . . . sent the case to a[n] ALJ[, . . . who] determined that Phillips' actions constituted prohibited discrimination on the basis of sexual orientation, not simply opposition to same-sex marriage as Phillips contended. . . .

[The ALJ rejected Phillips' free speech and free exercise arguments. With respect to the latter, c]iting this Court's precedent in Employment Div., Dept. of Human Resources of Ore. v. Smith, 494 U.S. 872 (1990), the ALJ determined that CADA is a "valid and neutral law of general applicability" and therefore that applying it to Phillips in this case did not violate the Free Exercise Clause. . . .

The Commission affirmed the ALJ's decision[, issued a cease and desist order, and ordered staff training and quarterly compliance reports. On appeal, the Colorado Court of Appeals affirmed the Commission's legal determinations and remedial order, and the Colorado Supreme Court declined review.]

II

A

Our society has come to the recognition that gay persons and gay couples cannot be treated as social outcasts or as inferior in dignity and worth. . . . The exercise of their freedom on terms equal to others must be given great weight and respect by the courts. At the same time, the religious and philosophical objections to gay marriage are protected views and in some instances protected forms of expression. . . . Nevertheless, . . . it is a general rule that such objections do not allow business owners and other actors in the economy and in society to deny protected persons equal access to goods and services under a neutral and generally applicable public accommodations law. See Newman v. Piggy Park Enterprises, Inc., 390 U.S. 400, 402, n. 5 (1968) (*per curiam*); see also Hurley v. Irish-American Gay, Lesbian and Bisexual Group of Boston, Inc., 515 U.S. 557, 572 (1995) . . . .

. . . [I]t can be assumed that a member of the clergy who objects to gay marriage on moral and religious grounds could not be compelled to perform the ceremony without denial of his or her right to the free exercise of religion. . . . Yet if that exception were not confined, then a long list of persons who provide goods and services for marriages and weddings might refuse to do so for gay persons, thus resulting in a community-wide stigma inconsistent with the history and dynamics of civil rights laws that ensure equal access to goods, services, and public accommodations.

It is unexceptional that Colorado law can protect gay persons, just as it can protect other classes of individuals, in acquiring whatever products and services they choose on the same terms and conditions as are offered to other members of the public. . . . Petitioners conceded, moreover, that if a baker refused to sell any goods or any cakes for gay weddings, that would be a different matter . . . .

Phillips claims, however, that a narrower issue is presented. He argues that he had to use his artistic skills to make an expressive statement, a wedding endorsement in his own voice and of his own creation[, which] . . . he could not express in a way consistent with his religious beliefs.

Phillips' dilemma was particularly understandable given [that at the time] . . . Colorado did not recognize the validity of gay marriages performed in its own State. . . . [Thus,] there is some force to the argument that the baker was not unreasonable in deeming it lawful to decline to take an action that he understood to be an expression of support for their validity when that expression was contrary to his sincerely held religious beliefs, . . . even one planned to take place in another State.

At the time, state law also afforded storekeepers some latitude to decline to create specific messages the storekeeper considered offensive. Indeed, while enforcement proceedings against Phillips were ongoing, the Colorado Civil Rights Division itself endorsed this proposition in cases involving other bakers' creation of cakes, concluding on at least three occasions that a baker acted lawfully in declining to create cakes with decorations that demeaned gay persons or gay marriages. [The *Jack* cases.]

. . . [A]ny decision in favor of the baker would have to be sufficiently constrained, lest all purveyors of goods and services who object to gay marriages for moral and religious reasons in effect be allowed to put up signs saying "no goods or services will be sold if they will be used for gay marriages," something that would impose a serious stigma on gay persons. But, nonetheless, Phillips was entitled to the neutral and respectful consideration of his claims in all the circumstances of the case.

B

The neutral and respectful consideration . . . was compromised here, however. The . . . Commission's treatment of his case has some elements of a clear and impermissible hostility toward the sincere religious beliefs that motivated his objection.

That hostility surfaced at the Commission's formal, public hearings . . . . At several points during its meeting, commissioners endorsed the view that religious beliefs cannot legitimately be carried into the public sphere or commercial domain, implying that religious beliefs and persons are less than fully welcome in Colorado's business community. One commissioner suggested that Phillips can believe "what he wants to believe," but cannot act on his religious beliefs "if he decides to do business in the state." . . . A few moments later, the commissioner restated the same position: "[I]f a businessman wants to do business in the state and he's got an issue with the—the law's impacting his personal belief system, he needs to look at being able to compromise." . . . Standing alone, these statements . . . might mean simply that a business cannot refuse to provide services based on sexual orientation, regardless of the proprietor's personal views. On the other hand, they might be seen as inappropriate and dismissive comments showing lack of due consideration for Phillips' free exercise rights and the dilemma he faced. In view of the comments that followed, the latter seems the more likely.

[At a later Commission hearing,] another commissioner . . . said far more to disparage Phillips' beliefs. The commissioner stated:

> "I would also like to reiterate what we said in the hearing or the last meeting. Freedom of religion and religion has been used to justify all kinds of discrimination throughout history, whether it be slavery,

whether it be the holocaust, whether it be—I mean, we—we can list hundreds of situations where freedom of religion has been used to justify discrimination. And to me it is one of the most despicable pieces of rhetoric that people can use to—to use their religion to hurt others."

. . .

To describe a man's faith as "one of the most despicable pieces of rhetoric that people can use" is to disparage his religion in at least two distinct ways: by describing it as despicable, and also by characterizing it as merely rhetorical—something insubstantial and even insincere. The commissioner even went so far as to compare Phillips' invocation of his sincerely held religious beliefs to defenses of slavery and the Holocaust. This sentiment is inappropriate for a Commission charged with the solemn responsibility of fair and neutral enforcement of Colorado's antidiscrimination law—a law that protects discrimination on the basis of religion as well as sexual orientation.

The record shows no objection to these comments from other commissioners. And the later state-court ruling reviewing the Commission's decision did not mention those comments, much less express concern with their content. Nor were the comments by the commissioners disavowed in the briefs filed in this Court. For these reasons, the Court cannot avoid the conclusion that these statements cast doubt on the fairness and impartiality of the Commission's adjudication of Phillips' case. Members of the Court have disagreed on the question whether statements made by lawmakers may properly be taken into account in determining whether a law intentionally discriminates on the basis of religion. See Church of Lukumi Babalu Aye, Inc. v. Hialeah, 508 U.S. 520, 540–542 (1993); *id.,* at 558 (Scalia, J., concurring in part and concurring in judgment). In this case, however, the remarks were made in a very different context—by an adjudicatory body deciding a particular case.

Another indication of hostility is the difference in treatment between Phillips' case and the cases of other bakers who objected to a requested cake on the basis of conscience and prevailed before the Commission.

. . .

. . . The Commission ruled against Phillips in part on the theory that any message the requested wedding cake would carry would be attributed to the customer, not to the baker. Yet the Division did not address this point in any of the [*Jack*] cases with respect to the cakes depicting anti-gay marriage symbolism. Additionally, the Division found no violation of CADA in the other cases in part because each bakery was willing to sell other products, including those depicting Christian themes, to the prospective customers. But the Commission dismissed Phillips' willingness to sell "birthday cakes, shower cakes, [and] cookies and brownies," . . . to gay and lesbian customers as irrelevant. The treatment of the other cases and Phillips' case could reasonably be interpreted as being inconsistent as to the question of whether speech is involved, quite apart from whether the cases should ultimately be distinguished. In short, the Commission's consideration of Phillips' religious objection did not accord with its treatment of these other objections.

[T]he Colorado Court of Appeals . . . relegated its complete analysis of the [claimed disparate treatment] issue to a footnote[, finding no impermissible discrimination] ". . . against a Christian patron on the basis of his creed" . . .

because "the Division found that the bakeries . . . refuse[d] the patron's request . . . because of the offensive nature of the requested message." . . .

A principled rationale for the difference in treatment of these two instances cannot be based on the government's own assessment of offensiveness. . . . [I]t is . . . the role of the State or its officials to prescribe what shall be offensive. . . . The Colorado court's attempt to account for the difference in treatment elevates one view of what is offensive over another and itself sends a signal of official disapproval of Phillips' religious beliefs. The court's footnote does not, therefore, answer the baker's concern that the State's practice was to disfavor the religious basis of his objection.

C

. . .

In *Church of Lukumi Babalu Aye, supra*, the Court made clear that the government . . . cannot impose regulations that are hostile to the religious beliefs of affected citizens and cannot act in a manner that passes judgment upon or presupposes the illegitimacy of religious beliefs and practices. The Free Exercise Clause bars even "subtle departures from neutrality" on matters of religion. . . . Here, that means the Commission was obliged under the Free Exercise Clause to proceed in a manner neutral toward and tolerant of Phillips' religious beliefs. . . .

. . . It hardly requires restating that government has no role in deciding or even suggesting whether the religious ground for Phillips' conscience-based objection is legitimate or illegitimate. On these facts, the Court must draw the inference that Phillips' religious objection was not considered with the neutrality that the Free Exercise Clause requires.

. . . [T]he State's interest could have been weighed against Phillips' sincere religious objections in a way consistent with the requisite religious neutrality that must be strictly observed. The official expressions of hostility to religion in some of the commissioners' comments—comments that were not disavowed at the Commission or by the State at any point in the proceedings that led to affirmance of the order—were inconsistent with what the Free Exercise Clause requires. The Commission's disparate consideration of Phillips' case compared to the cases of the other bakers suggests the same. For these reasons, the order must be set aside.

III

. . .

The outcome of cases like this in other circumstances must await further elaboration in the courts, all in the context of recognizing that these disputes must be resolved with tolerance, without undue disrespect to sincere religious beliefs, and without subjecting gay persons to indignities when they seek goods and services in an open market.

The judgment . . . is reversed.

■ JUSTICE KAGAN, with whom JUSTICE BREYER joins, concurring.

. . . I write separately to elaborate on one of the bases for the Court's holding.

. . . The Court partly relies on the "disparate consideration of Phillips' case compared to the cases of [three] other bakers" who "objected to a requested cake on the basis of conscience." . . . As the Court states, a "principled rationale for the difference in treatment" cannot be "based on the government's own assessment of offensiveness." . . .

. . .

What makes the state agencies' consideration yet more disquieting is that a proper basis for distinguishing the cases was available—in fact, was obvious. . . . CADA . . . makes it unlawful for a place of public accommodation to deny "the full and equal enjoyment" of goods and services to individuals based on certain characteristics, including sexual orientation and creed. . . . The three bakers in the Jack cases did not violate that law. Jack requested them to make a cake (one denigrating gay people and same-sex marriage) that they would not have made for any customer. In refusing that request, the bakers did not single out Jack because of his religion, but instead treated him in the same way they would have treated anyone else—just as CADA requires. By contrast, the same-sex couple in this case requested a wedding cake that Phillips would have made for an opposite-sex couple. In refusing that request, Phillips contravened CADA's demand that customers receive "the full and equal enjoyment" of public accommodations irrespective of their sexual orientation. . . . The different outcomes in the Jack cases and the Phillips case could thus have been justified by a plain reading and neutral application of Colorado law—untainted by any bias against a religious belief.[*]

. . . Colorado can treat a baker who discriminates based on sexual orientation differently from a baker who does not discriminate on that or any other prohibited ground. But only, as the Court rightly says, if the State's decisions are not infected by religious hostility or bias. . . .

■ JUSTICE GORSUCH, with whom JUSTICE ALITO joins, concurring.

. . .

. . . [T]wo of our colleagues have written separately to suggest that the Commission acted neutrally toward his faith when it treated him differently from the other bakers—or that it could have easily done so consistent with the First Amendment. (Ginsburg, J., dissenting); (Kagan, J., concurring). But, respectfully, I do not see how we might rescue the Commission from its error.

. . .

The facts show that the two cases share all legally salient features. In both cases, the effect on the customer was the same: bakers refused service to persons who bore a statutorily protected trait (religious faith or sexual orientation). But in both cases the bakers refused service intending only to honor a personal

---

[*]   Justice Gorsuch disagrees. In his view, the Jack cases and the Phillips case must be treated the same because the bakers in all those cases "would not sell the requested cakes to anyone." That description perfectly fits the Jack cases—and explains why the bakers there did not engage in unlawful discrimination. But it is a surprising characterization of the Phillips case, given that Phillips routinely sells wedding cakes to opposite-sex couples. Justice Gorsuch can make the claim only because he does not think a "wedding cake" is the relevant product. As [he] sees it, the product that Phillips refused to sell here—and would refuse to sell to anyone— was a "cake celebrating same-sex marriage." But that is wrong. The cake requested was not a special "cake celebrating same-sex marriage." It was simply a wedding cake—one that (like other standard wedding cakes) is suitable for use at same-sex and opposite-sex weddings alike. . . . A vendor can choose the products he sells, but not the customers he serves—no matter the reason. Phillips sells wedding cakes. As to that product, he unlawfully discriminates: He sells it to opposite-sex but not to same-sex couples. And on that basis—which has nothing to do with Phillips' religious beliefs—Colorado could have distinguished Phillips from the bakers in the Jack cases, who did not engage in any prohibited discrimination.

conviction. To be sure, the bakers *knew* their conduct promised the effect of leaving a customer in a protected class unserved. But there's no indication the bakers actually *intended* to refuse service *because of* a customer's protected characteristic. We know this because all of the bakers explained without contradiction that they would not sell the requested cakes to anyone, while they would sell other cakes to members of the protected class (as well as to anyone else). So, for example, the bakers in the first case would have refused to sell a cake denigrating same-sex marriage to an atheist customer, just as the baker in the second case would have refused to sell a cake celebrating same-sex marriage to a heterosexual customer. And the bakers in the first case were generally happy to sell to persons of faith, just as the baker in the second case was generally happy to sell to gay persons. In both cases, it was the kind of cake, not the kind of customer, that mattered to the bakers.

. . .

. . . In Mr. Jack's case, the Commission chose to distinguish carefully between intended and knowingly accepted effects. Even though the bakers knowingly denied service to someone in a protected class, the Commission found no violation because the bakers only intended to distance themselves from "the offensive nature of the requested message." . . . Yet, in Mr. Phillips's case, the Commission . . . concluded instead that an "intent to disfavor" a protected class of persons should be "readily . . . presumed" from the knowing failure to serve someone who belongs to that class.

. . . In the end, the Commission's decisions simply reduce to this: it *presumed* that Mr. Phillips harbored an intent to discriminate against a protected class in light of the foreseeable effects of his conduct, but it declined to presume the same intent in Mr. Jack's case even though the effects of the bakers' conduct were just as foreseeable. Underscoring the double standard, a state appellate court said that "no such showing" of actual "animus"—or intent to discriminate against persons in a protected class—was even required in Mr. Phillips's case. . . .

The Commission cannot have it both ways. The Commission cannot slide up and down the *mens rea* scale, picking a mental state standard to suit its tastes depending on its sympathies. . . . [I]t can't . . . apply a more generous legal test to secular objections than religious ones. See *Church of Lukumi Babalu Aye,* 508 U.S., at 543–544. That is anything but the neutral treatment of religion.

. . . [A]s the Court explains, it appears the Commission wished to condemn Mr. Phillips for expressing just the kind of "irrational" or "offensive . . . message" that the bakers in the first case refused to endorse. . . . In this country, the place of secular officials isn't to sit in judgment of religious beliefs, but only to protect their free exercise. . . . It is in protecting unpopular religious beliefs that we prove this country's commitment to serving as a refuge for religious freedom. . . .

. . . It is no answer . . . to observe that Mr. Jack requested a cake with text on it while Mr. Craig and Mr. Mullins sought a cake celebrating their wedding without discussing its decoration . . . See . . . (Ginsburg, J., dissenting). It is no answer either simply to slide up a level of generality to redescribe Mr. Phillips's case as involving only a wedding cake like any other, so the fact that Mr. Phillips would make one for some means he must make them for all. See . . . (KAGAN, J., concurring). These arguments . . . fail to afford Mr. Phillips's faith neutral respect.

. . . To suggest that cakes with words convey a message but cakes without words do not—all in order to excuse the bakers in Mr. Jack's case while penalizing Mr. Phillips—is irrational. . . . Words or not and whatever the exact design, it celebrates a wedding, and if the wedding cake is made for a same-sex couple it celebrates a same-sex wedding. . . . It is precisely . . . approval that Mr. Phillips intended to withhold in keeping with his religious faith. The Commission denied Mr. Phillips that choice, even as it afforded the bakers in Mr. Jack's case the choice to refuse to advance a message they deemed offensive to their secular commitments. That is not neutral.

. . .

The second suggestion fares no better. Suggesting that this case is only about "wedding cakes"—and not a wedding cake celebrating a same-sex wedding—actually points up the problem. . . . We are told . . . to apply a sort of Goldilocks rule: describing the cake by its ingredients is *too general*; understanding it as celebrating a same-sex wedding is *too specific*; but regarding it as a generic wedding cake is *just right*. The problem is, the Commission didn't play with the level of generality in Mr. Jack's case in this way. It didn't declare, for example, that because the cakes Mr. Jack requested were just cakes about weddings generally, and all such cakes were the same, the bakers had to produce them. Instead, the Commission accepted the bakers' view that the specific cakes Mr. Jack requested conveyed a message offensive to their convictions and allowed them to refuse service. Having done that there, it must do the same here.

. . . Neither the Commission nor this Court may apply a more specific level of generality in Mr. Jack's case (a cake that conveys a message regarding same-sex marriage) while applying a higher level of generality in Mr. Phillips's case (a cake that conveys no message regarding same-sex marriage). Of course, under *Smith* a vendor cannot escape a public accommodations law just because his religion frowns on it. But for any law to comply with the First Amendment and *Smith*, it must be applied in a manner that treats religion with neutral respect. That means the government must apply the *same* level of generality across cases—and that did not happen here.

There is another problem with sliding up the generality scale: it risks denying constitutional protection to religious beliefs that draw distinctions more specific than the government's preferred level of description. To some, all wedding cakes may appear indistinguishable. But *to Mr. Phillips* that is not the case—his faith teaches him otherwise. And his religious beliefs are entitled to no less respectful treatment than the bakers' secular beliefs in Mr. Jack's case. . . . It is no more appropriate for the United States Supreme Court to tell Mr. Phillips that a wedding cake is just like any other—without regard to the religious significance his faith may attach to it—than it would be for the Court to suggest that for all persons sacramental bread is *just* bread or a kippah is *just* a cap.

. . .

■ JUSTICE THOMAS, with whom JUSTICE GORSUCH joins, concurring in part and concurring in the judgment.

I agree that the . . . Commission . . . violated Jack Phillips' right to freely exercise his religion. As Justice Gorsuch explains, the Commission treated Phillips' case differently from a similar case involving three other bakers, for reasons that can only be explained by hostility toward Phillips' religion. . . . Although the Commissioners' comments are certainly disturbing, the discriminatory application of Colorado's public-accommodations law is enough on its own to violate Phillips' rights. To the extent the Court agrees, I join its opinion.

. . . I write separately to address his free-speech claim.

. . . [T]he Court of Appeals concluded that Phillips' conduct was not expressive and was not protected speech. It reasoned that an outside observer would think that Phillips was merely complying with Colorado's public-accommodations law, not expressing a message, and that Phillips could post a disclaimer to that effect. This reasoning flouts bedrock principles of our free-speech jurisprudence and would justify virtually any law that compels individuals to speak. It should not pass without comment.

. . .

. . . Colorado is punishing [Phillips] because he refuses to create custom wedding cakes that express approval of same-sex marriage. In cases like this one, our precedents demand " 'the most exacting scrutiny.' "

. . .

■ JUSTICE GINSBURG, with whom JUSTICE SOTOMAYOR joins, dissenting.

. . .

. . . The different outcomes the Court features do not evidence hostility to religion of the kind we have previously held to signal a free-exercise violation, nor do the comments by one or two members of one of the four decisionmaking entities considering this case justify reversing the judgment below.

I

. . . Jack['s] visit[s to] three Colorado bakeries . . . followed a similar pattern. He requested two cakes

> "made to resemble an open Bible. He also requested that each cake be decorated with Biblical verses. [He] requested that one of the cakes include an image of two groomsmen, holding hands, with a red 'X' over the image. On one cake, he requested [on] one side[,] . . . 'God hates sin. Psalm 45:7' and on the opposite side of the cake 'Homosexuality is a detestable sin. Leviticus 18:2.' On the second cake, [the one] with the image of the two groomsmen covered by a red 'X' [Jack] requested [these words]: 'God loves sinners' and on the other side 'While we were yet sinners Christ died for us. Romans 5:8.' " . . .

In contrast to Jack, Craig and Mullins simply requested a wedding cake: They mentioned no message or anything else distinguishing the cake they wanted to buy from any other wedding cake Phillips would have sold.

One bakery told Jack it would make cakes in the shape of Bibles, but would not decorate them with the requested messages; the owner told Jack her bakery "does not discriminate" and "accept[s] all humans." . . . The second bakery owner told Jack he "had done open Bibles and books many times and that they look amazing," but declined to make the specific cakes Jack described because the baker regarded the messages as "hateful." . . . The third bakery, according to Jack, said it would bake the cakes, but would not include the requested message.

. . . The Division found no probable cause to support Jack's claims of unequal treatment and denial of goods or services based on his Christian religious beliefs. . . . In this regard, the Division observed that the bakeries regularly produced cakes and other baked goods with Christian symbols and had denied other customer requests for designs demeaning people whose dignity the Colorado Antidiscrimination Act (CADA) protects. . . .

The Court concludes that "the Commission's consideration of Phillips' religious objection did not accord with its treatment of [the other bakers'] objections." . . . But the cases the Court aligns are hardly comparable. The bakers would have refused to make a cake with Jack's requested message for any customer, regardless of his or her religion. And the bakers visited by Jack would have sold him any baked goods they would have sold anyone else. The bakeries' refusal to make Jack cakes of a kind they would not make for any customer scarcely resembles Phillips' refusal to serve Craig and Mullins: Phillips would *not* sell to Craig and Mullins, for no reason other than their sexual orientation, a cake of the kind he regularly sold to others. When a couple contacts a bakery for a wedding cake, the product they are seeking is a cake celebrating *their* wedding—not a cake celebrating heterosexual weddings or same-sex weddings— and that is the service Craig and Mullins were denied. . . . Jack . . . suffered no service refusal on the basis of his religion or any other protected characteristic. He was treated as any other customer would have been treated—no better, no worse.[3]

The fact that Phillips might sell other cakes and cookies to gay and lesbian customers was irrelevant . . . . What matters is that Phillips would not provide a good or service to a same-sex couple that he would provide to a heterosexual couple. In contrast, the other bakeries' sale of other goods to Christian customers was relevant: It shows that there were no goods the bakeries would sell to a non-Christian customer that they would refuse to sell to a Christian customer.

Nor was the Colorado Court of Appeals' "difference in treatment of these two instances . . . based on the government's own assessment of offensiveness." Phillips declined to make a cake he found offensive where the offensiveness of the product was determined solely by the identity of the customer requesting it. The three other bakeries declined to make cakes where their objection to the product was due to the demeaning message the requested product would literally display. . . .[5] . . .

II

Statements made at the Commission's public hearings on Phillips' case provide no firmer support for the Court's holding today. Whatever one may think

---

[3]   Justice Gorsuch argues that the situations "share all legally salient features." But what critically differentiates them is the role the customer's "statutorily protected trait" played in the denial of service. Change Craig and Mullins' sexual orientation (or sex), and Phillips would have provided the cake. Change Jack's religion, and the bakers would have been no more willing to comply with his request. The bakers' objections to Jack's cakes had nothing to do with "religious opposition to same-sex weddings." (Gorsuch, J., concurring). Instead, the bakers simply refused to make cakes bearing statements demeaning to people protected by CADA. . . . Phillips did, therefore, discriminate *because of* sexual orientation; the other bakers did not discriminate *because of* religious belief; and the Commission properly found discrimination in one case but not the other. . . .

[5]   . . . [W]hile Jack requested cakes with particular text inscribed, Craig and Mullins were refused the sale of any wedding cake at all. They were turned away before any specific cake design could be discussed. . . . The Division and the Court of Appeals could rationally and lawfully distinguish between a case involving disparaging text and images and a case involving a wedding cake of unspecified design. The distinction is not between a cake with text and one without, see (Gorsuch, J., concurring); it is between a cake with a particular design and one whose form was never even discussed.

of the statements in historical context, I see no reason why the comments of one or two Commissioners should be taken to overcome Phillips' refusal to sell a wedding cake to Craig and Mullins. The proceedings involved several layers of independent decisionmaking, of which the Commission was but one. . . . What prejudice infected the determinations of the adjudicators in the case before and after the Commission? The Court does not say. Phillips' case is thus far removed from the only precedent upon which the Court relies, Church of Lukumi Babalu Aye, Inc. v. Hialeah, 508 U.S. 520 (1993), where the government action that violated a principle of religious neutrality implicated a sole decisionmaking body, the city council . . . .

> . . .

Page 1807. Add after Locke v. Davey:

Trinity Lutheran Church v. Comer
582 U.S. ___, 137 S.Ct. 2012, 198 L.Ed.2d 551 (2017).

■ CHIEF JUSTICE ROBERTS delivered the opinion of the Court, except as to footnote 3.

The Missouri Department of Natural Resources offers state grants to help public and private schools, nonprofit daycare centers, and other nonprofit entities purchase rubber playground surfaces made from recycled tires. Trinity Lutheran Church applied for such a grant for its preschool and daycare center and would have received one, but for the fact that Trinity Lutheran is a church. The Department had a policy of categorically disqualifying churches and other religious organizations from receiving grants under its playground resurfacing program. The question presented is whether the Department's policy violated the rights of Trinity Lutheran under the Free Exercise Clause of the First Amendment.

I

A

The Trinity Lutheran Church Child Learning Center . . . [was e]stablished as a nonprofit organization in 1980, . . . merged with Trinity Lutheran Church in 1985 and operates under its auspices on church property. The Center admits students [aged 2–5] of any religion . . . .

[The Center sought to replace the pea gravel surface below its playground equipment with a softer rubber surface by applying for a competitive grant from the Department.] When the Center applied, the Department had a strict and express policy of denying grants to any applicant owned or controlled by a church, sect, or other religious entity. That policy, in the Department's view, was compelled by Article I, Section 7 of the Missouri Constitution, which provides:

"That no money shall ever be taken from the public treasury, directly or indirectly, in aid of any church, sect or denomination of religion, or in aid of any priest, preacher, minister or teacher thereof, as such; and that no preference shall be given to nor any discrimination made against any church, sect or creed of religion, or any form of religious faith or worship."

In its application, the Center disclosed its status as a ministry of Trinity Lutheran Church and specified that the Center's mission was "to provide a safe, clean, and attractive school facility in conjunction with an educational program structured to allow a child to grow spiritually, physically, socially, and cognitively." [Among other things, the application described the playground's current safety hazards and noted that the benefits also would flow to the local community for use during non-school hours.]

[Though ranked fifth among 44 applicants, 14 of whom were ultimately awarded grants,] the Center was deemed categorically ineligible to receive a grant. In a letter rejecting the Center's application, the program director explained that, under Article I, Section 7 of the Missouri Constitution, the Department could not provide financial assistance directly to a church.

B

[In federal district court, Trinity Lutheran challenged the Department's "policy of denying grants to religiously affiliated applicants" as a violation of the Free Exercise Clause, but that court—relying on Locke v. Davey—rejected the claim, and the Eighth Circuit affirmed. The Supreme Court reversed, however.]

II

. . . The parties agree that the Establishment Clause . . . does not prevent Missouri from including Trinity Lutheran in the Scrap Tire Program. That does not, however, answer the question under the Free Exercise Clause, because we have recognized that there is "play in the joints" between what the Establishment Clause permits and the Free Exercise Clause compels. *Locke*, ...

The Free Exercise Clause "protect[s] religious observers against unequal treatment" and subjects to the strictest scrutiny laws that target the religious for "special disabilities" based on their "religious status." Church of Lukumi Babalu Aye, Inc. v. Hialeah, 508 U. S. 520, 533, 542 (1993) (internal quotation marks omitted). Applying that basic principle, this Court has repeatedly confirmed that denying a generally available benefit solely on account of religious identity imposes a penalty on the free exercise of religion that can be justified only by a state interest "of the highest order." McDaniel v. Paty, 435 U. S. 618, 628 (1978) (plurality opinion) (quoting Wisconsin v. Yoder, 406 U. S. 205, 215 (1972)).

In Everson v. Board of Education of Ewing, 330 U. S. 1 (1947), for example, we upheld against an Establishment Clause challenge a New Jersey law enabling a local school district to reimburse parents for the public transportation costs of sending their children to public and private schools, including parochial schools. In the course of ruling that the Establishment Clause allowed New Jersey to extend that public benefit to all its citizens regardless of their religious belief, we explained that a State "cannot hamper its citizens in the free exercise of their own religion. Consequently, it cannot exclude individual Catholics, Lutherans, Mohammedans, Baptists, Jews, Methodists, Non-believers, Presbyterians, or the members of any other faith, *because of their faith, or lack of it*, from receiving the benefits of public welfare legislation." *Id.*, at 16.

Three decades later, in McDaniel v. Paty, the Court struck down under the Free Exercise Clause a Tennessee statute disqualifying ministers from serving as delegates to the State's constitutional convention. Writing for the plurality, Chief Justice Burger acknowledged that Tennessee had disqualified ministers from serving as legislators since the adoption of its first Constitution in 1796, and that a number of early States had also disqualified ministers from legislative office. This historical tradition, however, did not change the fact that the statute discriminated against McDaniel by denying him a benefit solely because of his "*status* as a 'minister.'" . . . McDaniel could not seek to participate in the convention while also maintaining his role as a minister; to pursue the one, he would have to give up the other. In this way, said Chief Justice Burger, the Tennessee law "effectively penalizes the free exercise of [McDaniel's] constitutional liberties." . . . Joined by Justice Marshall in concurrence, Justice Brennan added that "because the challenged provision requires [McDaniel] to purchase his right to engage in the ministry by sacrificing his candidacy it impairs the free exercise of his religion." . . .

In recent years, when this Court has rejected free exercise challenges, the laws in question have been neutral and generally applicable without regard to religion. We have been careful to distinguish such laws from those that single out the religious for disfavored treatment.

    . . .

III

A

The Department's policy expressly discriminates against otherwise eligible recipients by disqualifying them from a public benefit solely because of their religious character. If [our] cases . . . make one thing clear, it is that such a policy imposes a penalty on the free exercise of religion that triggers the most exacting scrutiny. . . . This conclusion is unremarkable in light of our prior decisions.

Like the disqualification statute in *McDaniel*, the Department's policy puts Trinity Lutheran to a choice: It may participate in an otherwise available benefit program or remain a religious institution. Of course, Trinity Lutheran is free to continue operating as a church, just as McDaniel was free to continue being a minister. But that freedom comes at the cost of automatic and absolute exclusion from the benefits of a public program for which the Center is otherwise fully qualified. And when the State conditions a benefit in this way, *McDaniel* says plainly that the State has punished the free exercise of religion: "To condition the availability of benefits . . . upon [a recipient's] willingness to . . . surrender[ ] his religiously impelled [status] effectively penalizes the free exercise of his constitutional liberties."

The Department contends that merely declining to extend funds to Trinity Lutheran does not *prohibit* the Church from engaging in any religious conduct or otherwise exercising its religious rights. In this sense, says the Department, its policy is unlike the ordinances struck down in *Lukumi*, which outlawed rituals central to Santeria. Here the Department has simply declined to allocate to Trinity Lutheran a subsidy the State had no obligation to provide in the first place. That decision does not meaningfully burden the Church's free exercise rights. And absent any such burden, the argument continues, the Department is free to heed the State's antiestablishment objection to providing funds directly to a church.

It is true the Department has not criminalized the way Trinity Lutheran worships or told the Church that it cannot subscribe to a certain view of the Gospel. But, as the Department itself acknowledges, the Free Exercise Clause protects against "indirect coercion or penalties on the free exercise of religion, not just outright prohibitions." . . . As the Court put it more than 50 years ago, "[i]t is too late in the day to doubt that the liberties of religion and expression may be infringed by the denial of or placing of conditions upon a benefit or privilege." *Sherbert*, 374 U. S., at 404; see also *McDaniel*, 435 U. S., at 633

(Brennan, J., concurring in judgment) (The "proposition—that the law does not interfere with free exercise because it does not directly prohibit religious activity, but merely conditions eligibility for office on its abandonment—is . . . squarely rejected by precedent").

Trinity Lutheran is not claiming any entitlement to a subsidy. It instead asserts a right to participate in a government benefit program without having to disavow its religious character. The "imposition of such a condition upon even a gratuitous benefit inevitably deter[s] or discourage[s] the exercise of First Amendment rights." *Sherbert*, ... The express discrimination against religious exercise here is not the denial of a grant, but rather the refusal to allow the Church—solely because it is a church—to compete with secular organizations for a grant. Cf. Northeastern Fla. Chapter, Associated Gen. Contractors of America v. Jacksonville, 508 U. S. 656, 666 (1993) ("[T]he 'injury in fact' is the inability to compete on an equal footing in the bidding process, not the loss of a contract"). Trinity Lutheran is a member of the community too, and the State's decision to exclude it for purposes of this public program must withstand the strictest scrutiny.

B

The Department attempts to get out from under the weight of our precedents by arguing that the free exercise question in this case is instead controlled by our decision in Locke v. Davey. It is not. . . .

. . . Washington's selective funding program was not comparable to the free exercise violations found in the "*Lukumi* line of cases," including those striking down laws requiring individuals to "choose between their religious beliefs and receiving a government benefit." . . . At the outset, then, the Court made clear that *Locke* was not like the case now before us.

Washington's restriction on the use of its scholarship funds was different. [T]he State had "merely chosen not to fund a distinct category of instruction." . . . Davey was not denied a scholarship because of who he *was*; he was denied a scholarship because of what he proposed *to do*—use the funds to prepare for the ministry. Here there is no question that Trinity Lutheran was denied a grant simply because of what it is—a church.

The Court in *Locke* also stated that Washington's choice was in keeping with the State's antiestablishment interest in not using taxpayer funds to pay for the training of clergy; in fact, the Court could "think of few areas in which a State's antiestablishment interests come more into play." . . . The claimant in *Locke* sought funding for an "essentially religious endeavor . . . akin to a religious calling as well as an academic pursuit," and opposition to such funding "to support church leaders" lay at the historic core of the Religion Clauses. . . . Here nothing of the sort can be said about a program to use recycled tires to resurface playgrounds.

Relying on *Locke*, the Department nonetheless emphasizes Missouri's similar constitutional tradition of not furnishing taxpayer money directly to churches. . . . But *Locke* took account of Washington's antiestablishment interest only after determining . . . that the scholarship program did not "require students to choose between their religious beliefs and receiving a government benefit." . . . Washington's scholarship program went "a long way toward including religion in its benefits." . . . Students in the program were free to use their scholarships at "pervasively religious schools." . . . Davey could use his scholarship to pursue a secular degree at one institution while studying devotional theology at another. . . . He could also use his scholarship money to attend a religious college and take devotional theology courses there. . . . The only thing he could not do was use the scholarship to pursue a degree in that subject.

In this case, there is no dispute that Trinity Lutheran *is* put to the choice between being a church and receiving a government benefit. The rule is simple: No churches need apply.[3]

C

The State in this case expressly requires Trinity Lutheran to renounce its religious character in order to participate in an otherwise generally available public benefit program, for which it is fully qualified. Our cases make clear that such a condition imposes a penalty on the free exercise of religion that must be subjected to the "most rigorous" scrutiny. *Lukumi*, ... Under that stringent standard, only a state interest "of the highest order" can justify the Department's discriminatory policy. *McDaniel*, ... Yet the Department offers nothing more than Missouri's policy preference for skating as far as possible from religious establishment concerns. . . . In the face of the clear infringement on free exercise before us, that interest cannot qualify as compelling. . . .

. . .

. . . [T]he exclusion of Trinity Lutheran from a public benefit for which it is otherwise qualified, solely because it is a church, is odious to our Constitution . . . and cannot stand.

The judgment . . . is reversed, and the case is remanded for further proceedings consistent with this opinion.

■ JUSTICE THOMAS, with whom JUSTICE GORSUCH joins, concurring in part.

. . .

This Court's endorsement in *Locke* of even a "mil[d] kind," . . . of discrimination against religion remains troubling. See generally *id.*, at 726–734 (Scalia, J., dissenting). But because the Court today appropriately construes *Locke* narrowly, . . . and because no party has asked us to reconsider it, I join nearly all of the Court's opinion. I do not, however, join footnote 3, for the reasons expressed by Justice Gorsuch . . . .

■ JUSTICE GORSUCH, with whom JUSTICE THOMAS joins, concurring in part.

. . . I am pleased to join nearly all of the Court's opinion. I offer only two modest qualifications.

First, the Court leaves open the possibility a useful distinction might be drawn between laws that discriminate on the basis of religious *status* and religious *use*. Respectfully, I harbor doubts about the stability of such a line. Does a religious man say grace before dinner? Or does a man begin his meal in a religious manner? Is it a religious group that built the playground? Or did a group build the playground so it might be used to advance a religious mission? The distinction blurs in much the same way the line between acts and omissions

---

[3] This case involves express discrimination based on religious identity with respect to playground resurfacing. We do not address religious uses of funding or other forms of discrimination.

can blur when stared at too long . . . . Often enough the same facts can be described both ways.

Neither do I see why the First Amendment's Free Exercise Clause should care. After all, that Clause guarantees the free *exercise* of religion, not just the right to inward belief (or status) . . . . Generally the government may not force people to choose between participation in a public program and their right to free exercise of religion. . . . I don't see why it should matter whether we describe that benefit, say, as closed to Lutherans (status) or closed to people who do Lutheran things (use). It is free exercise either way.

For these reasons, reliance on the status-use distinction does not suffice for me to distinguish Locke v. Davey, ... [C]an it really matter whether the restriction in *Locke* was phrased in terms of use instead of status (for was it a student who wanted a vocational degree in religion? Or was it a religious student who wanted the necessary education for his chosen vocation?). If that case can be correct and distinguished, it seems it might be only because of the opinion's claim of a long tradition against the use of public funds for training of the clergy, a tradition the Court correctly explains has no analogue here.

Second and for similar reasons, I am unable to join the footnoted observation, n. 3, that "[t]his case involves express discrimination based on religious identity with respect to playground resurfacing." Of course the footnote is entirely correct, but I worry that some might mistakenly read it to suggest that only "playground resurfacing" cases, or only those with some association with children's safety or health, or perhaps some other social good we find sufficiently worthy, are governed by the legal rules recounted in and faithfully applied by the Court's opinion. Such a reading would be unreasonable for our cases are "governed by general principles, rather than ad hoc improvisations." . . . . And the general principles here do not permit discrimination against religious exercise—whether on the playground or anywhere else.

■ JUSTICE BREYER, concurring in the judgment.

I agree with much of what the Court says and with its result. But I find relevant, and would emphasize, the particular nature of the "public benefit" here at issue. . . .

The Court stated in *Everson* that "cutting off church schools from" such "general government services as ordinary police and fire protection . . . is obviously not the purpose of the First Amendment." . . . Here, the State would cut Trinity Lutheran off from participation in a general program designed to secure or to improve the health and safety of children. I see no significant difference. The fact that the program at issue ultimately funds only a limited number of projects cannot itself justify a religious distinction. Nor is there any administrative or other reason to treat church schools differently. The sole reason advanced that explains the difference is faith. And it is that last-mentioned fact that calls the Free Exercise Clause into play. We need not go further. Public benefits come in many shapes and sizes. I would leave the application of the Free Exercise Clause to other kinds of public benefits for another day.

■ JUSTICE SOTOMAYOR, with whom JUSTICE GINSBURG joins, dissenting.

. . . The Court today profoundly changes th[e] relationship [between church and state] by holding, for the first time, that the Constitution requires the government to provide public funds directly to a church. Its decision slights both our precedents and our history, and its reasoning weakens this country's longstanding commitment to a separation of church and state beneficial to both.

I

. . .

The Learning Center serves as "a ministry of the Church and incorporates daily religion and developmentally appropriate activities into . . . [its] program." . . . In this way, "[t]hrough the Learning Center, the Church teaches a Christian world view to children of members of the Church, as well as children of non-member residents" of the area. . . . These activities represent the Church's "sincere religious belief . . . to use [the Learning Center] to teach the Gospel to children of its members, as well to bring the Gospel message to non-members." . . .

. . .

II

Properly understood then, this is a case about whether Missouri can decline to fund improvements to the facilities the Church uses to practice and spread its religious views. This Court has repeatedly warned that funding of exactly this kind—payments from the government to a house of worship—would cross the line drawn by the Establishment Clause. . . . So it is surprising that the Court mentions the Establishment Clause only to note the parties' agreement that it "does not prevent Missouri from including Trinity Lutheran in the Scrap Tire Program." Constitutional questions are decided by this Court, not the parties' concessions. The Establishment Clause does not allow Missouri to grant the Church's funding request because the Church uses the Learning Center, including its playground, in conjunction with its religious mission. The Court's silence on this front signals either its misunderstanding of the facts of this case or a startling departure from our precedents.

A

The government may not directly fund religious exercise. . . .

Nowhere is this rule more clearly implicated than when funds flow directly from the public treasury to a house of worship. . . .

. . .

. . . The Church seeks state funds to improve the Learning Center's facilities, which, by the Church's own avowed description, are used to assist the spiritual growth of the children of its members and to spread the Church's faith to the children of nonmembers. The Church's playground surface—like a Sunday School room's walls or the sanctuary's pews—are integrated with and integral to its religious mission. The conclusion that the funding the Church seeks would impermissibly advance religion is inescapable.

True, this Court has found some direct government funding of religious institutions to be consistent with the Establishment Clause. But the funding in those cases came with assurances that public funds would not be used for religious activity, despite the religious nature of the institution. . . . The Church has not and cannot provide such assurances here. . . . The Church has a religious mission, one that it pursues through the Learning Center. The playground surface cannot be confined to secular use any more than lumber used to frame the Church's walls, glass stained and used to form its windows, or nails used to build its altar.

B

The Court may simply disagree with this account of the facts and think that the Church does not put its playground to religious use. If so, its mistake is limited to this case. But if it agrees that the State's funding would further religious activity and sees no Establishment Clause problem, then it must be implicitly applying a rule other than the one agreed to in our precedents.

. . .

III

Even assuming the absence of an Establishment Clause violation and proceeding on the Court's preferred front—the Free Exercise Clause—the Court errs. It claims that the government may not draw lines based on an entity's religious "status." But we have repeatedly said that it can. When confronted with government action that draws such a line, we have carefully considered whether the interests embodied in the Religion Clauses justify that line. The question here is thus whether those interests support the line drawn in Missouri's Article I, § 7, separating the State's treasury from those of houses of worship. They unquestionably do.

A

. . . Th[e] space between the two Clauses gives government some room to recognize the unique status of religious entities and to single them out on that basis for exclusion from otherwise generally applicable laws.

Invoking this principle, this Court has held that the government may sometimes relieve religious entities from the requirements of government programs. A State need not, for example, require nonprofit houses of worship to pay property taxes. . . .

Invoking this same principle, this Court has held that the government may sometimes close off certain government aid programs to religious entities. The State need not, for example, fund the training of a religious group's leaders, those "who will preach their beliefs, teach their faith, and carry out their mission," *Hosanna-Tabor*, 565 U. S., at 196. It may instead avoid the historic "antiestablishment interests" raised by the use of "taxpayer funds to support church leaders." Locke v. Davey, 540 U. S. 712, 722 (2004).

When reviewing a law that, like this one, singles out religious entities for exclusion from its reach, we thus have not myopically focused on the fact that a law singles out religious entities, but on the reasons that it does so.

B

Missouri has decided that the unique status of houses of worship requires a special rule when it comes to public funds. . . . Missouri's decision, which has deep roots in our Nation's history, reflects a reasonable and constitutional judgment.

1

This Court has consistently looked to history for guidance when applying the Constitution's Religion Clauses. . . .

. . .

. . . The use of public funds to support core religious institutions can safely be described as a hallmark of the States' early experiences with religious establishment. Every state establishment saw laws passed to raise public funds and direct them toward houses of worship and ministers. And as the States all disestablished, one by one, they all undid those laws.

[Justice Sotomayor recounted that history at length, and continued:]

The course of this history shows that those who lived under the laws and practices that formed religious establishments made a considered decision that civil government should not fund ministers and their houses of worship. . . .

2

In *Locke*, this Court expressed an understanding of, and respect for, this history. . . .

. . . Like the use of public dollars for ministers at issue in *Locke*, turning over public funds to houses of worship implicates serious anti-establishment and free exercise interests. The history just discussed fully supports this conclusion. As states disestablished, they repealed laws allowing taxation to support religion because the practice threatened other forms of government support for, involved some government control over, and weakened supporters' control of religion. . . . Inside a house of worship, dividing the religious from the secular would require intrusive line-drawing by government, and monitoring those lines would entangle government with the house of worship's activities. And so while not every activity a house of worship undertakes will be inseparably linked to religious activity, "the likelihood that many are makes a categorical rule a suitable means to avoid chilling the exercise of religion." . . . Finally, and of course, such funding implicates the free exercise rights of taxpayers by denying them the chance to decide for themselves whether and how to fund religion. If there is any " 'room for play in the joints' between" the Religion Clauses, it is here. *Locke*, ...

As was true in *Locke*, a prophylactic rule against the use of public funds for houses of worship is a permissible accommodation of these weighty interests. . . . Today, thirty-eight States have a counterpart to Missouri's Article I, § 7. The provisions . . . date back to or before these States' original Constitutions. That so many States have for so long drawn a line that prohibits public funding for houses of worship, based on principles rooted in this Nation's understanding of how best to foster religious liberty, supports the conclusion that public funding of houses of worship "is of a different ilk." *Locke*, ...

. . . Missouri will fund a religious organization not "owned or controlled by a church," if its "mission and activities are secular (separate from religion, not spiritual in) nature" and the funds "will be used for secular (separate from religion; not spiritual) purposes rather than for sectarian (denominational, devoted to a sect) purposes." . . . Article I, § 7, thus stops Missouri only from funding specific entities, ones that set and enforce religious doctrine for their adherents. These are the entities that most acutely raise the establishment and free exercise concerns that arise when public funds flow to religion.

Missouri has recognized the simple truth that, even absent an Establishment Clause violation, the transfer of public funds to houses of worship raises concerns that sit exactly between the Religion Clauses. To avoid those concerns, and only those concerns, it has prohibited such funding. In doing so, it made the same choice made by the earliest States centuries ago and many other States in the years since. The Constitution permits this choice.

3

. . .

. . . In all cases, the dispositive issue is not whether religious "status" matters—it does, or the Religion Clauses would not be at issue—but whether the government must, or may, act on that basis.

Start where the Court stays silent. Its opinion does not acknowledge that our precedents have expressly approved of a government's choice to draw lines based on an entity's religious status. . . . Those cases did not deploy strict scrutiny to create a presumption of unconstitutionality, as the Court does today. Instead, they asked whether the government had offered a strong enough reason to justify drawing a line based on that status. . . .

The Court takes two steps to avoid these precedents. First, it recasts *Locke* as a case about a restriction that prohibited the would-be minister from "us[ing] the funds to prepare for the ministry." A faithful reading of *Locke* gives it a broader reach. *Locke* stands for the reasonable proposition that the government may, but need not, choose not to fund certain religious entities (there, ministers) where doing so raises "historic and substantial" establishment and free exercise concerns. Second, it suggests that this case is different because it involves "discrimination" in the form of the denial of access to a possible benefit. But in this area of law, a decision to treat entities differently based on distinctions that the Religion Clauses make relevant does not amount to discrimination. To understand why, keep in mind that "the Court has unambiguously concluded that the individual freedom of conscience protected by the First Amendment embraces the right to select any religious faith or none at all." *Wallace* v. *Jaffree*, 472 U. S. 38, 52–53 (1985). If the denial of a benefit others may receive is discrimination that violates the Free Exercise Clause, then the accommodations of religious entities we have approved would violate the free exercise rights of nonreligious entities. We have, with good reason, rejected that idea, . . . and instead focused on whether the government has provided a good enough reason, based in the values the Religion Clauses protect, for its decision.

. . . The Court's desire to avoid what it views as discrimination is understandable. But in this context, the description is particularly inappropriate. A State's decision not to fund houses of worship does not disfavor religion; rather, it represents a valid choice to remain secular in the face of serious establishment and free exercise concerns. . . .

At bottom, the Court creates the following rule today: The government may draw lines on the basis of religious status to grant a benefit to religious persons or entities but it may not draw lines on that basis when doing so would further the interests the Religion Clauses protect in other ways. Nothing supports this lopsided outcome. Not the Religion Clauses, as they protect establishment and free exercise interests in the same constitutional breath, neither privileged over the other. Not precedent, since we have repeatedly explained that the Clauses protect not religion but "the individual's freedom of conscience," *Jaffree*, . . .— that which allows him to choose religion, reject it, or remain undecided. And not reason, because as this case shows, the same interests served by lifting government-imposed burdens on certain religious entities may sometimes be equally served by denying government-provided benefits to certain religious entities. . . .

Justice Breyer's concurrence offers a narrower rule that would limit the effects of today's decision, but that rule does not resolve this case. . . . To fence out religious persons or entities from a truly generally available public benefit—one provided to all, no questions asked, such as police or fire protections—would violate the Free Exercise Clause. . . . Missouri does not apply its constitutional provision in that manner. . . . The Scrap Tire Program offers not a generally available benefit but a selective benefit for a few recipients each year. In this context, the comparison to truly generally available benefits is inapt. . . .

. . .

Today's decision discounts centuries of history and jeopardizes the government's ability to remain secular. . . .

IV

. . .

The Court today dismantles a core protection for religious freedom . . . . It holds not just that a government may support houses of worship with taxpayer funds, but that—at least in this case and perhaps in others, see n. 3—it must do so whenever it decides to create a funding program. History shows that the Religion Clauses separate the public treasury from religious coffers as one measure to secure the kind of freedom of conscience that benefits both religion and government. If this separation means anything, it means that the government cannot, or at the very least need not, tax its citizens and turn that money over to houses of worship. The Court today blinds itself to the outcome this history requires and leads us instead to a place where separation of church and state is a constitutional slogan, not a constitutional commitment. I dissent.